PICTURING PETER BOGDANOVICH

PICTURING PETER BOGDANOVICH

MY CONVERSATIONS WITH THE NEW HOLLYWOOD DIRECTOR

PETER TONGUETTE

UNIVERSITY PRESS OF KENTUCKY

Scholarly publisher for the Commonwealth,
serving Bellarmine University, Berea College, Centre
College of Kentucky, Eastern Kentucky University,
The Filson Historical Society, Georgetown College,
Kentucky Historical Society, Kentucky State University,
Morehead State University, Murray State University,
Northern Kentucky University, Transylvania University,
University of Kentucky, University of Louisville,
and Western Kentucky University.

Editorial and Sales Offices: The University Press of Kentucky
663 South Limestone Street, Lexington, Kentucky 40508-4008
www.kentuckypress.com

Library of Congress Cataloging-in-Publication Data

Names: Bogdanovich, Peter, 1939– | Tonguette, Peter Prescott, 1983– interviewer, editor.
Title: Picturing Peter Bogdanovich : my conversations with the new Hollywood director / Peter Tonguette.
Description: Lexington : The University Press of Kentucky, 2020. | Series: Screen classics | Includes index.
Identifiers: LCCN 2020017976 | ISBN 9780813147314 (hardcover) | ISBN 9780813147321 (pdf) | ISBN 9780813147307 (epub)
Subjects: LCSH: Bogdanovich, Peter, 1939—Interviews. | Motion picture producers and directors—United States—Interviews. | Actors—United States—Interviews.
Classification: LCC PN1998.3.B64 A3 2020 | DDC 791.4302/33092—dc23
LC record available at https://lccn.loc.gov/2020017976

This book is printed on acid-free paper meeting
the requirements of the American National Standard
for Permanence in Paper for Printed Library Materials.

Manufactured in the United States of America.

Member of the Association
of University Presses

Contents

Prologue

"I Hadn't Realized It Was So Late in Ohio"

It may come as a surprise to those who know him for his great films, among them *The Last Picture Show, What's Up, Doc?,* and *Paper Moon,* but from 1991 to 1998 Peter Bogdanovich edited a calendar. It was not just any old calendar, either, but a revival of an ancient calendar, published to compete with the modern calendar that all of us Westerners unquestioningly make use of.

A little background might be helpful: as Robert Graves describes in book *The White Goddess*—his classic "historical grammar of poetic myth"—years were once divvied up differently than they are today. The months were shorter and more numerous. "This agricultural tree-calendar based on nature's cycles, and consisting of thirteen 28-day months and one extra day," Bogdanovich explained, "gave birth to the ancient phrase 'a year and a day.'"[1] The months were also called by other names—the names of trees, in fact. So, for example, instead of March, June, and December, there were Alder, Oak, and Elder.

For a whole host of personal and professional reasons, Bogdanovich cottoned to this calendar, and when he brought out his own version of it (originally titled *A Year and a Day Engagement Calendar,* later retitled *The White Goddess Engagement Diary*), he included a handy chart to aid in the conversion of any Gregorian date into a tree date.

Once when we were chatting, I mentioned to Bogdanovich that I had ascertained what my birthday would have been according to the old calendar.

"My birthday is March 27," I told him. "That equals Alder 10."

"Alder 10," he said, pausing thoughtfully. "That's good. That's the tree of foundations—and you're working on the foundation of me at the moment."

We laughed because we knew how true it was: I was, after all, writing a book about his films and had done plenty of thinking about the man who made them.

But in March 2014, busy with the completion of his newest film, *She's Funny That Way,* Peter Bogdanovich seemed to have forgotten my birthday and—momentarily, at least—that Ohio (where I lived) was several hours ahead of California (where he was then spending his time).

He was in Los Angeles, having dinner with his ex-wife and closest friend, Louise Stratten, whose sister, the late Dorothy Stratten, was the love of his life. Louise cowrote and coproduced *She's Funny That Way.*

It was about nine o'clock in the evening on the West Coast but just past midnight in Ohio. In my neck of the woods, the calendar had flipped to March 27—or Alder 10—when the phone rang. Absorbed in CNN's coverage of Malaysia Airlines Flight 370 (remember the wall-to-wall cable coverage that episode inspired?), I couldn't get to the phone from the sofa in time to pick up. The answering machine clicked on, and a short message followed: "Peter Bogdanovich calling Peter Tonguette. Hopefully you get this, Peter. Thanks."

I called back a few minutes later, and when I reached him, he was apologetic.

"I hadn't realized it was so late in Ohio," he said.

I told him that was okay. Then I asked what occasioned the call.

Rather jarringly turning my attention from the rat-a-tat-tat voice of CNN's Richard Quest to that of my favorite filmmaker, he told me he was curious for my opinion about a scene or two in *She's Funny That Way.* In the background, I could hear the rattle of plates and glasses; the murmur of orders being given.

"Sorry, Peter," he interjected, stating the obvious, "we're in a restaurant."

It would be a chicken breast and a piece of toasted rye bread for the Oscar-nominated director.

We didn't chat for long after that, but he said he was glad to hear a friendly voice and that we would talk again soon.

Well, this was a fine way to start my birthday. Not that he remembered it was my birthday—or, that evening, what time zone Ohio was in. There was no great meaning behind the call. Louise later told me it was her idea: Peter was just looking for someone to talk to who knew and admired his films—and, as he said, a friendly voice—and they happened to have my phone number.

Still. How, really, does it happen that Peter Bogdanovich—*Peter Bogdanovich!*—rings up a young journalist in the Midwest in the middle of the night?

Recalling his initial encounter with Alfred Hitchcock—one that ultimately led to a book not unlike this one, the famous *Hitchcock*—François Truffaut wrote: "It all began when we broke the ice."[2]

For Peter Bogdanovich and me, it all began with another phone call, about seventeen years ago . . . .

PART 1

"Call Me Peter, Peter"

The Giants were my delight, my folly, my anodyne, my intellectual stimulation.

— Frederick Exley, *A Fan's Notes: A Fictional Memoir*

But how seldom two imaginations coincide!

— Saul Bellow, *The Adventures of Augie March*

I dialed the number his assistant had given me.

Brrring.

No answer.

Brrring.

No answer.

Brrring.

No answer.

For some reason, calling Peter Bogdanovich for the first time for an interview made me feel like Tom Sawyer.

Could it have been because I was so young? Not Tom Sawyer young, but close enough. When I called Peter Bogdanovich on the night before Thanksgiving in 2003 (the date must have some sort of cosmic significance, but for the life of me I cannot imagine what it might be), I was several months' shy of my twenty-first birthday. I had a right to be nervous. If I measured myself against Peter Bogdanovich, as I often did, I was supposed to have *done* something by that age.

When he was twenty-one, he was already well on his way to the fortune and glory he would later gain as the director of a batch of extraordinary films that were all the rage—with both the critics and the public—in the early 1970s. The native New Yorker—born on July 30, 1939, to Borislav (a painter) and Herma (a homemaker and maker of frames)—started early. At the age of fourteen, while a student at the Collegiate School, he began penning frighteningly perceptive movie and theater reviews in his column "As We See It." This anticipated his subsequent career writing feature articles for *Esquire* and *New York,* among other august publications.

But the prodigy was not consumed with writing alone—oh, there was more.

Acting was his first passion. His "earliest performances," he wrote, were recitations of poetry and stories at dinner parties thrown by his parents: "After the meal they would ask me to recite . . . poems like Poe's 'Annabel Lee' or 'The Raven,' or Whitman's 'O Captain! My Captain!' or Robert W. Service's 'The Shooting of Dan McGrew'—or to read a short story like Poe's 'The Tell-Tale Heart.'"[1]

Soon, though, he moved out of the dining room and onto the boards.

In an introduction to Bogdanovich's collection of essays *Pieces of Time,* his editor at *Esquire,* Harold Hayes, noted with pride that Bogdanovich was all of fifteen when he became an acting student of Stella Adler—"having lied about his age and cut his gym class to make time available."[2] His classes with Adler—no matter the, ahem, fraudulent means through which they were obtained—resulted in appearances on stage and on live television, making him a seasoned trouper when he was not yet out of short pants.

More: "In 1959, at nineteen," Hayes continued, "he somehow managed to raise the money to stage an off-Broadway production of Clifford Odets' *The Big Knife.*"[3] Are you keeping track? Good: journalist, actor, stage director—and barely old enough to drive. He was not tranquil with his success, either. Hollywood beckoned. It would not be too many more years before he and his first wife—production and costume designer Polly Platt—headed from New York to California, armed with a little money, a plethora of contacts obtained through his writing career, and the general notion that they wanted to *make* movies—not just see them or write about them.

By the time he was twenty-one, then, Peter Bogdanovich had done his share of Big Things and was destined for even Bigger Things. Me? In between shoveling snow in my suburb of Columbus, Ohio, I was just trying to launch my writing career—not exactly the sort of thing that Harold Hayes would have considered worth commemorating in print.

Nonetheless, on that Thanksgiving Eve in 2003, I found myself dialing Peter Bogdanovich's number and waiting for him—or anyone—to pick up. I imagined the phone ringing off the hook in his handsome Upper West Side apartment, the one I had seen in a photograph when the *New Yorker* profiled him the previous year, just as his most recent film, *The Cat's Meow,* was about to come out.

On this night, however, it seemed that no one was home—or answering, anyway. I hung up. What to do? I had a backup plan. In case he did not pick up when I called at the appointed time, his assistant had given me a second number to try. It was, she told me, the number to his cell phone. I leaned back in my chair for a long moment. I grabbed the receiver and thought, *What the hell—why not?*

Brrring.

Brrring.

This time—improbably, because he still felt out of reach to me—he answered. "Yeah?" he said. He sounded impatient—a little testy. I did not know then that this was how he almost always answered the phone—"Yeah?"—no matter his mood, and that his tone was not unfriendly but quizzical. It suggested that he had . . . things . . . going on . . . *important* things. He simply wanted assurance that he was being interrupted for a damn good reason.

So: "Yeah?"

I gulped and began: Who I was. Why I was calling. When—*ahem*—we had been scheduled to talk.

He listened patiently, without saying a word in response, and I began to wonder if any of what I said rang a bell. Had his assistant bungled our phoner? When I finally stopped talking, he calmly explained that he was being driven home from the New York set of *The Sopranos*, the popular HBO television series on which he had the plum role of the Lorraine Bracco character's psychiatrist. Could I call him when he got home in fifteen minutes? He was, it turned out, perfectly polite, asking only that I give him some time—you know—to walk in the door and turn on the lights and have a sip of water before I started grilling him.

Shoot, I thought to myself. *I should have just waited.*

You may be wondering why I was calling Peter Bogdanovich in the first place.

Ostensibly, I was interviewing him for an article I was writing about his films, but I have to level with you: this was a bit of a ruse. In truth, I had loved his movies for years, and I simply wanted to talk about them with him. My mind was overflowing with questions: How did he cajole Ben Johnson into taking the part of Sam the Lion in *The Last Picture Show*? Why did he open *Paper Moon* with a close-up of its young star,

Tatum O'Neal? Was it just the way I saw it, or was *They All Laughed* more personal—more *him*—than anything else he'd ever done? If the only way I could ask him these (and many other) questions was by becoming a professional journalist and talking my way into an assignment to write an article about his work—well, so be it.

Let's face facts: I began writing about movies in the hope that my job would one day give me an excuse to talk to Peter Bogdanovich. There are worse reasons to select an occupation, right?

I was, to put it bluntly, a fan—but if you knew all that I did, you would be, too. What was there not to like? Following his detours in print and on stage, Bogdanovich jumped into moviemaking with gusto, and he met with such instantaneous success—laudatory reviews, big box office—that it was as though the public and industry had been waiting for him. *What took you so long?* they might have been asking.

By 1971, when *The Last Picture Show* was released, it had been a rough few years for anyone who prized classical filmmaking and its attendant virtues. Tapping into the antiestablishment mood of some in the country, films such as *Midnight Cowboy* and *Woodstock* seemed to be multiplying—like a virus. For all their differences, they had much in common: they were morally incoherent and visually ugly, bearing scant relation to the art form built by the likes of D. W. Griffith, John Ford, and Orson Welles.

Into this noxious environment stepped Peter Bogdanovich, and the contrast could not have been more striking. Pauline Kael was never his most sympathetic critic, but she got one big thing right. "He has a real gift for simple, popular movies," she wrote. "He can tell basic stories that will satisfy a great many people, and this is not a common gift."[4] Introducing Bogdanovich's book *Pieces of Time,* Harold Hayes quoted a studio executive expressing a similar sentiment: "People don't want to be reminded of their problems. They want to be diverted and entertained. They want a *Paper Moon* by Bogdanovich, not a reprise on the tragedy of Bobby Kennedy."[5]

Recognizing an ally, veteran directors saw that Peter Bogdanovich was part of their tradition—"one of us," as the cabal in Tod Browning's great horror film *Freaks* says. But these were no freaks—these were the *normal* people, and Bogdanovich joined their ranks eagerly. He became a friend to Ford and Welles and many others, and the only thing that stood in the way of an apprenticeship with Griffith was that the maker of

Intolerance and *Broken Blossoms* had died in 1948, when the future filmmaker was nine. Bad timing.

Director George Stevens, he said, sought him out and gave him a pat on the back: "You know what it's about. These guys don't know what it's about. That's why we need you."[6] Well, George Stevens wasn't D. W. Griffith, but, still, he was the man who had made *Shane* and *Giant* and *A Place in the Sun.* "These guys" meant, of course, Bogdanovich's peers—those much-honored filmmakers who emerged at about the same time he did, including Martin Scorsese, Francis Ford Coppola, and William Friedkin—but the most honest of them knew that Stevens spoke the truth. "The last person to make classical American cinema was Peter," Scorsese said. "To really utilize the wide frame and the use of the deep focal length. He really understood it."[7] Observed writer Judy Stone in the *New York Times* in 1968: "Peter is under 30, but he doesn't identify with his own generation."[8]

Howard Hawks immodestly pointed out that Bogdanovich, in his capacity as a journalist, "sat on my set for two and a half years and on Ford's for two and a half years, so he learned a few things."[9] Yes, yes, Howard—he *had* studied well. But he also benefitted from a more hands-on opportunity that presented itself soon after he made it to California with Polly Platt: he was brought on as an assistant on Roger Corman's low-budget biker film *The Wild Angels.* So when Corman—as a kind of thank-you present—told Bogdanovich that could direct a movie, Bogdanovich was raring to go.

Rebellion was in the air in 1968, and it usually took the form of the young rising up against the old. In his debut film, *Targets,* Peter Bogdanovich reversed the equation, pitting a chivalrous senior citizen against a murderous postadolescent.

The hero of the story is Byron Orlok (Boris Karloff), a star of antediluvian horror epics. As the film opens, we find Orlok watching his current effort (actually recut scenes from the Karloff flick *The Terror*) in a dingy screening room in downtown Los Angeles. With its shots of crows shrieking and floods washing away damsels in distress, what we see of *The Terror* looks remarkably démodé, and by the time it is all over, Orlok—sitting stoop-shouldered in the third row—has decided to call it a career. With murder and mayhem having become daily realities, who in their right mind would be spooked by such stuff?

Before Orlok can slink away into the night, however, he has to answer to Sammy Michaels (expertly played by Bogdanovich), a greenhorn writer-director with whom he had promised to collaborate on a future project. Sammy implores Orlok to think twice about hanging it up, but Orlok refuses to budge. In their stubbornness, however, they prove themselves to be two of a kind: with his conservative dress and respectful manner, Sammy looks as out of place as Orlok in the Southern California of the late 1960s. About the worst you can say about Sammy is that he rudely tells Orlok to hush when the two find themselves watching one of Orlok's old films on television (another Karloff project—this one, though, far more creditable than *The Terror:* Howard Hawks's top-notch thriller *The Criminal Code*).

The character of Sammy makes for a ready-made contrast to Bobby Thompson (Tim O'Kelly), a Vietnam veteran who, apropos of nothing, morphs into a serial killer. Like Sammy, Bobby is in his late twenties and sports a clean-cut appearance, but in every other way he is Sammy's shadow. A dim fellow with a toothy, heartless smile, we first see him as he purchases munitions at a gun store across the street from the screening room where Orlok and Sammy haggle. Orlok goes out of his way to call Sammy "a sweet boy," and one glimpse of Bobby explains why: in the world of *Targets,* civility and virtue are rare qualities indeed.

Yet the screenplay (written by Bogdanovich and Polly Platt, with uncredited rewrites courtesy of Samuel Fuller) avoids pinning Bobby's crimes on his war experience. After all, unlike many of his comrades, Bobby has returned home in one piece and seemingly none the worse for wear. What—we might ask—does he have to complain about? His placid family life is also exempted from blame: the single-story suburban house he shares with his parents and wife may be bland and uninviting, but so are many other houses, and few of them incubate mass murderers. "We tried to avoid a specific reason," Bogdanovich told Judy Stone. "We did a lot of research, and the most terrifying aspect of these crimes is that there is no answer. We can find no reason commensurate with the size of the crime."[10] Yet the not-so-subtle suggestion in *Targets* is that culture makes the difference: Sammy, with his appreciation of old movies, has it, whereas Bobby, forever gobbling Baby Ruths and listening to rock music, does not.

Bobby and Orlok encounter each other at the drive-in theater at which Orlok is to put in an appearance before sailing to retirement in England. Mayhem ensues when Bobby makes targets of those in the audience. With the police nowhere to be found, it is left to Orlok—unarmed and in a tuxedo—to confront Bobby. We suspect that their encounter will end in a blaze of bullets, but the film has a more clever—and more pointed—resolution in store for us. Cornered in a dark spot beneath the screen, Bobby sees Orlok loping toward him but becomes disoriented when he looks up to see a similar image of Orlok in *The Terror*. In his confusion, Bobby is left defenseless when Orlok approaches and slaps his face—an opprobrium far more humiliating than losing a gunfight. Bobby drops his rifle and curls up in a fetal position. Only a figure as virtuous as Byron Orlok could vanquish the likes of Bobby Thompson.

Peter Bogdanovich put his cards on the table with *Targets:* it matters whether movies have moral fiber or not. We imagine the young director concurring with the mother in Herman Wouk's great novel *Marjorie Morningstar,* then only about a decade old: "Marjorie's mother looked in on her sleeping daughter at half past ten of a Sunday morning," Wouk wrote, "with feelings of puzzlement and dread."[11]

"Puzzlement and dread"—three words that sum up Bogdanovich's perspective on the modern world. Modestly budgeted and not well distributed, *Targets* might have made a difference had it been seen by more audiences.

Then came the hits.

If you were distraught over the state of the movies in the late 1960s and early 1970s, *The Last Picture Show* surely came as a welcome change of pace. Critic Roger Ebert observed that the film did not just take place in the past but somehow was *of* the past. "'The Last Picture Show' has been described as an evocation of the classic Hollywood narrative film," Ebert wrote. "It is more than that; it is a belated entry in that age—the best film of 1951, you might say."[12] With its black-and-white photography and clean, traditional storytelling, who could disagree? Few did. Chosen for inclusion in the New York Film Festival, *The Last Picture Show* sold more tickets than some of the more au courant fare of 1971, such as *Shaft* and *Straw Dogs,* and was up for eight Academy Awards on Oscar night, winning a pair for the supporting performances by Ben Johnson and Cloris Leachman.

The film's much-ballyhooed first shot reveals the dilapidated facade and unoccupied ticket booth of the Royal Theater in Anarene, Texas, in 1951. One look at it, however, and we are surprised that anyone bothers to change the marquee. Panning past the theater and the shabby storefronts that surround it, the camera reaches an intersection, deserted except for

Cloris Leachman in *The Last Picture Show.* Courtesy Jerry Ohlinger's Movie Material Store.

a blinking streetlight dangling precariously from above. We wonder: Do any residents remain in Anarene to actually *go* to the movies?

But this thoroughly desolate-looking beginning is, in fact, a bit of sly humor from Bogdanovich. There is plenty of action taking place in Anarene—romances, affairs, au naturel pool parties—but it is going on in private. High-school student Sonny Crawford (Timothy Bottoms) is setting up house with his football coach's ashen-faced wife, Ruth Popper (Cloris Leachman), while his best friend, Duane Jackson (Jeff Bridges), is arranging motel-room assignations with his pretty, popular classmate Jacy Farrow (Cybill Shepherd), whom Sonny also desires.

The difference between exteriors and interiors—between respectability and immorality—is emphasized throughout the film. In a lovely early scene (absent in the original cut but later restored by Bogdanovich), we see Jacy as she drives Sonny and Duane home in her open-topped convertible. They peppily belt out the school song in the brisk autumn air, which is alive with feelings of friendship and innocence. Much later, however, when the class sings "Texas, Our Texas" at a graduation ceremony, the earlier scene's wholesome esprit de corps is obliterated by the private conversation Duane and Jacy carry on under their breath; having struck out during their previous tryst, he is imploring her to go to bed with him just one more time.

Now, a lesser director—a more conventional director—would be making a point about how the prim-and-proper 1950s were really no such thing. But in adapting Larry McMurtry's fine novel, Bogdanovich takes a more rigorous approach. Instead of reveling in the adolescents' behind-closed-doors antics, he casts his lot with the few adults in the story who disapprove of them, especially the rugged, tough-talking cowboy Sam the Lion (Ben Johnson).

Even the film's famous skinny-dipping scene has an unexpected tone of finger-wagging: the audience is saddened—*disheartened*—when Jacy capitulates after being pressured into getting undressed on the diving board. There is a devastating moment when, after hitting the water, she finds that the watch she is wearing—just given to her by Duane—has stopped. Jacy brings the watch close to her face to see if it is still working, shaking her wrist several times before realizing that it has died. Her expression suggests that she wonders if something inside her has died, too. Jacy's scruples are sadly transient: one of her prospective beaus smiles lustily at her from the opposite end of the pool, and she returns the look. Her watch is forgotten, as is her fleeting regret.

Director Leo McCarey—the master filmmaker behind *The Awful Truth* and *The Bells of St. Mary's*—once told Bogdanovich that he had long dreamed of making a movie that told the story of Adam and Eve. In fact, Bogdanovich, not McCarey, would be the better choice to direct a movie about the costs of eating from the tree of knowledge.

In the years following *The Last Picture Show*, Bogdanovich came to oppose the unchecked sex and nudity rampant in contemporary movies. "Could such legendary goddesses of the screen like Greta Garbo or Marlene Dietrich have maintained their hold on the collective imagination if they had been forced to bare all?" he later asked.[13] His unpopular but persuasive position is not far from that of literary critic George Steiner, who wrote that "sexual relations are, or should be, one of the citadels of privacy," but "the new pornographers subvert this last, vital privacy; they do our imagining for us."[14] Years later, when a tragedy in his personal life led Bogdanovich to testify in support of an antipornography ordinance in Los Angeles, he expressed regret over what relatively little skin was shown in *The Last*

Picture Show: "Believe me, if I had that scene to do over again, we'd just as soon not do it naked, because it wasn't really necessary."[15]

Who could reach Sonny, Duane, and Jacy? Certainly not their hapless English teacher (John Hillerman), who in a slightly pitiful scene recites a poem by John Keats. The camera pans across the classroom, but the power of the language fails to distract Jacy from looking at her compact or Sonny from looking out the window:

When old age shall this generation waste
Thou shalt remain, in midst of other woe
Than ours, a friend to man, to whom thou say'st
"Beauty is truth, truth beauty"—that is all
Ye know on earth, and all ye need to know.

No, the only one who can save them is Sam the Lion, who owns the Royal Theater and several other concerns in Anarene but whose primary function is as "the film's teacher, law-giver, fount of values," as the author Peter Biskind puts it in *Easy Riders, Raging Bulls.*[16] At one point, Sonny, Duane, and others solicit the services of an obese prostitute for Billy (Sam Bottoms), a dull-witted boy. When Sam learns that Billy was roughed up during this encounter, he scolds the group: "You boys can get on outa here. I don't want to have no more to do with you. Scaring a poor, unfortunate creature like Billy just so you could have a few laughs. I've been around that trashy behavior all of my life. I'm getting tired of puttin' up with it." Sonny feebly speaks up with an excuse, but Sam—in the scene's first close-up—cuts him off: "You didn't even have the decency to wash his face." Sonny gulps, and Sam turns away.

For critic Clive James, this was just about Peter Bogdanovich's best moment: "The great scene in his first great success, 'The Last Picture Show,' was when Ben Johnson told the normal boys off for their 'trashy behavior' in humiliating a half-wit."[17] Lincoln Kirstein once made the provocative remark that "ballet is about how to behave"—and cinema ought to be, too, though it seldom is. In their rare moral rectitude, Byron Orlok and Sam the Lion stand apart from the crowd.

Fittingly, *The Last Picture Show* reaches its climax not with the ill-fated elopement of Sonny and Jacy or even with Duane leaving town to serve in Korea. The story instead turns on the death of Sam the Lion. Even at this early stage in his career, though, Bogdanovich knew that a deathbed scene out of *Camille* would never cut it. The shock of Sam's death could be imparted only if it were revealed quickly—almost offhandedly.

Having returned from a jaunt in Mexico, Sonny and Duane are looking for Sam when they accost an old-timer snoozing in a car. "Hey, where is everybody?" Sonny asks. "Why'd Sam close the café?" Then the news comes—like a bolt of lightning. "Oh, yeah—y'all been gone, ain't ya?" the old guy says. "Been gone to Mexico. You don't know about it. Sam died yesterday morning." Sonny parks himself on the edge of the sidewalk as the talk moves on to the contents of Sam's will ("Craziest thing you ever heard. He left you the pool hall, Sonny. What do you think about that?"). The camera moves in closer as Sonny looks to the theater and then to the blinking streetlight; the breathtakingly subtle editing conveys a mind driven to distraction by grief.

Peter Bogdanovich often speaks about his preference for long takes, but when he decides he must make a cut, few directors are better at carving a scene into pieces. For example, in *The Last Picture Show* he hopscotches among the mourners at Sam's funeral—one person's reaction is shown, then another's. We see the waitress from Sam's café, Genevieve (Eileen Brennan), standing beside Sonny and Billy. While the three are grouped together in the same shot, each is inhabiting his or her own little world. The disparate nature of sorrow is the point of the image. Genevieve, clutching a handkerchief, cries openly; Sonny looks forlorn but keeps his emotions in check; and Billy is, as ever, uncomprehending.

Directly across from Sonny is Ruth Popper, who strains to make eye contact with her young lover. A spate of shots and reaction shots show Ruth smiling at Sonny and Sonny declining to smile back. Overcome with anguish over the loss of Sam, Sonny can't bring himself to be reminded of his dalliance with his middle-aged inamorata.

Finally, we see the Farrow family: Jacy and her parents, Gene (Robert Glenn) and Lois (Ellen Burstyn). Later, we learn that Lois and Sam were lovers, and the scene ends with Lois's point of view. From her perspective, we see Sam's casket being lowered creakingly into the earth. Then in a tender, lingering close-up, Lois punctuates her tears with a heavy sigh and shake of the head. She walks off in a wide shot—the first in the scene—as the others slowly scatter.

It is tempting to look at Bogdanovich's next film—*What's Up, Doc?*—as a peace offering to his rapidly growing audience: after putting them through the wringer with *Targets* and especially *The Last Picture Show,* he seemed determined to give them some belly laughs. A wild screwball comedy starring Ryan O'Neal as a dullsville musicologist and Barbra Streisand as wacky gal pal fit the bill.

Having traveled all the way from Iowa to San Francisco to attend a conference with his fellow musicologists, Howard Bannister (O'Neal), wearing a seersucker suit and a scowl and toting a plaid overnight case stuffed with igneous rocks, looks glumly bewildered as he waits for a cab. The rocks' ancient music-making properties are the subject of Howard's research, but their real purpose in the screenplay by Buck Henry, Robert Benton, and David Newman (taking off from a story by Bogdanovich) is as a metaphor for an academician weighed down by unwanted obligations. Foremost among these obligations is Howard's demanding, completely unlovable fiancée, Eunice Burns (Madeline Kahn), who when she is not scolding her intended is babying him in her high-pitched shriek of a voice. For example, even as Eunice counsels Howard to project manly virility when he meets Dr. Frederick Larrabee (Austin Pendleton)—the head honcho of a foundation that will award a $20,000 grant to a winning musicologist—she is tying his bowtie for him.

Howard first encounters wily, winsome Judy Maxwell (Streisand) at the drugstore inside the hotel where Howard and Eunice are staying. Emerging from behind some shelving, she asks, "What's up, Doc?"—but the question sounds more like a pass than a Bugs Bunny line. We already know that she is a one-woman wrecking crew: in an earlier scene, two motorcycles collide with each other as she innocently trots across the street. Yet we feel that Howard could benefit from a dose of character-building chaos. Tellingly, he wanders into the drugstore in search of aspirin to soothe a headache, but—in a good omen—he exits pain free, as if Judy's presence, while destructive, functions as a kind of elixir.

Judy has already started presenting herself as Howard's wife—a bit of wish fulfillment and a reminder that it is often the girls, not the guys, who do the romantic pursuing in Bogdanovich's films. Later that evening at Dr. Larrabee's dinner party, having rechristened herself Eunice Burns, or "Burnsy," Judy charms the pants off of the good doctor, in the process elevating Howard from dark horse to shoo-in to get the $20,000. The real Eunice has been delayed, and although Howard has grown increasingly petrified of her imminent arrival, at a key moment he elects to keep the charade going. At last, Eunice puts in an appearance—kicking, screaming, and insisting on the veracity of her identity—and the camera moves in on Howard: "I never saw her before in my life." Is it really a choice? Good times with Judy and big bucks from Dr. Larrabee or . . . what? Eunice? ("That's a person called Eunice?" Judy says earlier, as though the name itself is unpalatable.)

Of course, the deck is stacked. With brick-red hair and a wardrobe of housedresses, Kahn arguably makes one of the least-alluring screen debuts in history—not that the screenplay gives her much to work with in the sexiness department. At one point, we find her reading a book with the title *The Sensuous Woman* (for pointers?) before disgustedly putting it down.

The simple truth is that Eunice does not stand a chance next to Judy, and Streisand—covered up in a trench coat and cap at first—grows ever more sultry as the film goes on. The morning after inciting a disastrous chain of mishaps that culminates in the fire brigade being summoned to the hotel, Judy reveals herself to Howard—like a genie springing from a bottle—from underneath a sheet covering a piano. In the film's most romantic scene, Howard plays as Judy sings a slow rendition of "As Time Goes By." They end up on the floor together, the result of Judy trying to lay a kiss on Howard and Howard backing off, but for once it does not seem like another Bogdanovich pratfall. Really, it's almost as romantic as anything in *Casablanca.*

Of course, affaire de Howard and Judy is set against a serpentine backstory involving three other plaid overnight cases, each one of which gets confused with the other and all of which are being sought by a gallery of rogues, including an investigative reporter (Michael Murphy), a jewel thief (Sorrell Booke), and a government agent (Phil Roth). Everyone is tailing everyone else before the threads converge in a breakneck chase snaking through San Francisco. Near the end, a benevolent judge (Liam Dunn) is tasked with making sense of it all, but he would have saved himself a lot of aggravation had he bothered to ask if his own daughter—naturally, soon revealed to be Judy—was involved. By this point, however, Howard has realized that the unequivocal love she offers, even with its attendant danger, is just what the doctor—the doc?—ordered.

In some ways, *What's Up, Doc?* was even more old-fashioned than *The Last Picture Show;* it concerned itself with nothing but good clean fun. "This would have been heresy a few years ago, and it still may be," noted *Variety,* "but Peter Bogdanovich describes his latest (and third) feature,

'What's Up, Doc?,' as a 'G-rated screwball comedy without any socially redeeming values.'"[18] Heresy maybe, but a hit definitely. Save *The Godfather* and *The Poseidon Adventure,* no film made more money in 1972 than *What's Up, Doc?*. Even more significantly, it was beloved by the audiences who came to see it in droves.

New York Times critic Vincent Canby sarcastically observed that "the real mean age" of the audience he saw the film with at Radio City Music Hall was "about fifty-two and three months,"[19] but that is surely an exaggeration. After all, a few weeks after the film opened, Warner Bros. took out an ad in *Variety* announcing the attainment of a record that could have been achieved only with the help of an audience consisting of all age groups: a "new single-day all-time record" of $65,398 for the Music Hall.[20]

But what would be wrong if the film *did* speak to an older generation? When I was seventeen, I went to a revival screening of George Sidney's film version of Rodgers and Hart's musical *Pal Joey,* starring Frank Sinatra and Rita Hayworth, and after it was over, I found myself exiting the theater amid a sea of retirees. Not far from me was a husband and wife of perhaps eighty, and it occurred to me that they could very possibly have seen *Pal Joey* when it opened in October 1957! I lingered for a moment on the sidewalk and tried not to be too obvious as I listened to their conversation.

"That's the kind of movie that puts a spring in your step," the husband said.

"They don't make them like that anymore," the wife replied.

It was all I could do not to interrupt and concur that step-springing movies like *Pal Joey* were indeed a thing of the past—that is, unless Peter Bogdanovich was on the set to say "action" and "cut." He is a much better director than George Sidney, too.

"In the American cinema, he is the man of the hour," said one writer soon before the release of *What's Up, Doc?*,[21] and when *Paper Moon* was released in the spring of 1973, that hour was extended. Little more than a year had passed since *Doc* and only eighteen months since *The Last Picture Show,* but here was Peter Bogdanovich again—back in theaters with a smash.

This was no everyday occurrence. To put it into context, imagine that *Citizen Kane* had been a blockbuster and that Orson Welles followed it with two additional films of comparable critical and popular appeal—all in the space of less than three years. You might interject that *Citizen Kane* was a work of Important Cinema, whereas *The Last Picture Show, What's Up, Doc?,* and *Paper Moon* were . . . what, exactly? Granting that *Doc* was conceived and marketed as an overtly commercial work ("A screwball comedy. Remember them?" read the tagline), the remaining two-thirds of the triad fell somewhere in the middle of the highbrow–lowbrow spectrum: impeccably made and morally serious films that were nonetheless completely accessible.

Welles himself had the right idea when in conversation with Bogdanovich he labeled his young friend "a popular artist." At first, Bogdanovich bristled at the designation, but Welles explained that it was intended as a compliment. "*Shakespeare* was a popular artist. *Dickens* was a popular artist," Welles said. "The artists I personally have always enjoyed the *most* are popular artists."[22] Later, when several of Bogdanovich's films started to struggle commercially, he *remained* "a popular artist": they never failed with audiences for lack of trying. Bogdanovich *always* invited the strangers in the dark to see themselves in the story he was telling—even if, on occasion, only a handful of strangers showed up because of problems in marketing or distribution or both.

Before Bogdanovich agreed to direct *Paper Moon,* he came close to pulling off what would have been his greatest feat: to go along with his coming-of-age drama and his screwball comedy, he planned to direct a Western of unusual ambition. The news was heralded on the front page of *Variety* in February 1972: "Superstar western planned by Peter Bogdanovich for first of three pix for Warner Bros. will be his own original script, 'The Streets of Laredo' . . . with cast including John Wayne, James Stewart, Henry Fonda, Ryan O'Neal, Ben Johnson, Cybill Shepherd, and the Clancy Bros., Irish singing group."[23] After John Wayne got cold feet, and Bogdanovich saw no point in recasting a role conceived for a legend, the project was over—although the coauthor of the screenplay, Larry McMurtry, eventually spun a Pulitzer Prize–winning novel, *Lonesome Dove,* out of the material.

So Bogdanovich made *Paper Moon*—and as replacements go, he could have done much worse. An adaptation of Joe David Brown's novel *Addie Pray,* the film is—not unlike *What's Up, Doc?*—the story of one person in pursuit of another. Having made up her mind that lying, cheating, paternity-denying scalawag Moses Pray (Ryan O'Neal) is her father, orphaned eight-year-old Addie Loggins (Tatum O'Neal) spends the entire film trying to win his affection. *Paper Moon* takes the unfashionable but entirely convincing position that a daughter needs a father. That Moses is such a scoundrel certainly complicates the film's current of patriarchy. But for Addie, any father—even one as unreliable as Moses—is better than none at all.

Of course, it is clear from the start that Moses leaves a great deal to be desired. He meets his purported daughter for the first time at the burial of her mother, a prostitute with whom he had a liaison. Standing with Addie at the gravesite are a minister with a voice that hymns were written for ("Rock of Ages" is sung at the makeshift service) and a coterie of kind-hearted old ladies who stew over what will become of Addie. Pointedly, Moses is not among the initial mourners. He shows his face late, bearing flowers pilfered from a nearby tombstone, and initially hesitates when it is suggested that he look after Addie until she can catch a train to St. Joseph, Missouri, where a distant relative is said to live. With his cheap suit, wide-brim hat, and insincere smile, the character is quickly, and brilliantly, sketched by Bogdanovich and O'Neal.

Not long after Moses has been shamed into caring for Addie, we learn how he puts food on the table: as the proprietor of the respectable-sounding Kansas Bible Company, he pawns copies of the Good Book to poor souls who have never placed an order in the first place. Scouring newspaper obituaries, he shows up at the doors of women recently widowed, claims that a late husband had ordered a customized Bible, and insists that a balance is due. The moment when Addie realizes what Moses is up to is a gem of visual storytelling. Waiting in the car while Moses does his usual song and dance for a widow named Pearl, Addie spots a folded newspaper in the driver's seat. The name "Pearl" is circled in Pearl's husband's obituary, and when Addie snoops around in a trunk, she finds a stamp-and-ink set used to personalize the Bibles. The look of revulsion on Tatum O'Neal's face as she puts it all together is not only very funny but reflects her character's fundamental goodness.

Of course, Addie soon becomes Moses's willing and energetic partner, pulling off quick-change maneuvers in front of unsuspecting dime-store cashiers, but she also injects an element of fairness into their schemes. For example, Addie assesses the socioeconomic status of their dupes before determining how much is to be charged for a given Bible. A well-fed elderly woman clutching a strand of fat pearls ought to pay more; a gaunt mother surrounded by a half-dozen scrawny children will get a discount.

In fact, we feel that Addie, in teaming up with Moses, is motivated less by nascent criminality than by a fervent wish to be near her sole surviving parent. Having been orphaned once, she cannot let it happen again. Similar motives inspire Addie to outwit a loose woman with whom Moses has shacked up, Trixie Delight (Madeline Kahn, as jiggly as a bowl of Jello in her satin blouse). In a brilliantly orchestrated sequence, Addie frames Trixie in the hotel where Moses has temporarily installed the gang. With the assistance of Trixie's streetwise helpmate Imogene (P. J. Johnson—almost as good as Tatum O'Neal), Addie manages to entice a dopey front-desk clerk (Burton Gilliam, a one-of-kind bit comic player later reused in *At Long Last Love*) to meet Trixie in her room. When Moses finds the two of them in a compromising situation, he dumps Trixie, heartbroken over the betrayal.

Of course, we wish that Addie had a parent worthy of her—one like Byron Orlok or Sam the Lion or even "Frank D. Roosevelt," as Addie calls the thirty-second president of the United States. She goes on and on about FDR—not, we suspect, for his policies or programs but for his warm parental manner. But Addie takes what she can get, and when she is finally deposited in St. Joseph, we understand why she is not tempted by the care of a benevolent relative or the comforts of a normal home: she wants her pa, even if it means a life of crime.

While the characters in *Paper Moon* treat the Bible with a notable lack of reverence—as a floppy black book to be written in and thrown about—few films better or more entertainingly illustrate the Fifth Commandment to honor thy mother *and* thy father.

When Tatum O'Neal won an Academy Award for her performance in *Paper Moon*, her acceptance speech encapsulated the ascent of the film's maker: "All I really want to thank is my director, Peter Bogdanovich, and my father," she said—as though no one else really mattered. Was she wrong or just imprudent?

To be sure, over the course of his first four films, Bogdanovich had assembled a top-flight crew (including cinematographer László Kovács, designer Polly Platt, editor Verna Fields, and production associate Frank Marshall) and a lively group of actors (including both O'Neals, Madeline Kahn, Randy Quaid, Duilio Del Prete, and John Hillerman), and it is impossible to overstate the importance of their contributions. Yet audiences were coming to see the work of one artist, not a collective, and the studios knew that he was their biggest selling point.

When *What's Up, Doc?* opened in New York, the marquee gave the game away, as Bogdanovich later recalled: "The biggest kick I got was seeing my name on the marquee when I hadn't even asked for them to put it there. *My* name circled the marquee: PETER BOGDANOVICH'S COMEDY."[24] The message was loud and clear: the director was the one who mattered to the public. The same thinking accounts for the prominence Bogdanovich was given in the trailers for *What's Up, Doc?* and *Paper Moon* (and later for *Daisy Miller* and *Saint Jack*). There he is, front and center in behind-the-scenes footage—setting up shots, showing his performers how to play a given scene, and generally mugging for the camera.

"Hello," he says to the camera in the trailer for *What's Up, Doc?*, "I'm Peter Bogdanovich"—before pretending to forget the title of "this little picture we're making today." But none of the pictures were "little" as long as this was the guy who was directing them. The trailer for *Daisy Miller*, too, gets mileage out of the evolving Bogdanovich legend. A snippet from *Paper Moon* is shown before a voice-over solemnly intones: "Last year Peter Bogdanovich gave you the moon." We see a shot of the director behind the camera of his latest film, as the voice-over continues: "This year, Peter Bogdanovich has made a movie in color: *Daisy Miller*, starring Cybill Shepherd."

Paper Moon was the inaugural release of the Directors Company, a production company that Paramount Pictures put together for Bogdanovich, Francis Ford Coppola, and William Friedkin, affording them total control over their films if they kept their budgets reasonable. The idea, said studio president Frank Yablans, was to combine "such forceful talents as these with a climate where their creative skills can be utilized to their highest degrees."[25] Well, Coppola's contribution to the Directors Company was the interesting but commercially underwhelming film *The Conversation*, and Friedkin departed before making a film. In the end, *Paper Moon* was by far the transitory company's biggest hit.

Of course, there is more to Bogdanovich's story than the triumphant narrative sketched here so far: films that didn't go over with the public, films that were recut by studios, and even films that never found their way to the screen. In his book of interviews with directors, *Who the Devil Made It*, Bogdanovich quotes Josef von Sternberg on the subject of careers that start off smashingly but don't proceed as planned: "Yes, but there were a few pages after that."[26] And so there were for Bogdanovich.

Peter Bogdanovich directing Cybill Shepherd in *The Last Picture Show*. Courtesy Jerry Ohlinger's Movie Material Store.

But it was not only his career—fabled and fascinating as it was—that intrigued me. My mother, a movie buff, first told me about him, but she was aware of him mostly for his personal life, having followed his relationship with Cybill Shepherd—front and center in the media in the 1970s—which hastened the end of his marriage to Polly Platt. In fact, after I had seen *The Last Picture Show*, my mother proudly informed me that she had purchased the very issue of *Glamour* magazine in which Bogdanovich had reportedly first seen Shepherd's likeness. He was stumped about who to cast in the role of Jacy Farrow in *The Last Picture Show* and then he saw . . . well, the rest is history.

For my mother and eventually for me, the man who went on to live with the *Glamour* girl in a beautifully appointed house nestled in Bel Air was inseparable from the man who made the movies. When I was a teenager, I was a fan of many American films made in the 1970s—that was why my mother suggested I see Peter Bogdanovich's—but few of their directors had lives I actually wanted to live. Sure, I liked *The Last Detail*, but I could scarcely comprehend Hal Ashby's counterculture lifestyle. And I loved *Close Encounters of the Third Kind,* but I could not really connect with Steven Spielberg's nerdy obsession with film technology.

It was different with Peter Bogdanovich, whose life—especially up to the point we have reached so far, the release of *Paper Moon*—seemed both conventional enough to relate to and opulent enough to aspire to. Coming of age in Manhattan, he benefitted from his not-wealthy parents' willingness to scrimp and save in order to send him to the pricey Collegiate School and "a snazzy boys' camp," as he once put it,[27] as well as from their backing when it came to his artistic interests. In *Who the Devil Made It,* he wrote of the things he was taken to as a boy, including operas at the Met, shows on- and off-Broadway, and silent movies at the Museum of Modern Art.[28] The last item on the list is most crucial, but not for the obvious reason. Because many of the movies he and his father took in at the museum were silent, he explained, "seeing these pictures gave me also a better connection to, and understanding of, my father's past." He continued, "Which is why the young people's rejection of old movies . . . is also a rejection of family values and respect for age."[29]

Well, would any of his peers harp on the need for family values or bemoan a lack of respect for age? Doubtful. By contrast, it seemed to me, Peter Bogdanovich was cut from a different, more clean-living cloth—in spite of his transgressions. Yes, his marriage to Polly Platt was wrecked in the wake of his affair with Cybill Shepherd, but those facts alone don't tell the tale. His diaries from the mid- and late 1960s evince overwhelming tenderness for his wife, unconditional love for their two young children, Antonia and Alexandra, as well as surprising comfort with the pleasures of domesticity. That he was nuts about Shepherd threw a monkey wrench into what had been, to that point, an admirably conducted life, but it is a feeling comprehensible to anyone who has been swept off his or her feet. As Judy says in *What's Up, Doc?,* "Listen, you can't fight a tidal wave." Decades later, Bogdanovich struck a more sober tone: "I'd been a faithful husband for nine years, but I now felt powerless to stop the momentum." To put it another way, there were good times to be had with Shepherd, but they came at a cost. "I know my daughters have suffered," he added, "and I have tried to make up for it ever since."[30]

At least he looked back on the romance (and its fallout) with appropriately mixed emotions—and, besides, what is one divorce in Hollywood? My admiration for him was undiminished. For the most part, in the 1970s

Peter Bogdanovich was having a grand time the old-fashioned way. His services were required to fashion a montage in tribute to Charlie Chaplin at the Academy Awards in 1972. He got a call to host *The Tonight Show* when Johnny Carson was away. He concocted a musical inspired by a book of Cole Porter lyrics that Cybill Shepherd happened to give him one Christmas. In *Easy Riders, Raging Bulls,* Peter Biskind paints the following picture of Peter Bogdanovich in this period: "He had become a bit of a dandy, wearing candy-striped shirts with white collars, occasionally improved by an ascot. He sported a gold signet ring with his initials on it. He relished invitations to the White House, didn't mind a bit that it was Nixon who was doing the inviting."[31] If Biskind is trying to be sarcastic in this passage, he fails, at least as far as I am concerned. (He also gets one detail wrong: Bogdanovich wears a bandana, not—as widely reported—an ascot.) I don't know about you, but all of this sounded pretty good to me, including the visit to the Nixon White House. *What is so bad about that?* I thought. *My parents voted for Nixon in '72.*

Politics? Not for him. In fact, he chastised those "politically minded" stars who declined to attend the American Film Institute's tribute to John Ford due to Nixon's presence there. "Jane Fonda, I believe, even picketed," he wrote a few years later. "But then, that was her main occupation those days, as well as her privilege, though one might wish she would stop mixing politics with art quite so ferociously."[32] He thus shared the dismissive attitude toward youthful protest that Judy expresses in *What's Up, Doc?* After learning that Judy has been kicked out of college for blowing up a classroom, Howard asks, with a hint of concern, "Political activism?" "No," she corrects him. "Chemistry major."

In his documentary *Directed by John Ford,* there is a justly famous sequence in which Bogdanovich is heard firing questions at the director of *Stagecoach* and *The Searchers,* who is posed in front of a vista in Monument Valley but is in no mood to answer. I always loved one question in particular: "Would you agree that the point of *Fort Apache,*" he asks, "was that the tradition of the army was more important than one individual?" Well, as both Bogdanovich and Ford knew, there is more than this to *Fort Apache,* but still . . . even to ask such a question is so wonderfully out of touch with the zeitgeist of the early 1970s! "The tradition of the army"—what a phrase!

Better still are Bogdanovich's on-screen conversations with Ford's frequent collaborators, John Wayne, Jimmy Stewart, and Henry Fonda.

Peter Bogdanovich shows Ryan O'Neal how it's done on the set of *What's Up, Doc?* Courtesy Jerry Ohlinger's Movie Material Store.

Their thoughts are, of course, wonderfully insightful, but equally instructive are the glimpses we get of a youthful, dark-haired Bogdanovich, seen in over-the-shoulder shots at the edge of the frame before the camera moves in on the interview subjects—the slow dolly in being one of his signature visual tropes here and throughout his work. As Wayne tells an anecdote or Stewart cracks a joke, we see Bogdanovich chuckle, as if to confirm how close he is—how sympathetic, how understanding—to these men, each of whom is old enough to be his father.

Wrote journalist Tad Friend in a *New Yorker* profile of Bogdanovich in 2002: "His films transported audiences to a time before drugs, race riots, and polyester pants—a time when you drove your jalopy with high hopes to the spring dance."[33] It is right to emphasize his films' nostalgic disposition, which comes across in offhand, incidental details such as the radios playing Hank Williams's song "Kaw-Liga" in *The Last Picture Show* and the copies of the *Saturday Evening Post* hovered over by characters in *Nickelodeon.* But he was no tortured soul finding distraction from life's miseries by making escapist fare: Peter Bogdanovich was, at this point in his life, as footloose and fancy free as his films were. As proof, consider a wonderful publicity still from *What's Up, Doc?*: on one side is Bogdanovich—smartly dressed in one of those candy-striped shirts Biskind mentions—acting out a scene for Ryan O'Neal, and on the other is O'Neal imitating him precisely. Why do I suspect that Bogdanovich would have been perfectly happy if O'Neal had called it a day and allowed the director himself to do the part?

The differences between Peter Bogdanovich and me were not insignificant. He had been a teenager in Manhattan in the 1950s; I was a teenager in Ohio in the 1990s and early 2000s. His father was a painter; my father was a banker. He had a younger sister; I had a younger brother. Undaunted, I followed in his footsteps as best I could. When I read in his book of interviews *This Is Orson Welles* that he was sixteen when he first saw *Citizen Kane,* I promised myself that I would see the film at the same age and preferably under similar conditions: in a musty old theater on a midweek afternoon, with the sound of raindrops gently tap-tap-tapping on the rooftop. Later, when I began interviewing him, I never asked if his first experience with *Citizen Kane* was anything like what I imagined it to be. What if I had it wrong? Could I stand the disappointment?

I was already fifteen and a half when I made my vow to see *Citizen Kane* at sixteen. I scanned the movie listings in the newspaper, hoping against hope to read that a print of *Citizen Kane* would be shown somewhere near where I lived. But I was fast running out of time, and when I saw that the film was going to air on the local public-television station one evening, I decided to sit down and watch. I had told my plans to my father, who wondered why I gave up on them so quickly. I said that Peter Bogdanovich would understand: it was important to see *Citizen Kane* as soon as humanly possible.

At some point, I learned that Bogdanovich had not actually graduated from the Collegiate School, where he had made such an impression with his column "As We See It." "He left high school at sixteen years of age without a diploma, because of a failed algebra exam," the author Andrew Yule writes in his biography *Picture Shows: The Life and Films of Peter Bogdanovich.* "At the graduation ceremony he was still duly summoned and solemnly presented with a bulky, face-saving envelope, just like the graduates. On opening it later, he found it contained a blank chunk of cardboard."[34] Well, my interest in movies outweighed my interest in homework—especially algebra—too.

In fact, history was repeating itself—as I now sought to emulate him, he had once sought to emulate others. "I just wanted to be like those people on the screen," he said to an interviewer in 1972. "I didn't think about their private lives or what it was like to have all that money. I just wanted to be the people. I wanted to look like Bill Holden, because I wanted to be a real American boy, and do all those wonderful things. And with a name like Bogdanovich, there wasn't much of a chance. I wanted my name to be Jim."[35] I was a step ahead of him for a change: at least we had the same first name.

It took three tries, but we finally connected on Thanksgiving Eve in 2003. I wondered how much his assistant had actually told him about what I was doing—I had explained to her in some detail that the article I was writing would focus on his lesser-known films, but such things have a way of getting lost in translation—because he seemed pleasantly surprised when my first questions were concerned with *They All Laughed,* his most personal film, an ebullient look at lovers and love affairs, shot in his hometown and peopled with some of his favorite performers, including Ben Gazzara, Audrey Hepburn, John Ritter, and Dorothy Stratten. My singular focus on this film was, I confess, partly by design: I knew how highly he thought of *They All Laughed* and that he was rarely asked about it. Because I had studied him so intently and sought to model myself on him so closely, when I finally had a chance to talk to him, I knew how to push his buttons.

Later in our conversation, he said, responding to a comment I made about the film, "*They All Laughed* was my best picture." Pause. Did he wonder if I would agree with such a statement? Without thinking about it, I said, "I think so, too"—though I instantly regretted blurting out the words so quickly. In rushing to share such an unconventional opinion, I feared appearing insincere, which I certainly was *not.* I adored *They All Laughed*—it was and remains my favorite film of his—even if I had calculated that asking him about it first, before *The Last Picture Show* or *What's Up, Doc?* or *Paper Moon,* would get us off on the right foot.

I quickly turned my agreement into a question.

"So, it's *your* personal favorite?" I asked, somewhat meekly.

"Oh God, yeah," he said. "By miles."

I moved on, upping the ante by prodding him to talk about his visual style—another topic I knew he felt passionately about, but most critics ignored. His photography is not flashy like Orson Welles's or picture-postcard perfect like David Lean's, but it is oh so very *purposeful.* If he dollies in here, he means to say, "Pay attention—what she is about to say is important"; if he cuts to a wide shot there, he means to say, "Look closely—this may be the end or the beginning of something."

Because he is partial to deep-focus photography, the care he puts into his images is always in evidence. Everything in the frame is sharply rendered for all to see; there are no soft areas for him to ignore. A good illustration is found in *Texasville,* the sequel to *The Last Picture Show,* in which even over-the-shoulder shots are remarkably clear and distinct; in some angles, it seems as though we see every strand of hair on the back of Jeff Bridges's head. And in *Noises Off,* his hilarious film version of Michael Frayn's farce about a maladroit theatrical troupe, one striking shot begins with six or seven people standing on a stage during a rehearsal. As most of them file out onto the stage, going to their places, the camera shifts to a two-shot with the show's beside-himself director (Michael Caine) and one of his stars (Marilu Henner) as they gossip. In a swift camera move, we are taken from a public world to a private one. To borrow what director Wes Anderson said of another shot in another of Bogdanovich's movies: "It's kind of stagey, but you don't mind at all because it's such an elegant idea."[36]

After a few questions on these topics, Bogdanovich expressed his appreciation.

"Nobody ever notices things like that, Peter," he said. "None of the critics ever write about that kind of stuff, but to me that's all about filmmaking."

"I haven't read too many interviews where you're asked about things like this, either," I said.

"They don't have a clue. All they can do is ask me who I was doing an homage to."

"I don't think I've asked a single question about that!"

"Thank you very much—I noticed."

Behind each shot in a Peter Bogdanovich film is a particular perspective. He did not invent the so-called shot reverse shot—that is, a shot of a character having a look at a particular person or thing and then a shot of that particular person or thing—but he took it to the *n*th degree. Think of the moment in *Mask* in which a close-up of Rusty Dennis (Cher) is intercut every few seconds with a medium shot of her intermittent boyfriend,

Gar (Sam Elliott), as he rides his motorcycle past her. Cher's head moves as Elliott speeds by, as does the camera when showing her angle of him. As an example of montage, this scene would have been the envy of Eisenstein—or Hitchcock. In fact, it often seems as though Bogdanovich took the principle at work in Hitchcock's *Rear Window*—with all of those close-ups of wheelchair-bound Jimmy Stewart intercut with wide angles of the devious doings of Raymond Burr—and applied it writ large. "Most pictures don't have a point of view in scenes," Bogdanovich complained. "They just have shots."[37] Not his.

One of the best examples of looking and reacting in his films is found in a scene in the film that followed *Paper Moon,* the underappreciated *Daisy Miller.* Adapted from the short novel by Henry James, the story concerns a pair of Americans whiling away their days in nineteenth-century Europe. Although Frederick Winterbourne (Barry Brown) is beguiled by Annie P. "Daisy" Miller (Cybill Shepherd)—of Schenectady, New York—he misapprehends her character: Daisy affects a flirtatious manner in order to incite jealousy in Winterbourne and thus win his hand. In the process, however, she burnishes a reputation as a heedless, careless foreigner—and thus turns off her would-be beau.

Things do not end well for either one of them, but we get a glimpse of what might have been when early in the film Daisy sings Winterbourne the song "When You and I Were Young, Maggie." At her family's room in a hotel in Rome, Daisy is accompanied on the piano by her Italian friend Giovanelli (Duilio Del Prete), and we see the two of them in a loosely framed two-shot as she begins to sweetly sing.

At the end of the second line in the song, Bogdanovich cuts to Winterbourne, who is sitting opposite Daisy and Giovanelli. The camera dollies in to a close-up of him. Bogdanovich holds on Winterbourne's rapt-looking face for a long moment before returning to an angle of Daisy and Giovanelli.

As Daisy continues to sing, Bogdanovich again cuts on a line change—finally giving Daisy a close-up of her own when she sings the next lines. The slight distancing effect of the long lens indicates that we are seeing Daisy from Winterbourne's enthralled point of view.

Up to this point, Daisy has been looking in the distance, singing to no one in particular, but on the word *daisies* in the song, she glances toward Winterbourne, and the heavens melt. A very tight close-up of Winterbourne confirms that his eyes and Daisy's have met. Their largely unspoken longing for each other is elegantly evoked in this beautiful ballet of glances.

To watch an entire film made up of such carefully worked-out moments spoiled other films for me—they seemed so slovenly by comparison. When Pauline Kael compared Robert Altman's *Nashville* (a great film, no doubt) to a movie orgy, she meant it as a compliment, but what is an orgy but messy and unruly—and so is *Nashville.* Looking at an Altman film after a Bogdanovich film is akin to opening your mouth underwater in a swimming pool: too much, too fast.

In hindsight, though, it is no mystery why *Daisy Miller* broke the streak that began with *The Last Picture Show,* accelerated with *What's Up, Doc?,* and concluded with *Paper Moon.* Although *Daisy Miller* was warmly reviewed in the *New York Times* (critic Vincent Canby called it "something of a triumph for everyone concerned"), and decades later it was included in *The* New York Times *Guide to the Best 1,000 Movies Ever Made,*[38] the film lacked the obvious commercial appeal of Bogdanovich's earlier films. It featured a much less sympathetic group of characters, too. In fact, Winterbourne is flat-out unlikeable—a milksop who is constitutionally incapable of seizing the day. Daisy, of course, is loveliness personified, and, as played by Shepherd, she is not merely a rogue commoner from across the ocean. She has manners, curtsying primly after singing "When You and I Were Young, Maggie," and her hesitation in blatantly pursuing Winterbourne speaks to her propriety.

At the film's end, Daisy is taken ill and perishes, further dimming its box-office chances. Yet the story's tragic turn inspired some of Bogdanovich's finest filmmaking. After learning that Daisy is ailing, Winterbourne enters the lobby of her hotel. The camera stays outside, observing the action that follows through a lace curtain hanging on a door. Winterbourne is halfway up the stairs when a desk clerk rushes over to tell him the news about Daisy—well, we assume that's what he tells him. We can't be certain because the voices are drowned out by Verdi's "La donna e mobile," which is being played by an organ grinder somewhere off-camera. Shell-shocked, Winterbourne turns around and walks toward us, opening the door with the lace curtain and letting it swing quietly back into place.

Just one scene later, Winterbourne is seen standing calmly—too calmly—above Daisy's grave. He even manages to look her intuitive younger brother (James McMurtry—son of Larry) in the eye. In fact,

Bogdanovich seems more affected by the situation than Winterbourne. He grasps, as Winterbourne never will, the gravity of losing a woman like Daisy Miller. The director's camera flees the scene, receding from the graveyard until everything grows dim in a cloud of white smoke—which could easily be mistaken for Daisy's spirit. "I'm a classicist," Bogdanovich told critic Rex Reed, stating the obvious. "I like well-made films with beginnings, middles and ends, in which acting and writing are important instead of camera angles."[39] He seemed to delight in needling his contemporaries for their devotion to faddish film techniques. "I'm afraid it's largely a twentieth-century critical fashion to value originality as the main criterion of a work of art," he wrote in the early 1970s.[40]

Some saw such proclamations as signs of his arrogance, but they were, in truth, merely indicators of his self-assurance. From watching the great films and studying what it was that made them great, he trained himself how to make them. "I think that Peter had so much confidence," Louise Stratten told me, "and that he had such a knowing from a very young age of what he wanted to do and that he was so brilliant at it that he could direct things with his left hand and backwards and with his eyes shut. He could direct circles around so many people."

That confidence—particularly in his ability to tell a story with visuals alone—led him to decline the services of film composers on all but a handful of his films: his images would sink or swim on their own. In the most literal sense of the word, there is a lot of silence in his films. Instead of a full orchestra, we hear the wind in *The Last Picture Show* and the hubbub of a big city in *They All Laughed.* The penultimate scene in *Saint Jack* is startlingly quiet—in the hush of a balmy Singapore night, one man follows another, and the scene's tension is heightened a hundredfold by the absence of extraneous sound effects or ambient noise, let alone music. And perhaps the pivotal scene in *The Cat's Meow* depicts two characters playing a game of charades—silently acting out their feelings for each other.

At the same time, Bogdanovich will find almost any excuse for his characters to listen to the radio or to play a record, allowing him to gracefully fudge his "no music" rule. When watching his films, you stop counting the number of times a car whizzes by and music briefly blasts from a rolled-down window. But the music is fleeting, coming and going with the car, achieving the desired effect (a musical comment on a scene without resorting to a score) ever so quickly.

He occasionally uses the same device to nonmusical ends, as in the first shot of his expertly crafted made-for-television sequel to *To Sir, with Love*, which no less an authority than hard-to-please *New York* magazine television critic John Leonard described as "a bad idea that turned into a pretty good TV movie."[41] In the opening shot of *To Sir, with Love II*, a taxicab carrying Sidney Poitier pulls up and idles in front of the camera just long enough for us to hear a snatch of a radio broadcast: "This is Peter MacIntosh for the BBC in London. The weather forecast today . . . ." The words fade as Poitier's cab drives away, but the locale of the first scene in the film has been clearly and quickly established.

Then came the flops.

Referring to the films that followed Bogdanovich's earlier trio of triumphs, critic David Thomson once wrote, "Three-in-a-row struck back,"[42] and so they did in the form of *Daisy Miller, At Long Last Love,* and *Nickelodeon.* Sure, these films had their stray defenders—*Daisy Miller,* as noted, was admired by several important critics; *At Long Last Love* eventually accumulated a devoted following, including Roger Ebert and Woody Allen; and *Nickelodeon* did acceptable business. But what of the man who just a few years earlier had made millions laugh and cry?

Well, he was there, all right, and that was part of the problem: *At Long Last Love* and *Nickelodeon,* in particular, were the most personal projects he had yet undertaken, the former his first original screenplay since *Targets* and the latter his long-promised story of filmdom's origins. They were inward-looking films, not readily accessible to the masses in the manner of their predecessors, but if some audiences yawned, that didn't make these films any less revealing.

Set in the Manhattan of the 1930s, *At Long Last Love* uses the songs of Cole Porter—including "You're the Top," "From Alpha to Omega," and "Find Me a Primitive Man"—to tell of the romantic dalliances of four strangers whose paths cross: an idle scion (Burt Reynolds), an heiress with a cash-flow problem (Cybill Shepherd), an Italian émigré who has come to America to make a million (Duilio Del Prete), and a brassy singer (Madeline Kahn). The film unfolds in a succession of nightclubs, country clubs, movie palaces, and palatial estates. Some of the characters are better off than others, as fortunes are made, lost, and reacquired over the course of the story, and the emphasis on the finer things in life is undeniable. The stock-market crash is treated as comic fodder, and the lower orders are represented almost exclusively by an indecorous maid (Eileen Brennan), a straight-laced butler (John Hillerman), and an acerbic doorman (M. Emmet Walsh), none of whom seems to be sweating it.

The sets and costumes—rendered in inky black-and-white by production designer Gene Allen and costume designer Bobbie Mannix, but photographed in creamy color by László Kovács—resemble a live-action version of a cartoon panel by Peter Arno of the *New Yorker*. For some viewers, the results were unappealing. Critic Barry Putterman, in an otherwise sympathetic account of Bogdanovich's career in the second volume of the great auteurist survey *American Directors,* wrote of the film's "extremely icy detachment"—a not uncommon view.[43] Bogdanovich may have been celebrating wealth, but he did so not because he felt entitled to it, but because he hadn't always had it. In another context, he once quoted Cary Grant about the joys of staying at a hotel with all expenses paid: "The first thing you must do," Grant told Bogdanovich, "is kick off your *shoes* and let a lot of minions pick them up!" The remark, Bogdanovich wrote, spoke volumes about Grant—and, perhaps, about himself: "Only someone who had to earn this comfort through hard or intense labor would make that sort of comment."[44] Similarly, *At Long Last Love* conjures a world of affluence and leisure in part because its writer-director finally had a taste of such things. After years of striving, didn't he have a right to screen out poverty and drudgery? Even the name of the film's production company reflected Bogdanovich's ascent: Copa de Oro (Cup of Gold), after the street in Bel Air on which his house sat.

At Long Last Love has nothing of the hurried, racing feel of Bogdanovich's other Depression-era comedy, *Paper Moon,* in which the just-scraping-by characters are always on the run—an appropriate choice because, as abstract expressionist Willem de Kooning is supposed to have said, "the trouble with being poor is that it takes up all your time." By contrast, Michael (Reynolds), Brooke (Shepherd), Johnny (Del Prete), and Kitty (Kahn) have nothing *but* time, and they fill it by frequenting the racetrack, driving drunk after a night of dancing, and going shopping at Lord & Taylor. The film's extraordinarily long takes not only capture the cast's spirited live singing and dancing in real time but also a sense of living without pressure or deadlines. Take the scene in which Michael and Kitty sing "You're the Top" in his high-rise apartment—following the song's prominent use in *What's Up, Doc?,* it was now something of an anthem in the films of Peter Bogdanovich: the shot begins on a close-up of champagne glasses on a tray, follows Rodney as he brings the drinks into the living room—where Michael and Kitty sit, hands entwined, on a sofa—and continues as the twosome start to move, dollying in or dollying out as the choreography permits. No cut? No hurry.

Yet Bogdanovich insists that even those who have everything are in need of something more—as Brooke says, plaintively, "What's a million dollars without love?" Although Brooke likes Michael and Kitty likes Johnny, Michael likes Kitty and Johnny likes Brooke—a state of romantic dissatisfaction beautifully evoked in "I Loved Him (but He Didn't Love Me)," which Brooke sings about Michael and Kitty sings about Johnny during a long walk in what is supposed to be a gorgeously green Central Park.

The song repeated most often throughout the film is indeed "You're the Top," but the story's actual theme is best expressed in "Friendship." In spite of their differences, the characters come to bravely accept their unhappiness, emerging as chums at the Old 400 dance that concludes the film. There, in a magical moment, the men find themselves dancing with their ideal mate—Michael with Kitty and Johnny with Brooke—before a bandleader commands them to "change partners!" The couples oblige, the women resigning themselves to their fate. "I think she's more lovely now than ever I see her," Johnny tells Kitty of Brooke, who replies with a tight-lipped "Yup." "I think she's more beautiful now than I've ever seen," Michael tells Brooke of Kitty, who replies with an even more tight-lipped "Mm-hmm." To improve upon a line by F. Scott Fitzgerald: *And so they waltz on, borne back ceaselessly . . . into the penthouse.*

In its own way, *Nickelodeon* was as show-offy as *At Long Last Love:* in telling of the evolution of moviemaking, the story stopped in its tracks in 1915, the year of the premiere of *The Birth of a Nation*—because Bogdanovich himself stopped there. "Ford, Hawks, Dwan, and these other directors have already done everything, and *they* were all influenced by Griffith," he told interviewers Eric Sherman and Martin Rubin in 1968. "Unless you're some sort of primitive talent, you have to know the history of what came before to be any good."[45]

In its original conception, as Bogdanovich described it to Sherman and Rubin, the project was to be set in Hollywood "from 1909 to the present" and had at its center "a Dwan-Griffith-like figure,"[46] but when he finally made *Nickelodeon*, he had whittled down the time period to 1910 to 1915. The film, then, would chart the glory days of the silent film: its guileless beginnings up to its arrival as an art form to be reckoned with. There were solid dramatic reasons for the decision, but also personal ones: Bogdanovich would celebrate *those* days because they were the ones *he* found most useful and inspiring.

The film centers on Leo Harrigan (Ryan O'Neal), a meek attorney who—following a series of accidents and misunderstandings—is put to work for studio boss H. H. Cobb (Brian Keith). Leo starts off as a scenarist before being recruited to take over for a director on location in rural California. He is reassured by cameraman Frank Frank (John Ritter) that the job demands little: "It's okay—any idiot can direct."

In fact, Leo cottons to directing, but not because he thinks he is making art. Instead, the former attorney is charmed by the misfits and amateurs who make up his cast and crew, including Frank, leading man Buck Greenway (Burt Reynolds), leading lady Marty (Stella Stevens), and juvenile script doctor Alice (Tatum O'Neal). And he is positively *smitten* with Kathleen Cooke (Jane Hitchcock), an aspiring actress who is the gang's newest initiate. A romance develops between Leo and Kathleen—later becoming a love triangle involving Leo, Buck, and Kathleen—that has a simplicity and sweetness echoing the best of silent cinema.

In fact, Leo and Kathleen's first meeting is a sentimentalized version of the meet cute in *What's Up, Doc?* Again, Ryan O'Neal finds himself hounded by a persistent woman. The difference? Where Barbra Streisand is bossy, Jane Hitchcock is bewitching. In the scene, Leo is about to step off a trolley car, in which he has just concluded what amounts to his first story conference with Cobb, when Kathleen steps aboard and stumbles. Leo, having dropped the contents of his suitcase inside the car, does not see Kathleen on the floor, although she spots him. Kathleen, we learn momentarily, is "blind as a rat," so her point-of-view shot of Leo (seen gathering up his things in a hurry) is appropriately fuzzy. Leo rushes past Kathleen, tuning out her repeated cries of "I beg your pardon" until after he has gotten off the car. She rushes to a window and asks if he is all right. Leo, mumbling to himself, stops in midstride. Kathleen asks, "What?" Leo says, "Lollapalooza"—Cobb had earlier asked that Leo's story be "a real lollapalooza"—and then, "Hello." The two speak for several moments until the car begins to pull away, the camera irising-out on Jane Hitchcock's face as it grows tinier and tinier. This time, Ryan O'Neal wants—rather than flees from—the girl.

For much of its duration, *Nickelodeon* is an appealing episodic comedy, recounting the haphazard means by which movies used to be made (e.g., story lines were tailored to what material was shot rather than the other way around) and the equally unplanned ways in which they were exhibited (e.g., a movie's reels were shown out of order and in combination with those from other movies). Many of the incidents are modeled on tales relayed to Bogdanovich by such directors as Allan Dwan, Leo McCarey (for whom Leo Harrigan is named), and Raoul Walsh. But the film ends up achieving a certain heft as it steadily builds toward one of the great scenes in Bogdanovich's filmography: the premiere on February 8, 1915, of D. W. Griffith's *The Birth of a Nation,* the artistry and scope of which leaves Leo simultaneously inspired and depressed. He is inspired because he recognizes the significance and power of *The Birth of a Nation* and depressed because he *also* knows that his middling one- and two-reelers do not deserve to be mentioned in the same breath.

In excerpting passages of *The Birth of a Nation* in *Nickelodeon,* Bogdanovich chose not to focus on the earlier film's virulent racism. Instead, he shows clips of its rousing battle scene and, in an impressive director's cut of *Nickelodeon* that also shifted the film from color to black-and-white, the indisputably great scene in which the Little Colonel (Henry B. Walthall) arrives home and is met by his sister (Mae Marsh) on their front porch. The relatives' delight at seeing each other turns somber when each actor gazes sadly into the distance. With its bittersweet tone—not to mention its moments of characters looking at and away from each other—this is a most Bogdanovichesque of scenes, even though it was directed by D. W. Griffith.

When *The Birth of a Nation* ends in *Nickelodeon,* Griffith takes the stage, and Leo—like everyone else—applauds enthusiastically. Yet as he rides home from the premiere, it is not his newfound artistic aspirations but his nostalgia for the camaraderie of making movies that convinces him to persist in his crazy trade.

Riding with Leo is the old troupe: Buck, Kathleen, and Frank, along with little Alice, who is driving. Most had gone their separate ways until being reunited for the premiere of Griffith's epic. "Might as well quit. Best damn picture that's ever going to be made has already been made," Leo says, referring to *The Birth of a Nation.* "I'm sick of this racket anyway. Get up at dawn, work all day, every night, six days a week."

Commiserating with him, Buck quickly agrees, but then Alice spots a glimmer of light in the darkness: a greenhouse converted into a movie studio, in which a World War I adventure is being shot. She stops the car and says, "Look at that," to which Leo pipes in, wistfully: "They're shooting a picture." Shooting a picture—is there a better way to spend a life? As they drive off, they bounce ideas off of each other . . . the moviemaking will go on, we feel, into the 1920s and perhaps even the 1930s.

In hindsight, both *At Long Last Love* and *Nickelodeon* were too self-congratulatory—of Bogdanovich's success in life, of his exemplary taste in film—to be large successes, but perhaps such a fate was for the best. If they had been hits, would Bogdanovich have ever taken stock and returned with a follow-up as fascinating as *Saint Jack?* Based on a novel by Paul Theroux, the film is one of Bogdanovich's finest, owing much to the gritty, unadorned style of *Targets.* In fact, the films have the same producer, Roger Corman. They share something else, too: a main character worthy of our admiration. Like Byron Orlok in *Targets,* Jack Flowers (Ben Gazzara) in *Saint Jack* is a virtuous figure in a corrupt world. Of course, the great irony of the story is that Jack is an American-born pimp who in the latter days of the Vietnam War makes Singapore his home. When we first meet him, Jack seems more like a rogue than a hero—we grin at his endless barking of orders to underlings and superiors alike and his sincere desire that his paying customers have a good time.

But make no mistake: in Jack's own seedy way, he is as solid, as dependable as Byron Orlok—or Sam the Lion or even John Ford. Jack proves his mettle when a charming CIA agent (Bogdanovich in a devilish performance) offers him $25,000 to surreptitiously photograph an encounter between a muckraking U.S. senator (former James Bond star George Lazenby) and a male prostitute. In a fix and desperate for money—thanks to rival houses of prostitution that have brought his business to an end—Jack goes along with the scheme up to a point but ultimately realizes he cannot go through with it.

Long before the film's genuinely suspenseful finale, though, we know that Jack is one of the good guys. His qualities are especially evident in the friendship he strikes up with a placid British accountant named William Leigh (Denholm Elliott), whose dreams are so different from Jack's: William fancies retiring "to a small Georgian house in the West country," accompanied by his wife and a little pond filled with trout. From their first encounter, Jack handles William kindly—almost gingerly; the Englishman's rackety cough, heard on the first of his three stops in Singapore, suggests some brewing illness. "What is it—your ticker?" Jack asks, afraid, perhaps, of the answer. Howard Hawks referred to some of his own films as "love affairs between two men," but no such love affair in a Hawks film was ever as tender as that between Jack Flowers and William Leigh in *Saint Jack.*

For Jack, William's certain death spells the end of everything decent. Coursing through the film is a tone of longing and regret. Before Jack is to entrap the senator, he waits in a lobby and looks at a wall of clocks displaying times around the globe—he pauses to ponder the time in New York, his hometown, looking pensive and sad. Even when Jack's girlfriend of the moment, Monika (Monika Subramaniam), says, upon parting, "I look for you in Ceylon," it sounds as if she is saying good-bye rather than making a promise for the future. At least Jack has his integrity—as did Bogdanovich, for whom *Saint Jack* was a comeback in miniature. Although the film was never meant to reach the mass audience that had flocked to *The Last Picture Show, What's Up, Doc?,* and *Paper Moon,* it won over critics and tastemakers—receiving the Critics' Prize at the Venice Film Festival, for example—and set the stage for the most significant film of Bogdanovich's career.

On Thanksgiving Eve in 2003, the time flew by, and before I knew it, I told Bogdanovich I had to put a new cassette in my tape recorder. I was prepared to ask one or two more questions and leave it at that.

"I'll tell you what," he said, as I fumbled with the machine, "if you want to talk to me some more on another day—that's okay, you know."

He almost sounded apologetic.

"When would be convenient for you?" I asked.

"I don't know. I have some free time tomorrow, basically, but I don't know how busy you are on Thanksgiving."

Was he kidding? The stuffing and cranberries could wait—I wanted to talk some more to Peter Bogdanovich.

I told him I was not doing anything special and would be available whenever he was. We set a time. He was beyond solicitous—in fact, he was the easiest, most congenial interview subject I had yet encountered in my short career.

As we were about to hang up, he even managed to make me feel a little less funny about calling him from the bleak, snowy Midwest.

"You're in Ohio?" he asked.

How did he know? Had his assistant told him?

"Yes," I said, not volunteering much.

"Where?"

"Columbus."

He repeated "Columbus"—and all I could think was "how far a-way" it was, as the song goes in the Rodgers and Hammerstein musical *South Pacific*.

But he went on: "There's a nice theater marquee there. We used it in *Noises Off*. I didn't go there, but they went and shot it for me. So I haven't been to your hometown."

He was referring to the Ohio Theatre, a 1920s-era movie palace in downtown Columbus that still runs prints of old movies in the summer. It was there that I first saw *Bringing Up Baby, Stagecoach, Strangers on a Train,* and so many others, on glistening 35mm prints—seeing most of them because Peter Bogdanovich had recommended them in books he had written or in interviews he had given. And the Ohio Theatre's marquee does indeed appear briefly in *Noises Off*. (You can be sure that I double-checked as soon as we hung up.) I didn't much care if Peter Bogdanovich had actually *been* here; what gave me a tiny thrill was that *my* theater was in one of *his* films. Two cheers for good old Columbus, Ohio.

He seemed curious about his far-flung fan.

"How old were you when you saw *They All Laughed?*" he asked.

I couldn't remember, but I said I might have been about fourteen.

"Where did you see it?"

Was he conducting audience research? I cringed when I had to tell him I didn't see it in a theater but instead picked it up on videotape—how *amateurish!*

"How interesting," he said, mysteriously. "What made you decide to buy it?"

Good question.

"I must have read about it somewhere," I said, and indeed I had: in an interview with Quentin Tarantino that had appeared some years earlier in the *New York Times Magazine*. "*They All Laughed* is a masterpiece, I think," Tarantino had told the reporter. "It captures a fairy-tale New York. It makes New York look like Paris in the 20's. It makes you want to live there."[47]

The matter resolved, I thanked him again for his time and said how much I looked forward to talking with him again tomorrow—Thanksgiving Day. That's when he said: "You seem to *know* the answers to some of this stuff."

This took me aback. Yes, I had asked questions that I thought he would find engaging and surprising, but they were still *questions.* And his films left me with oodles of them. I began to think that the man who made them was speaking in a secret language that had little to do with characters or plot or even visual style. The language was discernable, but only to those who cared enough to listen for it, and even then . . .

You want questions? I'll give you questions: Why was his production company in the early 1980s called Moon Pictures? Why does the lead character in *Mask* show a preternatural interest in and knowledge of Greek mythology? Why, in describing Audrey Hepburn in an article written in 1999, did Bogdanovich invoke the Irish goddess Brigit? Why does a wannabe songwriter in *The Thing Called Love* recite the poetry of Robert Graves? And what about that calendar? Why, for the better part of the 1990s, did Bogdanovich edit a calendar inspired by Graves's *The White Goddess?* And why in nearly every one of his films are the women always winsome and the men a few steps behind? What was he *getting* at?

The first time we spoke, I didn't ask every one of these questions, but I danced around them, and his closing comment to me—"You seem to *know* the answers to some of this stuff"—confirmed that he was grateful for my having done so. *At last,* he might have been thinking, *someone noticed.*

The answers begin—and end—with the model and actress Dorothy Stratten.

Bogdanovich met Stratten not long after his relationship with Cybill Shepherd had reached an end. They fell in love and in time were going to get married. "Dorothy was the finest, kindest, most decent human being I've ever known," he said. "She made me change for the better."[48] She was not only one of the stars of *They All Laughed*—his follow-up to *Saint Jack* and also starring Audrey Hepburn, Ben Gazzara, and John Ritter—but its primary inspiration. Although he conceived the project before he knew her well, the love he had for her came to animate the film.

They All Laughed tracks the comings and goings of John, Charles, and Arthur (Gazzara, Ritter, and Blaine Novak, respectively), private eyes of varying experience and professionalism in the employ of the Odyssey Detective Agency in Manhattan. As the film opens, the trio has been retained to keep track of two married women suspected by their husbands of committing (or contemplating) adultery. John and Charles end up losing their hearts to the women they have been hired to track—Angela (Hepburn) and Dolores (Stratten)—which not only compromises their integrity but complicates their relationships with a bevy of other gal pals, including spunky country-western singer Christy (Colleen Camp) and carefree cabbie Sam (Patti Hansen).

The cast is ample, packed with Bogdanovich's family, friends, and coworkers: his daughters, Antonia and Alexandra, were given roles, as was his secretary at the time (Linda MacEwen) and his assistant on the production (Sean Ferrer, Hepburn's son with Mel Ferrer). The glistening New York locations have a lot to do with the film's easygoing charm. The detectives weave their way through real crowds, on real sidewalks and streets, flitting in and out of such landmarks as the Plaza and Algonquin hotels, the Rizzoli Bookstore, and FAO Schwarz.

Yet it is Stratten, seemingly as beautiful inside as out, who dominates *They All Laughed.* In a film full of gesturing and motioning between detectives supposedly working incognito, Charles signals to Arthur early on that he is smitten with Dolores by placing his hand underneath his jacket and simulating a pulsating heartbeat. The shot of Stratten used to represent Charles's point of view of Dolores is simply staggering: her profile nonpareil, her hair a striking sheath of white blond, and her smile reserved—the latter feature suggesting a quiet, modest countenance. It is no overstatement to say that few actresses in film history have been photographed so exquisitely—maybe Carole Lombard in *Twentieth Century* or Grace Kelly in *Rear Window* or Marilyn Monroe in her last, unfinished film, *Something's Got to Give.*

It would be too easy to call Stratten "ethereal" (as some writers have), but in *They All Laughed* she offsets her beauty with a sturdy, earthy quality, as when she trudges down the steps of her townhouse, armed with a pair of suitcases, or when she goes skating at a roller rink. In the latter scene—one of the film's most charming sequences—Charles, ostensibly still on the case, has tracked Dolores to the rink, foolishly deciding to don skates in hot pursuit.

For most of the scene, the camera stays on Charles as he observes the lithesome, elegant Dolores skating gracefully, but at a key moment

Dorothy Stratten and John Ritter in *They All Laughed.* Courtesy Jerry Ohlinger's Movie Material Store.

Bogdanovich shifts to Dolores's perspective. The camera dollies back as she skates toward us, while Charles, visible behind her, skates to catch up. He starts mugging for her benefit, a silly-looking smile on his face, but before she can spot him, he tumbles to the floor—*splat.* Dolores exits frame, but Charles remains grounded, the ties to his skates in knots. The scene echoes the ending of *Bringing Up Baby,* in which Katharine Hepburn precipitates the collapse of Cary Grant's dinosaur—what a mess a gorgeous woman can leave in her wake!—but with a difference: unlike Hepburn with Grant, Stratten has not actively contributed to Ritter's fall. Her mere *presence* brings out the klutz in him.

Throughout the film, Dolores is made to be slightly unattainable—quick to take leave or rush off, as she does after her first kiss with Charles in a stairwell across from her townhouse. (Our heart aches as she darts back home—she is so close yet so far.) It is left to Charles's friend Christy to cut to the chase: dancing at a club with Charles, Christy sees him making eyes at Dolores, who is paired with her friend Jose (Ferrer). Much like the bandleader in *At Long Last Love,* Christy has the foursome "change partners"—Christy takes Jose, while she gives Charles to Dolores. The film's spirit is monogamous, though; among the main cast, no character would think of taking another character's girlfriend or boyfriend once who likes who has been established. Christy may be fond of Charles, and Jose may enjoy the company of Dolores, but each is willing to sacrifice so that true love—the kind that seems to exist between Charles and Dolores—might flourish.

The film contrasts the Charles–Dolores romance with that of an older detective—Gazzara's John, who has his sights set on Hepburn's Angela, the discontented wife of a globetrotting millionaire. Their affair is destined to end unhappily and does, but the film itself is unfailingly bright and peppy. In one appealing moment, Arthur and Sam trade slightly risqué barbs—she teases him about the trio of "chicks" who are after him, and he jokingly asks to take refuge by sleeping on her floor—but their conversation ends amiably, even respectfully.

"It's nice to meet you, Sam," Arthur says.

"You, too, Curly," Sam replies.

This exchange is incidental—fleeting, even—yet it powerfully communicates the characters' decency and civility.

By the final reel, Dolores has agreed to marry Charles, despite their barely having carried on a conversation. In a magical scene, Christy—knowing Charles and Dolores's feelings for each other better than they do—again orchestrates their coming together. As Christy sings "I Don't Think I Could Take You Back Again" on stage in a club, she motions Dolores from upstairs to descend to Charles's table downstairs. When we see Stratten emerge in white at the top of a staircase, she resembles a vision from on high. Her presence seemingly summoned by Christy, Dolores walks slowly and silently, as she might in a marriage procession, to Charles's table, and when she sits down, he gets to the point.

"Dolores?" he asks. "Will you marry me?"

"Okay," she says. "I will."

She adds, of course, that their marriage will have to wait until her divorce is a done deal. Here, in the film's single most significant scene, Stratten emanates a straightforward solidity—both in her firmness in answering "yes" and in her practicality in adding the bit about her divorce.

The suddenness of Charles and Dolores's engagement parallels Bogdanovich and Stratten's. "I think it was clear to Dorothy that it was *me* asking her to marry me . . . because I worked for a long time to get John to say it just the way I wanted him to say it," he said. "And Dorothy's answer was just the way I assume she would have answered it."[49]

The daughter of Dutch parents, Dorothy Ruth Stratten was born in Vancouver, British Columbia, in 1960. She achieved notoriety because of her appearance in the pages of *Playboy*, the dubious handiwork of the man who became her husband, Paul Snider. The Playboy mansion, which Bogdanovich visited for a time in his post-Shepherd funk, was the setting of his introduction to Stratten. It was 1978, and although he was left breathless by her beauty, and she was intrigued with him, they would not see each other again until the following year. As he wrote in his memoir of their relationship, *The Killing of the Unicorn,* he assumed she was attached (in fact, she had yet to marry Snider), while she was fed misinformation about him concerning his previous relationships and the supposedly dodgy state of his career.[50]

When they met again, it was not Bogdanovich but Stratten who made the first move. "In ancient courting customs," he reflected, echoing a pattern evident in many of his films, "it was the woman who pursued the man." One day at the mansion, Stratten spotted Bogdanovich, remembered their earlier encounter, and called his name: "I turned and saw the unfamiliar bleached hair before I saw anything else."[51] Her natural radiance, he learned, had been "improved" by *Playboy*, but that was not all that was troubling her.

Over the course of many subsequent days and nights together, Stratten revealed to Bogdanovich that she was profoundly unhappy in both her life and work—having deep reservations about her recent marriage and finding herself increasingly uncomfortable with posing for *Playboy.* Stratten sought out Bogdanovich the way someone lost at sea wires SOS; she had no family in the United States and desperately few allies.

Bogdanovich provided Stratten with answers to many of her problems. He gave her what ultimately became a major role in *They All Laughed* and suggested she avail herself of the many non-*Playboy* modeling and acting opportunities that would surely come her way. Above all, he loved her, and she him.

He came to feel, he wrote, "as though we had known each other all our lives,"[52] and the equality of their relationship is striking. Yes, he was older and more experienced. Yes, he showed her the sights when she arrived in New York for the first time to make *They All Laughed.* And, yes, she had come to him looking for help. But she was already a writer of poetry and an enthusiast of Thornton Wilder's *Our Town* (having acted in a production of it) and Fyodor Dostoyevsky's *Crime and Punishment,* having fully grasped their themes. They resolved to read Dostoyevsky's *The Idiot* at the same time because it was Bogdanovich's father's favorite book. "I'm sure I had preconceived ideas about Hef's Playmates," he said, "but Dorothy was very spiritual, very deep."[53] And she was already aware—far more than he was—of the resentment and wickedness of men, owing both to her family background (her father having left the scene early on and her mother enduring a subsequent failed marriage) and to her own experience with her abusive husband. "I hadn't had much exposure to men who consistently browbeat women, much less terrorized them," Bogdanovich wrote. "But Dorothy had seen little else from men all her life."[54] By this time, Stratten had a firm wish to get a divorce from Snider.

Both Bogdanovich and Stratten were a bit out of touch: two first-generation North Americans with a hankering for their roots. "D. R. was a small-town girl who tried, against her better instincts, to be a 'liberal, modern' woman," Bogdanovich commented in *The Killing of the Unicorn,* referring to her by a nickname. "Neither she nor I had ever really dealt with the difference between the Old World culture of our parents and the ruthless American way we found outside the home." The presence of *Playboy* in her life was an aberration, Snider's doing; when she met him, she was employed at a Dairy Queen and later took a job at the phone company. She told Bogdanovich that "hate" is what got her through posing for the magazine: "I mean that I hated all those men so much, and my hatred was so strong, it made a kind of invisible shield between them and me, and then I didn't feel as naked anymore." Even after she became famous the world over because of *Playboy,* she retained, at her core, an innocent quality entirely alien from it; Bogdanovich wrote of being struck, during one encounter, that she "looked as though she had stepped out of the nineteenth century."[55]

Peter Bogdanovich had lasting relationships with Polly Platt and Cybill Shepherd, but in Dorothy Stratten he found a mate for life, a woman whose beauty and character rose above that of anyone he had ever known. After filming ended on *They All Laughed,* the two enjoyed a honeymoonlike vacation in London. "The happiest moment of my life was with Dorothy in London, under the trees near the Thames," he said. "We started laughing from sheer happiness."[56] When Stratten made it back to Los Angeles, she felt she had to deal with her now-estranged husband, who had become a menace. She met with Snider at the residence they once shared, but she never returned to what was by then her new home—Bogdanovich's house on Copa de Oro.

On August 14, 1980, Paul Snider murdered Dorothy Stratten and killed himself later that same day. She was twenty.

The enormity of the disaster is difficult to fathom. Imagine having two long, loving relationships that came to unhappy ends. Imagine then meeting a person, in the least likely of places, whom you find you love more than anyone who came before her and who loves you back. Imagine discovering that the love is not passing, but strong, solid, and profound. Imagine winning that improbable lottery—and imagine having it snatched from you in an instant.

Could most men endure such a reversal? For a time, it seemed as though Peter Bogdanovich might not—yet he persevered.

He heeded the counsel of Merlyn in T. H. White's *The Once and Future King:* "The best thing for being sad . . . is to learn something. That is the only thing that never fails."[57] So at the age of forty-two he set about acquiring knowledge as never before. "Her death . . . was either the end of Life," he wrote, "or somehow had to be turned into the most profound form of comprehension, from which a new beginning might emerge."[58] He would reckon with the most obvious question—How did it come to be that Paul Snider murdered Dorothy Stratten?—and his research formed the basis of *The Killing of the Unicorn,* which was a cause célèbre when it was published in 1984.

But a more daunting question lingered: Why—not how, but why—did it happen? "I was trying to find out how we got to the place where somebody as pure and innocent and good as Dorothy could get killed," he said. "How could that happen? What was the world about that it could produce an incident like that? Was there ever a time when that couldn't have happened?"[59]

Ensconced in his house on Copa de Oro, still at work on *They All Laughed,* he retreated to his library in search of an answer. He pored over the collected works of, among others, Francis Bacon, Michel de Montaigne, and Ralph Waldo Emerson: "I went looking for clues anywhere and everywhere," he wrote.[60] No light bulb went off until he recalled Orson Welles advising him in the 1970s to familiarize himself with poet, novelist, and historian Robert Graves. Back then, Bogdanovich told me, he had asked

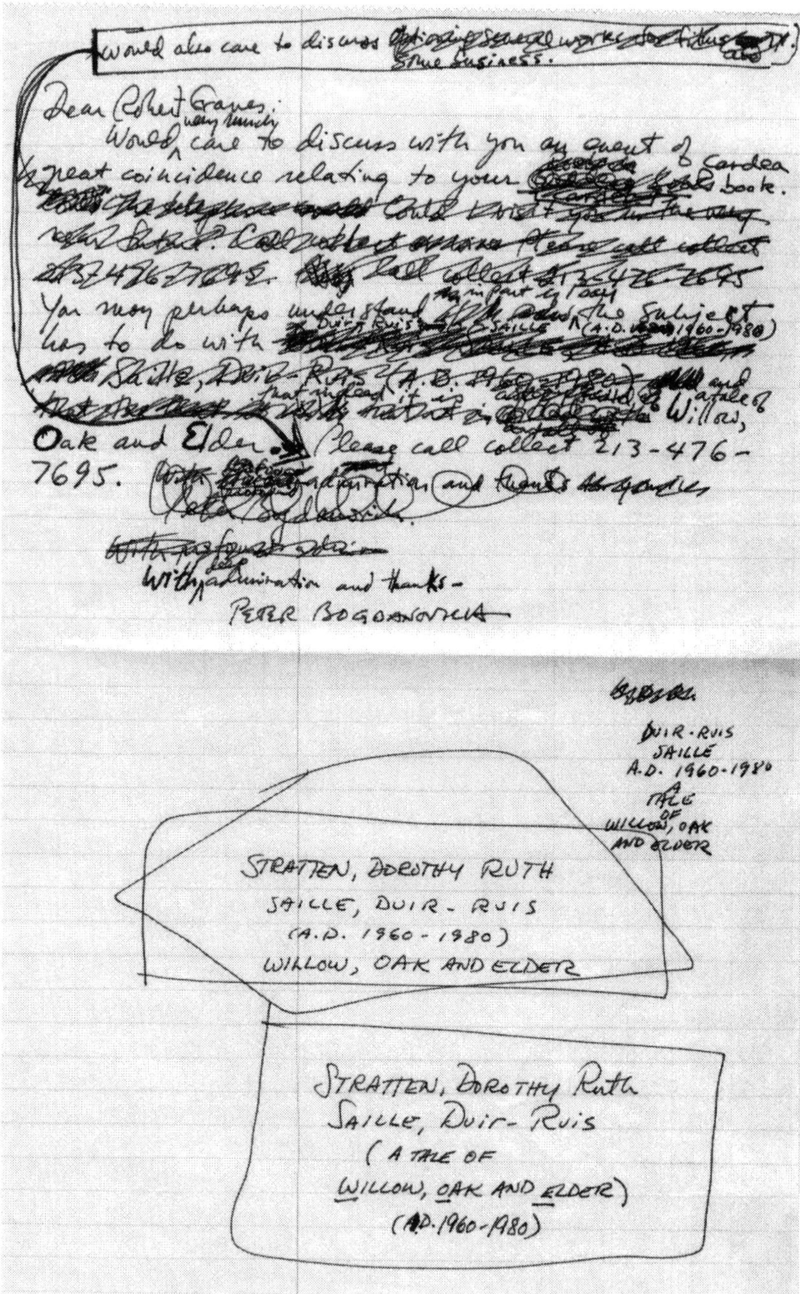
Would also care to discuss some business.

Dear Robert Graves:
Would very much care to discuss with you a great coincidence relating to your book.
You may perhaps understand the subject has to do with Duir-Ruis Saille (A.D. 1960–1980) a tale of Willow, Oak and Elder. Please call collect 213-476-7695.
With deep admiration and thanks –
PETER BOGDANOVICH

DUIR-RUIS
SAILLE
A.D. 1960–1980
A TALE OF WILLOW, OAK AND ELDER

STRATTEN, DOROTHY RUTH
SAILLE, DUIR-RUIS
(A.D. 1960–1980)
WILLOW, OAK AND ELDER

STRATTEN, DOROTHY RUTH
SAILLE, DUIR-RUIS
(A TALE OF
WILLOW, OAK AND ELDER)
(A.D. 1960–1980)

Peter Bogdanovich's draft mailgram to Robert Graves. Courtesy Lilly Library, Indiana University, Bloomington.

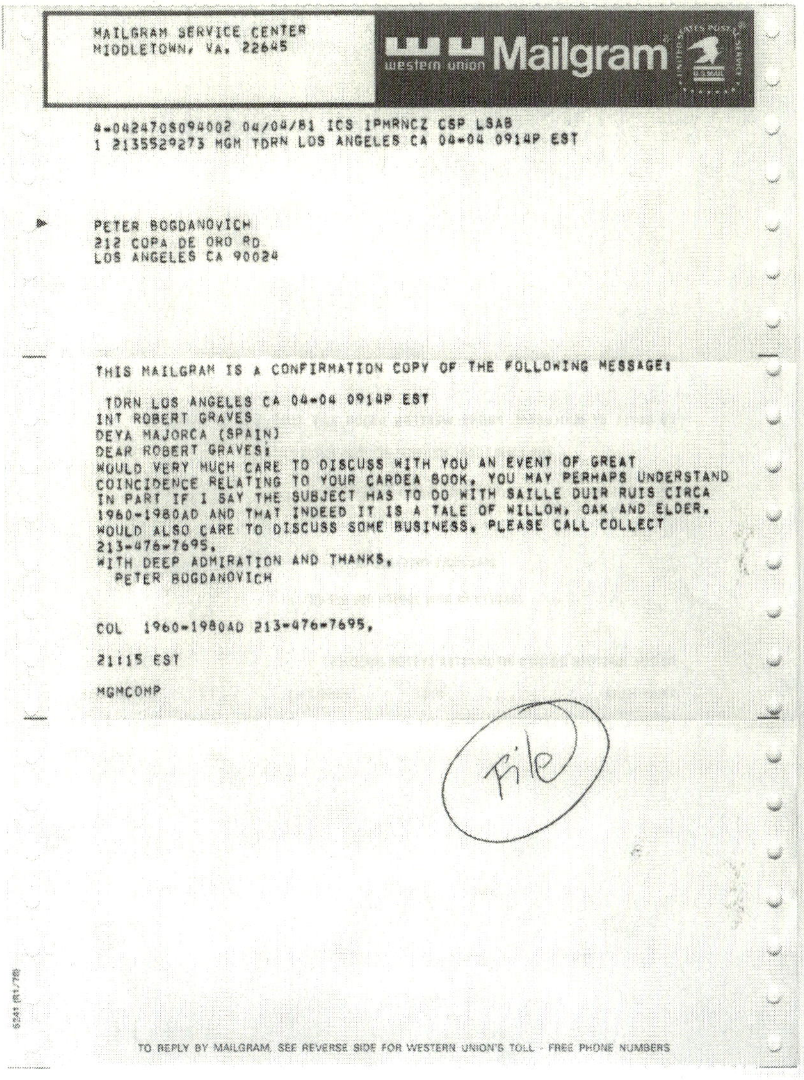

MAILGRAM SERVICE CENTER
MIDDLETOWN, VA. 22645

western union Mailgram

4-042470S094002 04/04/81 ICS IPMRNCZ CSP LSAB
1 2135529273 MGM TDRN LOS ANGELES CA 04-04 0914P EST

PETER BOGDANOVICH
212 COPA DE ORO RD
LOS ANGELES CA 90024

THIS MAILGRAM IS A CONFIRMATION COPY OF THE FOLLOWING MESSAGE:

TDRN LOS ANGELES CA 04-04 0914P EST
INT ROBERT GRAVES
DEYA MAJORCA (SPAIN)
DEAR ROBERT GRAVES:
WOULD VERY MUCH CARE TO DISCUSS WITH YOU AN EVENT OF GREAT COINCIDENCE RELATING TO YOUR CARDEA BOOK, YOU MAY PERHAPS UNDERSTAND IN PART IF I SAY THE SUBJECT HAS TO DO WITH SAILLE DUIR RUIS CIRCA 1960-1980AD AND THAT INDEED IT IS A TALE OF WILLOW, OAK AND ELDER. WOULD ALSO CARE TO DISCUSS SOME BUSINESS. PLEASE CALL COLLECT 213-476-7695.
WITH DEEP ADMIRATION AND THANKS,
PETER BOGDANOVICH

COL 1960-1980AD 213-476-7695,

21:15 EST

MGMCOMP

File

TO REPLY BY MAILGRAM, SEE REVERSE SIDE FOR WESTERN UNION'S TOLL - FREE PHONE NUMBERS

Peter Bogdanovich's mailgram to Robert Graves. Courtesy Lilly Library, Indiana University, Bloomington.

Cybill Shepherd to have a look at Graves's books *The White Goddess* and *The Greek Myths,* which deal with the belief systems of female-worshiping cultures. Reporting back to Bogdanovich, Shepherd summarized the books' basic thesis: "Well, before men were in charge, they say women were in charge."

Now, however, he grasped the full implications of Graves's insights for himself—as he would tell me, "The world that he resurrects in *The White Goddess* and *The Greek Myths* is a world where what happened to Dorothy wouldn't have happened." His studies gave him an appreciation for mythology, especially Greek mythology—"among the most ancient of Western religious histories," he noted[61]—that resulted in characters in his films for years to come referencing ancient gods and goddesses. He was advancing not a religious idea but a moral one: a society's health depends on what its citizens believe. Or, as he boldly asked near the end of *The Killing of the Unicorn,* would Dorothy Stratten's story have been different if "from the first civilizations of the Stone Age, the date had been known as 11,980 in the Year of Our Lady" instead of anno Domini 1980?[62]

It was not enough, though, to read Robert Graves. He had to *meet* Robert Graves. Perhaps he sensed that Graves would be the last in a series of elderly male mentors—like Welles and Ford and Hawks, but with a difference. What Graves offered was something infinitely more valuable than listening to a director explain this shot or that cut. Maybe, through absorbing the work of a writer who loved and venerated women, Bogdanovich could preserve the memory of the woman he loved and venerated.

So in April 1981—less than nine months after Dorothy Stratten was killed—Peter Bogdanovich sent a telegram to Majorca, Spain, home to Robert Graves, his wife, Beryl, and their children.

> DEAR ROBERT GRAVES:
>
> WOULD VERY MUCH CARE TO DISCUSS WITH YOU AN EVENT OF GREAT COINCIDENCE RELATING TO YOUR CARDEA BOOK. YOU MAY PERHAPS UNDERSTAND IN PART IF I SAY THE SUBJECT HAS TO DO WITH SAILLE DUIR RUIS CIRCA 1960–1980 AD AND THAT INDEED IT IS A TALE OF WILLOW, OAK AND ELDER. WOULD ALSO CARE TO DISCUSS SOME BUSINESS. PLEASE CALL COLLECT. . . .
>
> WITH DEEP ADMIRATION AND THANKS,
> PETER BOGDANOVICH[63]

The message was all riddles and codes. Only Graves, Bogdanovich reckoned, could decipher what he had written. "Dorothy's murder was still fresh in the public consciousness," Bogdanovich told me, "and I didn't want to come out and say it was about D. R. so I put it in code that I knew he would understand on sight."[64] "Saille Duir Ruis" were letter names for "Stratten, Dorothy Ruth" in the Ogham, or Old Irish, alphabet. The letters had a secondary meaning: "Duir, the Oak, is the Tree of Triumph; Saille, the Willow, is the Tree of Enchantment, but Ruis, the Elder, is the Tree of Doom, thus poetically encapsulating Dorothy's story."[65] In the end, although Graves no longer spoke to anyone, even his family, Bogdanovich made several voyages to Majorca to spend time in his presence, all the while burrowing deeper on his own into religion, mythology, and even numerology.

"I like the idea of boiling things down to a number," he said, "and seeing what it means."[66] The manuscript pages of *The Killing of the Unicorn*—the book he was writing during this time—are lined with scribbles alluding to the ancient thirteen-month calendar: "Wednesday," being derived from "Mercury," is connected with Hermes and thus to the concepts "wisdom" and "wise counsel." These fascinating jottings are the product of someone anxious to make order out of chaos.

There was practical work to be done, too. Leery of how 20th Century Fox would handle the distribution of *They All Laughed,* he formed his own company to put the film out. "Nobody was quite sure what to do with the film, and we all knew it needed special treatment," he told the *Los Angeles Times.* "So I formed a company called Moon Pictures—I chose the name because I felt the romance had gone out of movies and we needed more moonlight and we're distributing it."[67] Other films were to follow under the nascent company's banner, including yet-to-be-made adaptations of Graves's novels *The Golden Fleece, Watch the North Wind Rise,* and *Wife to Mr. Milton* as well as a new version of Thornton Wilder's novel *The Bridge of San Luis Rey.*

"I'm a widower," Bogdanovich told an interviewer in 1982, "I don't do much of anything."[68] But this was not so; between writing, editing, traveling, and, of course, reading, he engaged in a torrent of activity in the first years after Dorothy Stratten's death. How easy it would have been for him to give up or lose heart. No one would have blamed him if he had retired from public life. Instead, he toiled—and not always profitably. *They All Laughed* would have been better served if Fox *had* remained its distributor; the film's box-office failure meant the end of Moon Pictures and Bogdanovich's ambitions for it. And *The Killing of the Unicorn,* although an undeniably potent and deeply moving work, generated mountains of bad publicity.

WED. METIS. WISE COUNSEL. WISDOM. HERMES. MERCURY (4)
DEC. 74 = (5) || 12/14 = (8) = 13 = (4) [10] : 17 = (8) 25 (7)
ELDER 20 = (2) || 13/20 = (6) = (8) : 16 : (7) : 23 : (5)

(2) ... The evening will be forever,
Yet time was not enough.

(1)
(#) For our lone story, D.R. had written to me, in a poem, less than three months before she was killed, the most eloquent summation:

Manuscript page from *The Killing of the Unicorn*. Courtesy Lilly Library, Indiana University, Bloomington.

But his motives were unimpeachable. "I was completely foolhardy, naïve," he later told the *Los Angeles Times,* referring to the distribution of *They All Laughed.* "I'm not sorry I did it because I did it for love and dedication. But people would come to me and say 'You're running out of money' and I'd just laugh."[69] Dedication to Dorothy Stratten trumped love of money.

Though he resisted directing again, that, too, changed, when he made *Mask* in 1985. Despite all the knocks that life had given him, he kept on shooting—*for her.*

We talked on Thanksgiving Day and again a week before Christmas and yet again the first week of the New Year.

Several months passed. It was now March 2004, and just before I was to file my now finished article with my editor, I sent Bogdanovich a copy to peruse. Earlier, I had told him that I wanted him to see (and sign-off on) what I had used from our interviews. "You remind me of myself," he said. "That's what I used to do."

After he had a chance to look the piece over, he called me.

"It's probably one of the better things ever written about me," he said.

I thanked him.

"I'm not going to be like Orson and change my answers *and* your questions," he reassured me, referring to the postinterview editing Orson Welles had performed on *This Is Orson Welles.*

I felt relieved.

"But," he went on, "I'm not sure you gain anything by quoting the whole song."

My article, you see, began with a discussion of the scene in *Daisy Miller* in which Cybill Shepherd sings "When You and I Were Young, Maggie," and as a kind of tone setter I quoted the entire song at the top.

He was right, and on the whole I could not complain. He was very complimentary. He gave me several other pieces of advice that I have always tried to remember. He pointed out that I had the unconscious habit of using the same word twice in close succession. And he said that I ought to read Robert Graves and Alan Hodge's guide for good writing, *The Reader over Your Shoulder,* which I promptly did. I reference it still.

We went through my article a page at a time, as he made gentle suggestions, and—as promised—he only very rarely changed his remarks. He seemed pleased.

Before we hung up, he told me that he was going to send me a signed copy of *The Killing of the Unicorn.* It was, he said, a kind of thank-you gift for what I had written about him. I was surprised—not that he was grateful for my efforts but that he was sending me *this* book, the one in which he revealed so much of himself so openly, rather than, say, *Pieces of Time* or *Who the Devil Made It.* I was, in fact, sure that he would not have given this particular book—so personal, so painful—to someone who had not asked the right questions and therefore had understood a little about who he was. The book meant, perhaps, that I was not just another interviewer or—worse—just another *fan.*

From the beginning, I worried about being seen that way. Ironically, one of the films he was thinking about making when I first got to know him was an adaptation of a novel by Sam Kashner called *Sinatraland.* "The book is a short novel in the form of letters from a fan of Sinatra's to Sinatra," Bogdanovich told me. "Part of the plot is whether he answers them or not, although he doesn't seem to answer them." He explained that *Sinatraland* would be different from *The Cat's Meow* and *The Mystery of Natalie Wood*—his two recently completed movies about Hollywood—because it offered an outsider's rather than an insider's perspective about show business.

Of course, Peter Bogdanovich was once a fan, too, finagling ways to meet directors by interviewing them. Through his insight and understanding, though, he often emerged as a friend or protégé. He knew the drill, then, of beginning life as a fan and ending up as something *more* than a fan.

The great director King Vidor once said: "The friends we meet through the language of artistic expression we have known a long time before we first see them face to face."[70]

By 1985, when *Mask* was released, tough times had come for directors of Bogdanovich's epoch. Hal Ashby, six years removed from *Being There,* was about to begin his final film. Francis Ford Coppola was distracting himself with minor-league projects such as *Rumble Fish* and *Peggy Sue Got Married.* Martin Scorsese was working with, of all people, Tom Cruise on *The Color of Money.*

Bogdanovich, though, struck back in spite of the woe that had engulfed him since August 1980: *Mask*—his first effort since *They All Laughed*—was a film with rare sentiment and feeling (rare, that is, for those unfamiliar with *The Last Picture Show* or *Paper Moon*). Yet when offered the script in 1983, he was ambivalent about taking it on.

"I said I didn't really want to get into it," he recalled, "but the more I did, the more I found it interesting, and I thought it had something to say, particularly about the transcendence of a certain kind of death."[71]

That he stressed the project's spiritual dimension is, at first blush, puzzling. After all, this film is unusually preoccupied with the physical world—namely, the disfigurement of Rocky Dennis (whose face was deformed due to a condition present since birth) versus the normalcy of his family and friends. Eric Stoltz played Rocky, and Cher played his mother, Rusty. Writing in *Film Comment,* critic Armond White praised the film for what he called its "brave studies of difference," with Bogdanovich employing Welles-like "deep-focus effects for closeup two-shots of the deformed Rocky next to some pretty character."[72] Throughout, we are invited to wonder how we would feel if we looked as Rocky does: Would we have the courage to go outside? Would we have the nerve to attend school and stand up to the whispers? Would we care if we wore a coat and tie instead of blue jeans to a graduation ceremony?

Point of view is used particularly skillfully in a scene following Rocky's graduation, when the boy spots Lisa (Alexandra Powers)—a pretty, kind-hearted classmate—standing across from him in a parking lot. We see her waving to him and him waving back. In a closer angle, we see Lisa mouthing the words "Have a great summer" before being whisked away by her handsome kith and kin. As Lisa disappears, Rocky looks on sadly; her tiny gesture is equivalent to a girl offering a handshake instead of a kiss.

But for all of the care given to documenting the tangible miseries of Rocky's life, *Mask* is indeed concerned largely with what cannot be seen. There is a powerful passage included in the dazzling director's cut of the film (which also replaces songs by Bob Seger with those by Bruce Springsteen) in which Rocky, reacting to the death of an old biker named Red (Harry Carey Jr.), chooses not to weep but instead stoically insists that his late friend has achieved a kind of liberation. "Red," Rocky says, "is everywhere now."

For his part, Rocky intuits that his own time on earth is short. Perhaps that is why late in the film the camera cranes down oh so slowly to Rocky as he dances with Diana (Laura Dern), the blind girl he has fallen for at a summer camp. Music by the Beatles—"I Want to Hold Your Hand" and "Girl"—is heard, and then Rocky and Diana say the words to "Auld Lang Syne." The film itself seems to pause so that Rocky can take in the quiet perfection of the moment—perhaps it is a moment he will add to his list of "things that are good," a litany as affecting as Emily's "good-bye, world" monologue in Thornton Wilder's *Our Town.* While Emily mourns "clocks ticking" and "new-ironed dresses and hot baths," Rocky romanticizes such passing pleasures as "ice cream and cake, and a ride on a Harley." And "the sun shining on my face." The list is read by Rocky in a posthumous voice-over as Rusty and Gar stand near his grave, but its tone is hopeful rather than melancholic.

Where did this rush of spiritual feeling come from? Bogdanovich says he was not raised in a religious home—"Mom was Jewish and dad was Serbian-Greek Orthodox, although we had no religious training at all"[73]—and his films prior to *Mask* seldom referred to questions of the afterlife. Yet the absence of Dorothy Stratten forced him to consider ways in which she might still be with him—a wish not unlike the painful, hopeful sentiment offered in Graham Greene's *The End of the Affair:* "People can love without seeing each other, can't they."[74]

In fact, in *The Killing of the Unicorn* Bogdanovich writes of a series of small, omenlike incidents that made a believer of him. There was the time when the lights in his office fluttered after he read a few lines from Noel Coward's *Private Lives,* a play that held special significance for him and Stratten. And the time when a stray calico cat found its way into his living room, where he was writing a song about Stratten—the same type of cat pictured on a card Stratten had once given him.[75]

Not insignificantly, it was during this period—so pregnant with signs and signals—that Bogdanovich began to write a screenplay, his first since *They All Laughed,* which was eventually titled *Wait for Me.* The protagonist is movie director Charles Benedict, who is contending, not unhappily, with the ghosts of those he has loved and lost—especially the ghost of his cherished sixth wife, Cynthia. Is it a mere coincidence that there are seven letters, including a *y*, in the names "Cynthia" and "Dorothy"? And that *C* comes right before *D*?

An early version of *Wait for Me* was mentioned in *Variety* in January 1983 as a vehicle for John Cassavetes, who was, the trade paper reported, set to appear "as a film director whose three wives, two alive and one dead, intervene in the making of the man's new picture."[76] Cassavetes may be gone, and the screenplay's three wives may have become six, but Bogdanovich still intends to make *Wait for Me.*

He found that one way to cope was to remind himself of the person who was missing. So, starting with *Mask,* he made a point to reference Dorothy

Stratten—and the ways in which she altered his vision of the world—in every film he subsequently made, big or small, comedy or drama, original screenplay or adaptation.

There were only spotty laughs to be found in his first film after *Mask*, a would-be farce called *Illegally Yours*, which was directed under trying circumstances. A few weeks before shooting began, producer Dino De Laurentiis axed the screenplay without ever finding a suitable replacement. As it stands, Rob Lowe—looking fairly disinterested—plays the dweeby Richard Dice, who carries a longtime torch for Molly Gilbert (Colleen Camp). Complications ensue when Molly is put on trial for murder, and Richard is called to serve on the jury. Little of the hackneyed setup is convincing. But, perhaps to distract himself, Bogdanovich filled the cast with veterans of *They All Laughed*—in addition to Camp, Linda MacEwen and George Morfogen make return appearances. And a role was written for Dorothy Stratten's younger sister, Louise (credited as L. B. Straten).

Lowe was given bits of dialogue that reflected his director's present interests: digressions on numerology and quotations from the poetry of William Blake ("Why was Cupid a boy, / And why a boy was he? / He should have been a girl, / For aught that I can see"). Even amid the wreckage of *Illegally Yours* were hints of what was on Bogdanovich's mind.

His next film, *Texasville*, had more going for it from the start. Drawn from Larry McMurtry's sequel to *The Last Picture Show*, the film featured the memorable spectacle of a majority of the original cast, aged almost twenty years, reconvening in Archer City, Texas. *Texasville* is a wise, witty look at a community coming apart at the seams. In the distressed and depressed 1980s, we encounter Duane (Jeff Bridges) working as an oilman burdened by debt; Sonny (Timothy Bottoms) beset by memories of past picture shows; and Jacy (Cybill Shepherd) in a state of lamentation, having traded her youthful zest for middle-age doldrums following the death of her little boy, Benny. Her situation in particular tethers *Texasville* to *Mask* in its insistence on the truth of eternal life. Observing some children playing in a field, Jacy cries out (in words carefully preserved from McMurtry's novel), "Look at those kids—just look at those kids. *It's like Benny's here.* Maybe the ones that live carry the lives of the ones that die."

Women, Bogdanovich said in a conversation with John Ritter shortly after the death of Dorothy Stratten, are "essentially superior" to men,[77] and his later films make an article of faith out of that position. *Texasville* concerns itself largely with the unknowability of the "fairer sex"—as though women are too good to fully decipher. "What do you and Jacy talk about all day?" Duane asks his wife, Karla (Annie Potts), referring to her bull sessions with Jacy at the Dairy Queen. Later, after a late-night argument with Duane, Karla reflects on the differences between the sexes. As Duane sulks in the background, Karla lies in bed watching television, her head held aloft by a heap of pillows. She says, "You don't understand a thing about women, and you never will." Duane will have none of it, asking, "How many things are there to know about anybody?" Karla says there are only "three or four" things to know about Duane but a million things to know about her.

The camera moves in on Potts as she continues, in words again taken almost verbatim from McMurtry's novel: "They don't have names, Duane. They can just be feelings. Like these little plants I read about in *National Geographic.* They only bloom one hour in twenty years. I have little feelings like that. One might only bloom once during our whole marriage. You could be sitting right there, two feet away, and never notice it."

Duane turns to a window to ponder the darkness outside, but the light from the bedroom casts a reflection. As we watch him watch himself—gray-haired, overweight, wearing a scowl instead of a smile—we wonder if Karla has it wrong. Are there *even* "three or four" things to know about Duane?

Four years after *Texasville,* Bogdanovich made another great film about the secrets of married life: *Song of Songs,* based on a short story by Harry Mark Petrakis and shown on Showtime's *Picture Windows* series. The main character, Ted (George Segal), commits adultery but feels secure that his wife, Angie (Brooke Adams), has never strayed. His illusions are challenged late in the story, but we are given a hint early on: Angie is shown looking for an extended moment at a man with whom, it turns out, she has been carrying on a relationship for many years (a part played, rather amusingly, by Bogdanovich). The shot, seemingly arbitrary, sets the stage for the revelations to come.

Sometimes the references to Dorothy Stratten are large and abstract, other times tiny and specific.

In *Texasville,* for example, a car radio blasts "One Day since Yesterday" —a song from *They All Laughed* that Bogdanovich and Earl Poole Ball wrote in tribute to Stratten. In *The Thing Called Love,* a Nashville-set story of prospective singer-songwriters, allusions to Robert Graves and ancient courtship practices are folded into the script. In their love scene, Miranda Presley (Samantha Mathis) looms over James Wright (River Phoenix) and recites a poem by Robert Graves—verse as a romantic turn-on. Later, on a sojourn to Memphis, James proposes to Miranda, his sense of the dramatic undiminished by the fact that they are standing in a convenience store. Like Bogdanovich, James is a devotee of the past. When Miranda insists that "you don't just get married" on a whim, James refers to "the old Irish trial marriages," in which a union could be dissolved twelve months after it was entered into by the parties repeating "I divorce you" three times. In *The Cat's Meow,* the typeface used for the opening titles is called "Dolores"—the name of the character played by Dorothy Stratten in *They All Laughed.*

And in *Noises Off,* Louise (L. B.) Stratten—who was Bogdanovich's wife from 1988 to 2001 and remains his best friend and ally—makes a surprise appearance in the film's jubilant finale, in which the troupe's accursed play comes together just in time for a Broadway opening night. We see Frederick Dallas (Christopher Reeve) and Belinda Blair (Marilu Henner) kissing lustily; Garry Lejeune (John Ritter) and Brooke Ashton (Nicollette Sheridan) doing the same; and Lloyd Fellowes (Michael Caine) and Poppy Taylor (Julie Hagerty) showing off their engagement rings. And then we see Louise Stratten, casually outfitted in overalls, playing a stagehand who has been paired with stage manager Tim Allgood (Mark Linn-Baker)—she, too, is given a happy ending.

Louise Stratten appeared in many small parts—more than bits but not quite leads—in most of the films Bogdanovich made in the 1990s: a pregnant housewife in *The Price of Heaven* (a.k.a. *Blessed Assurance*); a police officer in *Naked City: A Killer Christmas;* a football player's wife in *A Saintly Switch.* In *Song of Songs,* Louise and Peter even share the screen for a charming moment—she plays his girlfriend, and the smile he casts her way in their one scene together is genuine. The best of their collaborations is *A Dime a Dance,* which serves as the couple's most direct comment on the Dorothy Stratten tragedy: in this stylish though brutal adaptation of a Cornell Woolrich short story, Louise portrays one of the victims of a cold-blooded murderer of dance-hall girls. In the film's haunting opening scene, Bogdanovich dissolves from a high-angle shot of the killer "dancing" with the body of the slain woman to a similarly positioned high-angle shot of the dance hall itself, filled with carefree bodies

River Phoenix in *The Thing Called Love*. Courtesy Jerry Ohlinger's Movie Material Store.

in motion. Yet—in a hint of what is yet to come in *Wait for Me*—Louise's character reappears throughout *A Dime a Dance*, remembered in flashbacks that are strangely more vivid than the present-day scenes.

These were television projects, made in the years after offers for feature films had tailed off, and they were enhanced mainly by how seriously Bogdanovich took them. No matter the quality of their scripts (some were excellent, others just so-so), he brought his lunch pail and hard hat to work, shooting and staging each with inventiveness and panache.

On these "jobs of work," Louise was like a good-luck charm. She was a fine, versatile actress, yes, but through her mere presence she must have also brightened the set for her director and husband. As the sister of Dorothy Stratten, she was a tangible reminder of an earlier, better period—and a help in moving forward, too.

In the fall of 2004, several months after my article was published, I finally met Peter Bogdanovich face-to-face.

By then, I had moved with my family from Ohio to suburban Maryland. One day I received a flyer in the mail promoting a screening of *They All Laughed* at the American Film Institute (AFI) Silver in Silver Spring, Maryland, with Peter Bogdanovich in attendance to sign copies of his latest book, *Who the Hell's in It.*

I felt as if someone had picked the lock to my brain. Who but me would think to show *this* film and not one more famous, such as *The Last Picture Show?* Not only would I finally meet the director whose work I so admired, but it would be at a screening of my favorite of his films. And then there was the perfect timing: our meeting would be preceded by my having written an article on him. There was a reason for me to be there as something other than a . . . *fan.*

As it turned out, the book signing was to take place in a dreary, second-story conference room at the AFI Silver—all neutral carpeting and fold-up chairs. Of course, I arrived early, so only a few staff members were present to greet me. I remember wondering if Peter Bogdanovich would show—I had become accustomed to having his assistant call me with last-minute postponements of our previously scheduled interviews. No one else seemed worried. A woman with the AFI Silver said kiddingly that she knew what my priorities were: movies, *not* politics. Indeed, I was missing a presidential debate between Bush and Kerry in order to be there—or was it a vice presidential debate between Cheney and Edwards? *Whatever.*

See?—she was not wrong.

But, lo and behold, Peter Bogdanovich soon walked through the door, followed by his assistant. We made eye contact for only a second or two because, of course, he had no idea who I was, having only *heard* me on the other end of a phone line, and he was immediately besieged by the small group that had by now gathered in his absence. He sat down at a long table beside a row of windows, surrounded by books stacked in neat piles, and I walked over to him. As I handed him *Who the Hell's in It* (my father, who could not make it, had purchased a copy for me in advance), I introduced myself, my mother, and my brother—the witnesses to my Big Day. All of a sudden, the four of us started . . . chatting.

My mother asked him if he would do his impression of Cary Grant for the audience after the screening. He said he would. He did.

She also said that we weren't long for Maryland—that we would be moving soon, returning to Ohio.

"You don't like it here?" he asked, puzzled.

"Not much," she said.

I interrupted—trying to explain: "Well, Ohio is home, you know? Like when you returned to New York after living in California." There I was, forever putting my little self in his big shoes.

He laughed and said that he understood what I meant, but that he had lived in California for several *decades* before he came back to New York—not less than twelve months.

A line was forming behind us. He took a long time to write the inscription in my book. The AFI staffers must have looked as though they wondered why because, after a few moments of scribbling, he felt compelled to explain who I was. If I had any doubt about what he thought of what I had done, though, all I had to do was read what he wrote:

October 5, 2004

For Peter,

Thank you so much for the great effort and time and words on my work—
it has meant a great deal to me—!

All the best to you in everything you do—

Peter Bogdanovich

He handed me back the book, and we shook hands. I noticed the block letters on his signet ring: PB. PT had finally met PB.

As the night wore on, it began to feel like a scene out of one of his movies. First, there was Peter Bogdanovich himself. Of course, I knew that he often acted out the scenes in his movies for his actors, so it came as no surprise to me that he had some of the jauntiness of John Ritter in *They All Laughed* and a dose of the cynicism of Ben Gazzara in *Saint Jack.* But as I stood and talked to him, I was surprised at how many other performances from his films came to mind. His dry, knowing tone reminded me here and there of the way Cybill Shepherd speaks in *At Long Last Love*—the way she says, with a touch of sarcasm in her voice, to the serenading Duilio Del Prete, "You . . . sing!"

Since Bogdanovich was accompanied by his assistant, I was reminded that he had cast an assistant from an earlier era (Linda MacEwen) in *They All Laughed.* She was delightful in the movie, and as I watched his current assistant flitting around the conference room, I wondered if she, too, would show up on the big screen one day. *Am I witnessing history?* I thought. *The next Linda MacEwen?*

After *They All Laughed* was shown (to enthusiastic audience response), he walked on stage, sat in a spindly director's chair, and began fielding questions from the audience. I was in the very last row. I could not help myself and raised my hand. I asked him to explain how he planned the amazing scene in the film in which Colleen Camp sings "I Don't Think I Could Take You Back Again" over a succession of intricately edited shots showing looks between Camp and the other actors. In fact, he had already explained to me in scrupulous detail how he put the scene together: while on the set, without the benefit of a storyboard or any other advance planning, he carefully matched each line in the song to a particular shot.

So I knew the answer to my question. More important, he knew I knew the answer.

He sighed to the audience at the AFI Silver and said, looking directly at me, "Well, Peter, you have a bit of an advantage because you know the story already. . . ." Nonetheless, he recounted a simplified version, but not before he introduced me as the author of a fine new article on his films—"He spent a lot of time on it," he said coolly, as though my industriousness counted for more than my perceptions—and the audience oohed and ahhed at this *kid* being singled out by a big-shot director.

The night was as magical as I hoped. I couldn't resist looking to his life to give my own the appropriate context. I remembered something he wrote about first seeing George Cukor's classic comedy-drama *Holiday,* starring Cary Grant and Katharine Hepburn as two glorious misfits among the well-to-do. "After the film, as I walked home on the dark Manhattan streets," he wrote in *Who the Devil Made It,* "I was feeling buoyant, happier than I could ever remember, positive about the vast possibilities of life."[78]

That night, walking into the brisk air, I was feeling those feelings and thinking those thoughts.

Incidentally, I happen to think that no film by another director is closer in spirit to Peter Bogdanovich's work than Cukor's *Holiday.* Its joyful, life-affirming spirit calls to mind *What's Up, Doc?* and especially *They All Laughed,* in which the characters are perfectly happy to shuck rules in the name of love.

Over the years, I asked him quite a bit about *Holiday.*

"It's kind of a rebellious film in a quiet way," he told me one time. "It had a big impression on me. It certainly made me feel good."

Later, he told me that he watched *Holiday* with Dorothy Stratten when they were making *They All Laughed.*

"We saw a double-bill of *Holiday* and *It Happened One Night,*" he said. "The only other film we saw together was *The Shining,* which I hated. She wanted to see it. She said, 'Promise me we won't leave,' because I used to get up and leave if I didn't like a picture. I sat through it—for her. I hated it."

"But did she like *Holiday?*" I asked.

"She loved it."

In 2003 and 2004, when I first knew him, Peter Bogdanovich was still in what the *New Yorker* condescendingly called "movie jail"—that is, television. The medium was generous to him, though: in the eleven months that passed from our first interview in November 2003 to our meeting at the AFI Silver in October 2004, he finished editing *The Mystery of Natalie Wood* for ABC, directed *Hustle* (a gripping, effective drama about Pete Rose) for ESPN, and went behind the camera for an episode of *The Sopranos* for HBO. His work was never less than sturdy and sound—it was like Allan Dwan going to work for pay cable.

Still . . . he wanted more than simply to put his camera in the right spot. There was much he wanted to *say.* His anxiousness to make another personal film—one in which he picked up threads begun in *Targets* and *The Last Picture Show* and *At Long Last Love* and *Saint Jack* and *They All Laughed,* one in which he dealt directly with Dorothy Stratten and his life since her death—was evident from one of our first conversations in 2003, when I asked him if he had ever met King Vidor.

"I knew him," he said. "Not well, but I knew him enough to say he was one of the nicest men I ever knew."

We proceeded to talk about Vidor's films for a few minutes—I had just seen the amazing *Our Daily Bread* and was taken with the famous, Eisenstein-influenced finale in which the farm collective takes up ditch digging to help irrigate their crops—and then he told me that he almost made a film with Vidor. "He was going to direct it, and I was going to produce it," he said. "He'd wanted to do it for years. It was the story of James Murray, the leading guy in [Vidor's film] *The Crowd,* and what happened to him. It was a very sad story. We were going to do it for a million-and-a-half for the Directors Company at Paramount, and then, of course, the Directors Company fell apart for various reasons."

How depressing to learn that Vidor had a chance—a *real* chance—to make a film after he retired but missed out because of politics or pettiness or whatever it was that spelled the end to the Directors Company. I told Bogdanovich that although Vidor was in his late seventies when they were talking about his movie about James Murray, I had the sense—from having seen an elderly but vigorous Vidor interviewed in various documentaries—that at the time he still had the spirit and the spunk to direct.

"He could have made a picture," Bogdanovich said. "So could Ford. So could Hawks."

But none of them did.

"You just have to keep fighting, that's all," he continued. "It's a good sign that Roman Polanski won the Oscar at sixty-nine." Polanski had won the Best Director Award for his masterful Holocaust drama *The Pianist* earlier that year.

I pressed him on this a little, knowing that it would not be very many years before he, too, was sixty-nine. Did he have a movie like *The Pianist* up his sleeve? Was a comeback in the offing?

"You just have to keep acting young, and they forget how old you are," he said. "That's the thing to do—don't let yourself look old. Everything is perception anyway."

As it turned out, he was not sixty-nine but seventy-three when he finally was given his chance. He spent the summer of 2013 in New York, shooting *She's Funny That Way.* Many were banking that he still had what it took: filmmakers Wes Anderson and Noah Baumbach were the first to lend their support to the project, and a whole bunch of star actors followed suit, including Owen Wilson and Jennifer Aniston.

In the film, naive theater director Arnold Albertson (Wilson) balances a happily mundane family life (a wife and two kids) with occasional trysts with high-class prostitutes, whom he invariably asks to forsake their profession. Arnold puts his money where his mouth is, though: he ponies up $30,000 to help each woman turn over a new leaf.

Alas, Arnold pulls this stunt one too many times when he encounters Izzy Patterson (Imogen Poots), a prostitute who happens to be an actress on the side. Izzy takes her $30,000, gets her first apartment, buys time with a therapist (Aniston), and proceeds to audition for Arnold's new production, a rather salty play titled *A Grecian Evening.* This comic collision is captured in a series of reaction shots that are vintage Bogdanovich. When Izzy clomps on stage, script pages in hand, she is first recognized by another actor cast in the show, Seth Gilbert (Rhys Ifans), who has previously seen Arnold and Izzy in flagrante delicto. Izzy then recognizes Arnold and trips, which prompts Arnold to look up—he is seated near the foot of the stage with good-hearted playwright Joshua Fleet (Will Forte)—to see this lady of the night standing (or stumbling) before him.

When Bogdanovich and Louise Stratten first hatched the script for *She's Funny That Way* in the late 1990s, they probably thought it was the stuff of a sex farce. When he got around to making the film, however, the tone had shifted to something less madcap and more romantic. Now, the story sidelines Arnold, making his fumbling attempts at concealing or explaining away his infidelities seem more pathetic than comic. (At one point, he lamely explains to his wife that his largesse to prostitutes renders him a feminist—*kind of, sort of.*)

In fact, Izzy is the film's omniscient narrator, recounting her own story her own way to a journalist (Illeana Douglas). What's more, she parlays her $30,000 into a career that Arnold can take little credit for: yes, she wins and keeps the part in *A Grecian Evening*, but the show is a flop, and she ultimately prospers on-screen, not onstage, and becomes romantically involved with neither Arnold nor Josh but with a top film director. "Only a man capable of deep love could celebrate a wild girl's pilgrim soul with so much joy," Clive James wrote of Barbra Streisand's Judy in *What's Up, Doc?*[79] In *She's Funny That Way*, an even wilder girl's soul is celebrated with even more joy because *she* is the author of her fate.

Of course, the film is very funny—its cast filled out with Austin Pendleton as a judge gaga for Izzy, George Morfogen as a somewhat lethargic detective retained by the judge, and Cybill Shepherd as Izzy's loudmouthed mother—and it is very possible that it will kick off a fresh series of Bogdanovich comedies. If *She's Funny That Way* might be considered a contemporary *What's Up, Doc?*, how wonderful it is to contemplate a fresh *Paper Moon* or a new *They All Laughed*. In fact, his first project after *She's Funny That Way* was a delightful documentary tribute to Buster Keaton, released in 2018, *The Great Buster*. But the texture of *She's Funny That Way*—the way Izzy's journey is taken seriously and, in a scene set among the unicorn tapestries at the Cloisters, is placed in the context of the centuries' old battle of the sexes—suggests that Bogdanovich yearns to do more than simply generate guffaws.

We should never forget the easy appeal of his early comedies or the charmed life he led while making them. But let us affirm the view expressed by Larry McMurtry, who once said about Bogdanovich, "Peter wanted to do romantic comedies and be Ernst Lubitsch—but his personality is in the great Serbian manner and, in fact, tragic."[80] The progression from whimsy to sadness in his films has a certain inevitability, just a matter of living long enough to experience a loss—or two or three. How could Bogdanovich's personality be anything but "in fact, tragic"?

Consider the lines McMurtry wrote about his greatest protagonist, Emma Greenway, in his novel *Terms of Endearment*. On her deathbed, Emma seems to yearn to be in the company of those already departed. "Once, picking up a copy of the *Iliad* that Melba had given her, she chanced upon the phrase 'among the dead,' and found it comforting," McMurtry writes. "Even counting people she knew, there were a lot of dead to be among."[81]

As the losses accumulate, the time nears for Peter Bogdanovich to finally film *Wait for Me*—the screenplay he first conceived in the early 1980s, about a ghost-beset director. But for people like Bogdanovich and Emma Greenway, ghosts are not scary but essential: life is unthinkable without them. Describing *Wait for Me* to broadcaster Charlie Rose in 1997, Bogdanovich said earnestly, "I'm very interested in ghosts." Rose laughed, saying, "Imagine my surprise." Amazingly, however, Rose had no follow-up question to such a strange and provocative remark.

Well, what can I say? I never made that mistake.

In the fall of 2010—seven years after we were first in touch—Peter Bogdanovich and I began doing a new series of interviews for this book. He was never very guarded with me, but he became even less so. More than once, he suggested that I begin taping our calls as soon as he answered the phone, in case he had an insight worth preserving amid our chitchat. He kidded me: when I would remind him from time to time that it had been seven (then eight, then nine, then . . .) years since we first spoke, he feigned incredulousness. "Really?" he asked. "Jesus, you're getting old—I'm not, of course, at all!"

During this time, he was living in North Carolina, teaching kids younger than I about filmmaking at the University of North Carolina School of the Arts as he waited for the go-ahead to make *She's Funny That Way.* He had a fair amount of free time, so about once a month—usually on a Sunday afternoon—I dialed a number to reach him, this time in the provinces rather than in the Big Apple. Sometimes I caught him in the middle of watching a movie on television—*The Third Man* or *Adam's Rib* or *Battling Butler*—and he would ask me to call back after it was over. At those moments, he seemed like every other serious movie buff you've ever known: a good movie can't just be switched *off.* More often, there was music playing in the background—usually Louis Armstrong or Frank Sinatra or something classical, maybe Mozart.

One day, after years of my referring to him as "Mr. Bogdanovich," he said, "Call me Peter, Peter."

The year 2010 had been unspeakably terrible for me: in January, my father had died unexpectedly. The pain and sorrow and loneliness had not lessened as the year went one—and it still has not. Heartache does not change. Peter knew this. He, too, had lost his father unexpectedly and when he was at an age not very much older than mine at the time. I was twenty-six; he had been thirty-one.

So that day when he asked me to throw out the "Mr." and start using "Peter," he was giving me more than just a pat on the back. He was, I think, expressing solidarity with someone who had experienced something as terrible as losing a parent at a young age. Few people, in my experience, understand as well as he does how horribly wrong life can go.

His concern should surprise no one familiar with his work. As Clive James put it, "His movies. . . . were marked from the beginning by a rare compassion for those blasted by fate."[82]

That I can find my way around his films so easily is a sign of his greatness as an artist. In appealing to the masses, he nonetheless manages to connect with the individual audience member, convincing each of us that what is happening on screen reflects our own lives. How often have I felt like Rocky in *Mask* at the moment when the sweet girl tells him to have a great summer. How often have I walked down a city street in the springtime, lulled along by jabbering pedestrians and traffic noise, and thought of *They All Laughed.* And how often in recent years have I recalled the funeral of William Leigh in *Saint Jack.* We grow fond of this character over the course of the movie, and although his death is not a total surprise, we are nevertheless devastated by it, and we want to say a nice, long good-bye to him. The film instead reminds us that no hymn, no matter how beautiful, lasts forever. Before we know it, the service is over, and the mourners get on with their day. But William Leigh, of course, cannot.

How I long to see *Wait for Me;* how very much I find myself identifying with Charles Benedict, who misses his loved one and wishes to hear from her. This is no longer academic for me, just as it surely is not for the millions of other potential audience members.

Orson Welles was right. Few artists are capable of reaching so many as Peter Bogdanovich.

Somewhere in the middle of working on this book, I received an email from Bogdanovich out of the blue. He said that he had found a copy of the one project of his that, for some reason, I had never managed to see: a television pilot called *Prowler* from 1995, starring Scott Bakula as a Los Angeles police officer. He had described the show to me in an email the previous year: "It was for WB TV but didn't sell—too dark, but Scott refused to allow any humor into the proceedings, much as I tried and the studio tried. It was OK—certainly uncompromising but very depressing, I thought."[83]

So he mailed me a copy of *Prowler.* Inside was a handwritten note he had jotted on a yellow legal pad:

Dear Peter—

Here it is—the final piece of the puzzle!?!@!*

Best, Peter

I think he was being humorous—after all, what could an unsold TV pilot tell me about him that I didn't already know?—but when I sat down to watch, my opinion changed.

In many ways, *Prowler* was quite ordinary, enhanced here and there by a felicitous camera move or a nice cut. But one thing stood out: the Scott Bakula character is a widower. This is more than just an incidental detail. The recent loss of his wife comes up again and again in the story, inspiring a rather poetic monologue from the character near the end: "I didn't feel anything for a long time. I lost myself in my job—lucky I had it. And then small pieces of life started to sneak up on me, like windows opening, letting in a color or a sound . . . ."

I never asked Peter if it was his idea for the character to have lost his wife, but I always assumed it was. I picture him in a script conference or on the set, finding yet another way to refer to the death of Dorothy Stratten, the signal event of his life.

This reminds me: over the past several years, I have begun to repeat some of my father's phrases or sayings in casual conversation. I will be talking to someone and say something he said. The person hearing it does not know my reason for saying it, but that does not matter. It is a way of summoning the person you miss. In the end, this is what Peter Bogdanovich has been doing for more than three decades: alluding as a way of remembering—and not caring if more than one or two or ten people know it.

Who would have guessed that *Prowler* really *was* the final piece of the puzzle?

Near the end of one of our last conversations for this book, I told him that I wished that my father knew what was happening in my life—what I was doing on this or that day or this or that hour. I asked him if he ever wondered whether the people we lose know what has become of us.

"I believe they do know," he said.

"I'm glad to hear that you do because I do, too," I said.

"I often think about that, and I'm sure they do know. I think spirits hang around the people they love."

"Isn't that, after all, what *Wait for Me* is all about?"

"Yes, that's exactly what it's all about. I did it as a fantasy and a comedy, but I meant every word of it."

"At this point in your life, there really isn't a more important picture you could make for yourself—and for a lot of other people, too."

"Than *Wait for Me.*"

"Thank you so much for answering all of these questions over the past years."

"Oh, that's all right, Peter. You'll probably come up with a few more."

PART 2

Q&A

The questions and answers that follow are taken from interviews I conducted with Peter Bogdanovich in November and December 2003; January 2004; September, October, and December 2010; January, February, March, May, June, July, November, and December 2011; January and July 2012; November 2013; September 2014; October 2015; and April 2019.

Beginnings

Peter Bogdanovich (PB): I never would have come to America if it hadn't been for Hitler. My mother was pregnant with me, and the war was looking like it was going to happen. My father was prescient about these things. My mother's family was Jewish, my father's family was Greek Orthodox. He had nothing to worry about himself, but her family was in deep shit, and he went to Paris and got visitor visas for her entire primary family: her mother, her father, and her brother and sisters. He got visitor visas to go to New York to see the World's Fair, which was starting in 1939, which is when the war broke out. They took the *Ile de France,* and they came over in May of '39. My mother was pregnant, and I was born full term in July of '39. The war started in Poland in August.

I grew up with a European family and spoke a foreign language first. My father painted at the same place where we lived, so I was surrounded by composition and color my whole life from birth. And he had a lot of intellectuals around, writers, other painters, and musicians. It was an egghead background.

Peter Tonguette (PT): *Even as a young man, you revered older people.*

PB: I think I told you that story where I was sitting at a dinner table with George Cukor and Dennis Hopper. Dennis turned to George and said, "We're going to *bury* you." George said, "Yes, yes, of course." I thought, "What a fucking shitty thing to say."

PT: *And yet you yourself were younger than Hopper, weren't you?*

PB: I was.

PT: *Hopper's contempt couldn't be excused by his age, then—he should have had some respect!*

PB: Some cultural background, which he lacked. Jerry Lewis made an interesting comment about me. He said that Peter interviewed all of those old directors because he was looking for his father. I thought that was a very perceptive remark. My father was a wonderful man, but he wasn't very talkative. He didn't go into great detail. I mean, my favorite review of *Targets* was a look he gave me. It wasn't anything he said. It was just a look he gave me after he saw it. It sort of said, "He got it, and it was brilliant." But he didn't say anything. He just nodded somberly.

PT: *You came by your taste in movies innocently.*

PB: I didn't even know I'd seen any Howard Hawks pictures, and it turned out that two of them were two of my favorite movies. When I was ten, if you'd asked me what my favorite movies were, I would have said *Red River* and *I Was a Male War Bride.* I had no idea they were by the same director.

PT: *But at some point you began studying them consciously, right?*

PB: Well, I learned how to direct movies by looking at other directors' work and seeing how they used the grammar of the medium. I didn't do a homage to this person or that movie. I was just using techniques that were part of the vocabulary of movies. Just like Griffith introduced close-ups and inserts. Hitchcock remembered the ride to the rescue in *Orphans of the Storm*—it's very much like a Hitchcock sequence.

PT: *What was the Bogdanovich Tape Broadcasting Company?*

PB: Those were my first productions. I didn't do that many of them; there are only about two, I think. They were a lot of work. I would tape off of the radio a dramatic radio show. Both times it was a show called *Suspense.* It would begin, "You're always right with Autolite. Autolite presents *Sus-pense!* Tonight's guest: Richard Widmark." Or whoever it was. It was a movie star every week who would do the lead. They were usually quite good.

I taped one called "Mate Bram," which was about a ship, and a guy gets drunk and kills people and doesn't remember it. There were nine characters in it. I taped it with a tape recorder I got for Christmas or my birthday. I said I wanted a tape recorder because a rich school friend of mine in sixth grade had a Revere tape recorder—one of those big mothers that they used to make. I saw it at his house, and I wanted one.

So I recorded the show, and then I would transcribe the whole thing on a small portable typewriter they'd gotten me. Actually, I think I did it by hand first, and then I typed it. It was like a script. Then I would do all the voices and reenact the thing. But I'd do it my own way with my own choice of music. I played all the parts—including the women. And I would do all the sound effects, either with things in the room or orally. My parents used to hear me making these noises and throwing things. They'd be amused. It took quite a while to do it. I kept breaking the tape. I had to paste it together with Scotch tape because I didn't know how to splice, so there were sound bumps in it.

The other one I did was only four characters—two people caught in an elevator with somebody trying to kill them. I remember that was a very suspenseful show. It had a radio playing in it, and it was playing very up-tempo, counterpoint music. And I did another one for my mother when she was in the hospital in April of 1952. She was in the hospital giving birth to my sister [Anna Thea Bogdanovich]. I took the comic book of *Snow White and the Seven Dwarfs*, and I acted it out for her, the whole comic book. I played it over the phone to her on Easter.

PT: *Growing up, who were some of your favorite writers?*

PB: Oh, Steinbeck and Saroyan and Hemingway and Fitzgerald—those guys. And then Chekhov and Tennessee Williams. Dylan Thomas. I like Dickens a lot, too. My parents were well read. My mother read *War and Peace* every couple of years—the whole damn book.

PT: *You told an interviewer about a short story you wrote when you were a student at the Collegiate School. You said it was about "a female fan of Frank Sinatra who gets jilted by him."*[1]

PB: It's called "Premiere." It was one of the first things I wrote. I wrote it for my English class, and the teacher, Henry Adams, thought it was great and used it as a model in class. We published it in the school newspaper, which was a glossy kind of paper. It's called the *Collegiate Journal.*

PT: *Was "Premiere" your first publication?*

PB: Yes, of any kind. It was the first time I wrote a short story. I think I wrote about five or six short stories in all.

PT: *Do you think that "Premiere" was the best of them?*

PB: No, I think the best of them is called "Times Square, You Know?" It's very Saroyanesque, but it's quite good. It's all about going down to Forty-Second Street to see a double bill of *Tobacco Road* and *The Grapes of Wrath* and what happened to me. It's really exactly what happened. It's written in a very colloquial style. It also reflects on the movies, my feeling about the movies that I've seen, and how it relates to the people on the street that I see. The short story was written when I was a junior or senior. I wrote it in one burst after I came back from seeing the two movies, and then it was published in the *Collegiate Journal.* In fact, the first screenplay that I ever did was based on that short story, and I think it's lost, unfortunately. We were going to make it as a short, and the producer had all the copies—I never held on to one. The script was done right after I got out of high school.

I did a lot of writing in those years, between the time I was about fourteen until I was about twenty. I wrote five full-length plays. I can't imagine that they're any good. They were rather derivative.

PT: *People have the idea that the only writing you did was as a critic.*

PB: No, I started with creative writing. I did start writing reviews fairly soon for the school paper. That's what started me as a critic. I never was really a regular reviewer, except for my school paper and for *Ivy* magazine, a short-lived Ivy League slick magazine.

PT: *Your column for the* Collegiate Journal *was called "As We See It." I noticed that your inaugural review was of the play* End as a Man, *starring Ben Gazzara, who, decades later, starred in* Saint Jack *and* They All Laughed.

PB: I know, isn't that interesting? That was an amazing coincidence. I told that to Ben when we were working on something. The first review I ever wrote was about him in *End as a Man.*

PT: *And your last "As We See It" was a review of the film based on* End as a Man*—also starring Gazzara.*

PB: *The Strange One.*

PT: *You shared a byline on "As We See It" with another student, Vladimir Lehovich.*

PB: I don't know how it started because Vladimir didn't write anything. It was called "As We See It," and somebody said, "Who's 'we'?" So I said to Vladimir, "You want to write it so we can say 'we'?" He said, "Okay. What do we do?" I said, "You don't have to do anything. I'll write it."

PT: *Later, the byline changed to "Peter Bogdanovich and Friend"—who was that?*

PB: "Friend" was supposed to be Suzy Tucker, my girlfriend. Everybody knew I had a girlfriend, so they thought she was writing it with me.

PT: *But in fact it was all you.*

PB: The whole column was always me.

PT: *Were you influenced by any critics or reviewers in writing the column?*

PB: Not in high school. I did read *Cue* magazine, which had short reviews. The magazine is gone now. *Cue* basically just listed what was on, like *Time Out.* I used to check it all the time to see what was playing, and I'd read the short review. Brevity was always a big thing.

PT: *Did you enjoy your time at the Collegiate School?*

PB: The only thing I enjoyed was the Drama Club the first year, and then I got kicked out the second year. That's a long story. I didn't particularly like high school. I liked my teacher of English, Henry Adams. He was a great teacher and a terrific guy. We read some pretty good stuff in that four-year class.

I was chomping at the bit because at fifteen I went away to summer stock. At sixteen, I was skipping the Collegiate Recreation Activities—CRA—and I was going across town to Stella Adler's. I was a kid, but I did as much as I could. I did two live television shows and summer stock for four years. Then I produced and directed *The Big Knife.*

PT: *You've said that your stage productions resembled movies, especially Agatha Christie's* Ten Little Indians, *which you put on during a summer-stock season in Phoenicia, New York.*

PB: That was very much of a movie staging. I didn't think about it at the time. The first act, like any Agatha Christie play or like most plays period, is the longest act. It's about forty-five pages, and it's all exposition, the entire thing. People introducing themselves to each other, everybody saying who they are, what they do, why they're there. Very, very necessary—and very, very boring. [*Laughs.*] So I just broke every single rule you can imagine: I paced it fast, I had people walking upstage on their lines, I had people crossing on other people's lines. Things you're not supposed to do. And it was absolutely riveting. We played forty-five pages in twenty-five minutes. It just zipped along. You could see the audience was into it because they were all leaning forward. They had to pay attention because we weren't taking our time with it at all. It was fast. It was great. Overlapping dialogue. We'd have lines coming in over each other and people crossing at the wrong time. There are nine characters, and they're all in that first act. I staged it like an Orson Welles production.

The ending of *Ten Little Indians* the play is different from the ending of the source of *Ten Little Indians,* which is a novel she wrote called *And Then There Were None.* So in rewriting the script—I changed it from off the coast of England to off the coast of Maine; and I made it American, changing the "should's" to "would's"—I rewrote the ending completely to match the ending of *And Then There Were None.* In *Ten Little Indians,* the girl and her lover remain alive; in *And Then There Were None,* everybody dies. The lover gets killed, and it ends with her walking upstage to hang herself. So we did that ending. People were just devastated. To break the mood, we had the curtain come up for the curtain calls, and the only person who came out was the guy who drove the boat at the very beginning, who just dropped them off on the island. He came out, stood there, looked from left to right, nobody appeared, shrugged his shoulders, and the curtain came down! It was a big laugh. Then the curtain went up again, and everybody came out for curtain calls.

In the second or third act, there's a scene where a gun goes off on stage. Somebody shoots somebody. The lights are supposed to be out on the stage. In other words, the lights go out on stage in the living room or wherever the hell they are, and there's a gunshot, and then the lights are relit, and you see who's been killed. So I did something you're not allowed to do. I went to the ushers and told them that exactly one minute before the shooting, turn off the exit lights in the theater. What happened was, the lights went out onstage, and the exit lights were already out. So it was absolutely pitch black! You couldn't see your hand in front of your face. It was *black.* And the audience got very, very uneasy because they didn't know what had happened. They just suddenly realized that they were in the fucking dark and a gunshot went off. It was like a one-frame cut. It was just a flash, and you could see the silhouette of bodies. Then the lights went on, and people *screamed!* It was against all fire regulations!

PT: *You probably couldn't get away with that today.*

PB: I don't think you could get away with it on Broadway! The ending was very dramatic. We had a player piano that we established that only plays "Ten Little Indians." I stole a couple of lines from [Welles's film] *Touch of Evil:* at one point, he says, "All of us are guilty, guilty, guilty." The triple "guilty." And at the end, when the main killer gets shot—George Morfogen was playing it—I said with each shot I wanted him to cross further stage left. And, at the end, with the last shot, I wanted him to throw himself into the piano so it starts to play. George said, "Well, how am I supposed to do that with each shot?" I said, "Well, you stagger." I did it for him, and then he saw what I meant. That was the end of the heavy. Then the lover dies, and she walks upstage toward the shadow of a noose coming out of a doorway. It was the best physical production we did that summer. The audience loved it. It sold out every night.

PT: Ten Little Indians *was part of a season of four plays you directed in Phoenicia.*

PB: The best were *Ten Little Indians, Once in a Lifetime,* and *Camino Real.* The production of *Rocket to the Moon* was not particularly interesting. The play is a little difficult to do, and the leading girl was not that good—she was a guest star. It was okay, it wasn't great. But the other three were memorable.

PT: *Around this time, you began writing for* Esquire. *You were one of the so-called New Journalists.*

PB: I knew a lot of people at *Esquire.* That's where I met [Robert] Benton and [David] Newman and Gay Talese. Tom Wolfe came into *Esquire* after I was there. I remember Harold Hayes saying he found a new writer named Tom Wolfe. I said, "Thomas Wolfe?" He said, "No, Tom Wolfe."

PT: *In a way, he was doing the same sort of thing you were doing.*

PB: We were all doing a kind of New Journalism, which was subjective objectivity.

PT: *In your later books—particularly* Who the Hell's in It*—you are still working in that style.*

PB: That's very much like the pieces I did; only it's better, I think.

PT: *Some of your original* Esquire *pieces are very good, though.*

PB: The Bogart piece got a lot of attention when it came out. It was a tremendous success. I did a lot of radio interviews about that. It sort of heralded the Bogart cult.

Three for Corman

The Wild Angels (1966, American International Pictures)
Director: Roger Corman; screenplay: Charles Griffith; assistant to director: Peter Bogdanovich

Voyage to the Planet of Prehistoric Women (1968, American International Pictures)
Director: Derek Thomas (Peter Bogdanovich); screenplay: Henry Ney; producer: Norman D. Wells

Targets (1968, Paramount Pictures)
Director: Peter Bogdanovich; screenplay: Peter Bogdanovich; story: Polly Platt and Peter Bogdanovich; producer: Peter Bogdanovich

PT: *You got your first exposure to moviemaking as an assistant to Roger Corman on* The Wild Angels.

PB: I rewrote 80 percent of the script—I'm not exaggerating—for $300 and no credit. Then I directed for three weeks the second unit, including things that were not second unit because they involved the stars. I directed the whole sequence on the motorcycle with Bruce Dern, when he kills the cop. I directed Peter Fonda and Nancy Sinatra in a couple of scenes on the beach and one scene with Peter where he starts his bike—a big, elaborate sequence. I did action stuff in Palm Desert. I also helped Roger with some of the sequences I didn't direct. He asked me to sort of design the setups.

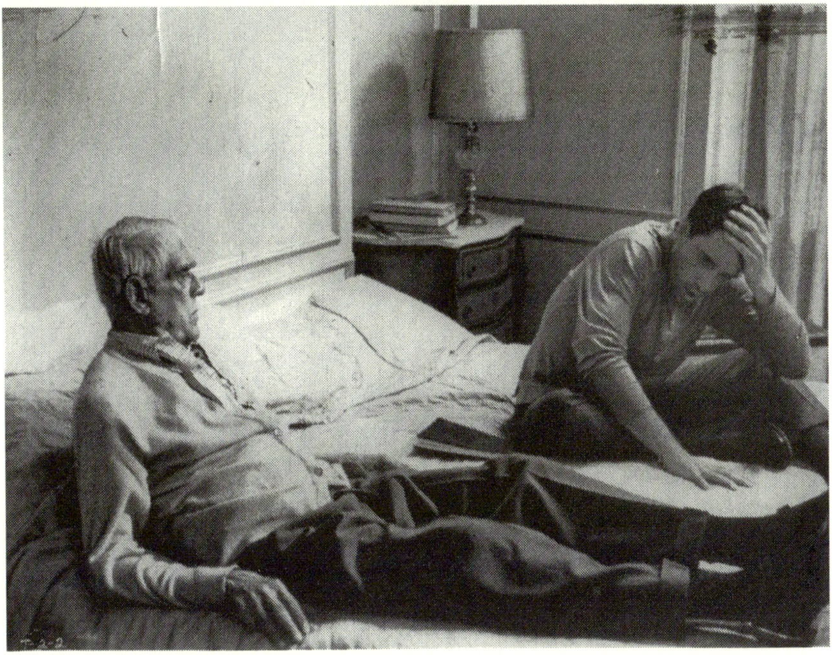

Boris Karloff and Peter Bogdanovich in *Targets*. Courtesy Jerry Ohlinger's Movie Material Store.

So I had a lot to do with the picture, and it was the biggest success of his career. It cost $300,000, and it grossed $6 or $7 million. What people don't realize is that *The Wild Angels* was the beginning of the New Hollywood—unless you count Cassavetes's *Shadows*. But as far as the New Hollywood that made money, that was the beginning of it. It was a very unorthodox film in its day. It led directly to *Easy Rider*. It was sort of the first of the off-Hollywood exploitation pictures, though it had more serious pretensions.

Anyway, it was a hit. Roger immediately called me and asked me if I would like to make a picture of my own as a way of paying me back and also giving me the chance of making a movie. He said, "Look, Boris Karloff owes me two days of work. I want you to shoot for two days with Karloff. You can shoot twenty minutes in two days. I've shot whole pictures in two days!" Which he has. "Then take twenty minutes of Karloff footage from the picture I made with him called *The Terror*—it's not a great picture, but you can find twenty minutes in there. Now you've got forty minutes of Karloff. So I want you to work with some other actors for ten days and shoot forty minutes. Then we'll have a new eighty-minute Karloff picture. Are you interested?" I said, "Well, yeah, sure." And he also threw in, "Oh, by the way, I'll pay you $6,000, and you can give some of it to your wife—she can work with you." I said, "Oh, thanks a lot."

PT: *This became* Targets, *but didn't he have something else in mind for you to do first?*

PB: He said, "And one more thing. I bought a Russian science-fiction film called *Storm Clouds of Venus,* and Curtis Harrington dubbed it for me. AIP won't buy it unless we put some women in it. So I'd like you to take Mamie Van Doren—I made a deal with her—and three or four other women down to Leo Carrillo Beach. It's a good match for the Black Sea. Shoot some stuff with them and put it into the picture. It won't take you more than a few days." Well, that took longer than *Targets!*

PT: *This was released as* Voyage to the Planet of Prehistoric Women. *Is your footage in the finished film?*

PB: Anything with Mamie Van Doren. It's about ten minutes.

PT: *Did you try to put any style into it?*

PB: Well, I tried to do it as best I could. Roger said, "Look, we can't have any sound. I don't want to spend money on sound." I said, "What are we going to do about the dialogue?" He said, "Well, have them communicate through telepathy." So we shot it that way. Everybody at the studio said, "What the fuck is going on?" Roger said, "We'll have to put some thought voices in." Things like: "Moana, go over and get the fish." The studio looked at it again and said, "What the fuck is going on?" [*Laughs.*] So then I had to narrate the whole thing. I wrote a narration for one of the astronauts. I stole the last line from *The Lady from Shanghai* as a kind of joke: "Maybe someday I'll forget her—maybe I'll die trying." And I spoke it. People have said that I directed the picture. I had nothing to do with 90 percent of it. I just found places to put the women in.

In the meantime, while we were doing all of that with Mamie and so on, we were working on *Targets.* The first problem was not the script, but what the fuck to do with it. What do you make Karloff? Is he going to be the heavy in a Victorian castle? How do we integrate that with something contemporary, or do we have to do a Victorian horror piece? I wasn't about to do that. So we had a devil of a time trying to figure out what to do with Boris. *The Terror* is one of the worst movies ever made. It's unspeakably bad. The sequences that are in *Targets* from *The Terror*—the opening sequence and the other little bits and pieces here and there—are not at all the way they are in the picture. It's totally recut by me. Things that last a second or two in my cut go on for hours. It's about three reels condensed into three minutes. That's why it looks kind of promising because it's vastly abbreviated.

We couldn't figure out what the hell to do. We thought of all sorts of ridiculous things, like that he stalks people in supermarkets. We couldn't even think of anything. One day I was shaving, and I had a thought in my mind as a joke of how to begin the picture. I was laughing to myself. You start the picture with the end of *The Terror.* The lights come up, and Boris Karloff is sitting in the projection room, right next to Roger Corman; he turns to Roger and says, "Roger, that is by far the worst film ever made." Then I thought to myself, "That's not a bad idea. Then he would be an actor." The joke became the reality. If he's an actor, then *The Terror* is a movie he was in, and we don't have to do a story related to that at all.

A few months before, Harold Hayes said, "You know, you ought to make a movie about that guy in Texas who shot all those people." I said, "I don't want to make a movie about that." He said, "Well, it'd make a good movie." So when we had the idea about Boris being an actor, we thought, *What if he's an actor who's retiring because his kind of stuff isn't relevant anymore, and we crosscut with this kid who ends up shooting people?* He kills his mother and his wife and so on, like Charles Whitman. Harold suggested it, and we remembered it. Once we solved Karloff, we knew we had to have another story, and it's a horror picture, so what is horrible today? Well, this kid in Texas, shooting people randomly.

PT: *You were setting side by side outmoded movie horror with modern horror.*

PB: Modern horror is much more awful.

PT: Targets *is very much a film of its moment. I sense you had strong feelings about what was going on in the country in the late '60s.*

PB: I thought that we were entering into a pretty decadent era. The violence reflected the fucked-up-edness of the period. *Targets* is a very savage film. Unfortunately, it's still relevant.

Initially, I killed Karloff off in the middle of the picture because I didn't know what else to do with him. We only had him for two days. Then I asked Sammy Fuller to read it. We had a script called *Before I Die*, and Sammy read it and said, "Come over to the shack." That meant, come over to his house. "Come over to the shack. We'll go over it." So I went over, and he said, "Why do you kill Karloff in the middle of the picture?" I said, "Well, we only have him for two days." He said, "Never think about that! Never think about limitations while you're writing a script! Write what you want! You'll figure out how to do it later."

Well, that was a huge point. You can't kill your star off in the middle of the picture. Then Sammy asked if we had any footage from *The Terror* in which Karloff is in a tuxedo. I said we did. "Great! You've got him in a tuxedo for a personal appearance." He gave me the idea of the kid seeing Karloff coming toward him on the screen and coming toward him in reality, which is a great coup de theâtre. I mean, I don't believe it for a minute, but it works. I sweated to make that work.

PT: *Fuller didn't want to be credited—why?*

PB: We talked for about two or three hours. Sammy paced up and down, and we discussed things. I'd write down what he said. When it was over, I said, "Jesus, Sammy, you've rewritten the whole script. You should get credit for this." "No credit, no credit." "But, Sammy, you've had so much great input on this." "No credit, no credit." "Why not?" "If you give me credit, they'll think that I did the whole thing." "You practically did, Sam." "No credit, no credit." My character in the picture is named Sammy Michaels. That was a tip of the hat to Sammy—his full name was Samuel Michael Fuller.

PT: *Were you able to get more days with Karloff to pull this off?*

PB: Well, I handed in the script, and Roger called me. He said, "It's the best script I've ever had to produce." I said, "Really?" He said, "It's excellent. But you can't possibly shoot Karloff in two days. You'll have to cut stuff out." I said, "Roger, you just said it's the best script you've ever produced. How can I cut things out? It will make it less good." He said, "Well, I'm not going to pay Karloff for extra time." I can't remember what happened, but he did eventually pay for three more days. I can't remember how I convinced him. I talked to the agent, and the agent loved the script, and Boris loved the script. What would it cost to get him for five days?

PT: *So you ultimately had five days with Karloff.*

PB: Five full days and nights. We shot half the picture in five days! [*Laughs.*]

PT: *One of the most impressive scenes is when Karloff reads the "appointment in Samarra" monologue, which is taken from W. Somerset Maugham. How did that come about?*

PB: There was a TV showing of Chuck Jones's *How the Grinch Stole Christmas!*, which Boris narrated. It was on about two weeks before we were going to start shooting. I'd never seen it. I liked Chuck Jones's stuff. Boris narrated it brilliantly. He had a great voice. When it was over, I said, "How can I make a movie with Boris Karloff without having him tell a story? How can I let that opportunity go by?" But what's he going to tell? I'd always remembered this quote about the appointment in Samarra, which John O'Hara used for the epigraph for the beginning of his novel *Appointment in Samarra*. It's written by Maugham, from a play of his. I hadn't read the play, but I'd remembered the quote. I thought, *Maybe I'll have him do that*. It seemed to go with our story. We basically stole the speech from Maugham. I think we paid the estate twenty-five bucks or something.

When we were shooting it, there were four or five other people in the scene. I went over to Boris, and I said, "Do you want some cards off-camera?" He said, "Idiot cards?" "Well, I thought it might be a little difficult . . . ." "No, no, no, I have the lyrics, I have the lyrics." That meant he knew the lines. I said, "Well, what do you think if I start on you and pan around to the other people listening and end up on you as you finish?" He looked completely disgusted but didn't say anything. He just said, "Yes, you can do that, I suppose," but he looked completely horrified at the thought! [*Laughs.*] So I quickly thought, *He's thinking he should be on camera all the time, and he's right*. I said, "What about if I start way back there with all five of you in the shot, and I slowly move in on you through the whole thing?" He said, "That sounds better." I said, "Well, let's do that." "Fine."

The way the room was configured, we'd established a room-service tray, and it was in the way of the dolly. So we floated it out. As the camera passes the table, right at a certain moment, right when it just is out of camera range, two technicians would float the table out as silently as possible while the camera was moving forward. It had to be very precisely done. We started to shoot it, and on the first take they fucked up the table. So we started again. On the second one, although you can hear it on the track, it was fine, and we finished the take. I had said to Boris, "At the end, when the camera is in a big head, think about your own death." He said, "All right." So we moved in, moved in, moved in, pulled the table out, moved in, moved in, and then he says that last line. I said, "Cut! Print! God that was great!" And the entire crew—this is now about one o'clock in the morning in a small studio on Santa Monica Boulevard—burst into applause. Boris got tears in his eyes. His wife, Evie, was on the set, and she had tears in her eyes. She said to me, "Can you imagine how long it's been since a crew applauded for Boris?" It was a wonderful moment.

PT: *It's the high point of the film.*

PB: It's meant to be. Because it sort of says what's going to happen.

PT: *There is no editor credited on the film, so I always assumed you cut it yourself.*

PB: I had an editor, and he cut one scene together, the scene in the Polo Lounge with Karloff and the girl and the publicity man, and he cut it like a chase. It was so bad that we had to reorder the dailies. I fired him and took over and did it myself with an assistant.

PT: *Didn't you cut your own scenes on* The Wild Angels*?*

PB: I learned how to edit myself on *The Wild Angels.* Roger called me into his office and said, "The stuff you shot doesn't cut." I said, "What do you mean it doesn't cut?" Monte Hellman was the editor. Roger said, "Monte said it doesn't cut." I said, "Well, then he's cutting it wrong." So I went down and looked at it, and, of course, it was all cut wrong. I told Roger, "It's absolutely cut completely wrong. It's not the way I shot it." Roger said, "Well, then cut it yourself." I said, "Well, I don't know how to use the equipment." Roger said, "You don't know how to use a Moviola? Oh, for Chrissakes, go downstairs and talk to Dennis. He'll show you." So they sent the editing equipment out to my house in Van Nuys, and I edited it myself. I brought it in, they said it was fine, and that was it. I learned to edit in my head before I even shot it. All of the great directors I talked to—Ford and Hawks and Orson and Dwan—they all cut in the camera.

PT: *Verna Fields was the sound editor of* Targets *and later the picture editor of* What's Up, Doc?, Paper Moon, *and* Daisy Miller.

PB: She did a great job. All of that stuff on the freeway and at the drive-in [in *Targets*] was shot silent, so you can imagine the work that was involved with that. She did a brilliant, brilliant job.

By the time of *What's Up, Doc?,* I hired Verna to edit it. It was the first time that she worked as an editor on a big picture. She'd been a sound editor. I said, "Look, I'm going to mark it before you cut it. Before you make any cut, I have to mark it. This is the first picture that I'm not cutting myself. If I see some assembly that I haven't created, I'll be confused." I marked every frame. "S" means start—leave that frame in. "C" means cut—cut that frame out. That's how we did the whole picture. Because of digital, I don't have to work like that any longer. It's become too easy.

PT: *Polly Platt designed* Targets.

PB: Polly had never done production design on anything. She'd done costumes in the theater, but she'd never done any production design for a movie. We worked very closely on the color scheme. We had all warm colors for Karloff, and we had all cold colors for [killer] Bobby [Thompson (Tim O'Kelly)]. I was somewhat influenced by Norman Mailer's writing about the effect of the plastic society on people's psyches. The movie is a little bit about that. People said, "Well, why did he [Bobby] do that?" Well, look where he lived. In *Cannibals and Christians,* Mailer talks about how people are affected by the ugliness of society, by the ugliness of things around them.

PT: *Did you know Norman Mailer?*

PB: We were pretty good friends for a while. He liked some of my pictures, and I liked some of his writing. I remember the first connection I had with him. It was way back at the New Yorker Theater when Dan Talbot wanted to do a film festival, and he wanted to get literary figures to write program notes. So we got Jack Kerouac and Gay Talese. There were a bunch of them. I got in touch with Mailer, but I can't remember what movie he wrote about. It was around the time that he had stabbed his wife, Adele [Morales]. I don't think I met him until the '70s. We were quite friendly for a while. When he was in LA, he'd come over to the house with his girlfriend, and then she became his wife [Norris Church

Mailer]. Then we saw him in Brooklyn Heights, too, where he lived. The four of us would go out on the town—Norman and Norris and me and Cybill. But then I had a terrible parting of the ways with him.

PT: *Do you want to say what it was over?*

PB: Dorothy had been killed, and *They All Laughed* was playing in New York. He called me up and said, "I saw your picture. I wish you wouldn't write." And I saw red and said, "You know, Norman, I've been humoring you for years that I'm interested in what you think about movies, but you haven't got a fucking clue about anything about movies, so why should I give a fuck what you think?" He said, "Peter . . ." I said, "I don't give a *fuck* what you think, that's what I think." And that was it. I hung up on him. He approached me a few years later to play a part in *Tough Guys Don't Dance,* and I turned him down.

PT: *Did you regret the relationship ending?*

PB: Not particularly. It was so fucking insensitive of him to call me like that. I didn't miss him. I had a nice relationship with him for a while. He was very competitive with me.

PT: Targets *does not have a score.*

PB: When I was cutting it, and when I was finishing it, I liked the way it felt using music as a sound effect rather than as music. Since I had clips from *The Terror* at the beginning, I had the main titles covered, and I thought that the use of counterpoint in the music or an announcer talking or a news broadcast creates the feeling of another world going on beyond the movie. It gives you a kind of double view: there's a world outside the world of the movie. There is basically no score in *Rear Window,* either. That had an impact on me. In fact, I saw *Rear Window* when we were preparing *Targets.* I said, "What's the point? I'll never do anything that good."

Directed by John Ford (1971, American Film Institute)

> Director: Peter Bogdanovich; screenplay: Peter Bogdanovich; producers: James R. Silke and George Stevens Jr.

PT: *How did you come to make a documentary on John Ford for the American Film Institute?*

PB: It started around 1967 or '68. George Stevens Jr. called me and said that the AFI was planning to do a series of documentaries about filmmakers, and they wanted to know if I would like to do the first one on Frank Capra. I said, "Well, I'd like to do one for you, but I don't think Frank Capra should be first." "Who do you think should be first?" "Well, John Ford. I mean, he's more of the foundation than Capra. And I think he's a more important artist." So they said okay, and they financed it, along with the California Arts Commission.

I shot the interviews and picked the clips. They never paid for the clips, so the picture couldn't be shown for anybody paying a fee. They could only show it free, like at film festivals or on PBS. It was never really screened much, and it became legendary because nobody saw it! [*Laughs.*] The interviews with Wayne, Stewart, Fonda, and Ford and the narration by Orson were good, but overall I felt it was shallow, not rich enough, not personal enough, and I just didn't find it entertaining enough. I was always dissatisfied with it. I felt it was weak and always wanted to redo it.

PT: *You finally got the chance in 2006, when it ran on Turner Classic Movies.*

PB: We redid it completely and interviewed five or six more people, including myself. I think the contemporary voices—Scorsese, Spielberg, Walter Hill, Clint Eastwood—talking about Ford and the influence he had on them gave it a certain cachet. We just made it much more dense and much richer. I brought Frank Marshall in to give it a little more clout. He always wanted to work on it and hadn't worked on it before.

PT: *It's fitting that you brought Frank Marshall on board because you first met him at the house of John Ford.*

PB: Yes, at a birthday party for Ford's daughter, Barbara, in 1966.

PT: *I like Spielberg's story about meeting Ford as a teenager and being lectured by him about painting and composition.*

PB: It was a good anecdote.

PT: *I love the way you shot the original interviews with Wayne, Stewart, and Fonda. You had the camera on tracks so you could dolly-in when necessary.*

PB: I had never done a documentary, and I didn't really have any rules to break. What I did was I went out and saw the three actors some time before shooting the interviews. I had a tape recorder and talked with them for several hours. I got some stories and so on. I had those interviews transcribed and picked the stories that I wanted them to tell on camera. So I gave them a script, basically, of what they had said. I said, "Obviously, you are not going to read this, but it's to remind you of what you said." Knowing the stories, I knew when would be the time to move in. I laid the dolly track with Stewart on that long story about [*The Man Who Shot*] *Liberty Valance.* I had my hand down underneath the lens, and I just gave the signal when to dolly in. László [Kovács] shot the one with Jimmy. I think it's the best shot of the three. We did a dolly on Duke, and we did with Fonda also.

PT: *Didn't you move the camera back when Wayne stands up to illustrate a point?*

PB: We cut back.

PT: *Still, it's much more sophisticated than most talking-head documentaries.*

PB: I tried to make it more like a film. Fonda told me the story about going to meet Ford for the first time and standing in front of his desk while Ford said, "What the hell is all this shit about you not wanting to play Lincoln?" When he told me the story on the tape recorder, he stood up and acted it out. So when we went to shoot the film, I said, "Look, I've made a dolly track because when you told me the story, you stood up. You can do that again, and I'll just dolly back for you." He patted my hand, and he said, "You're a good director." [*Laughs.*]

PT: *Had you already made* Targets?

PB: I had made *Targets.* I think they called me right after it opened or right before it opened. I had definitely shot it.

PT: *Technically speaking, then,* Directed by John Ford *is your second film.*

PB: Technically, it would be my second film.

PT: *Now, for your interview with Ford, sitting outside in Monument Valley, there is no camera movement. It looks like you just locked the camera down.*

PB: Well, we were lucky to get him sitting!

PT: *What were you expecting when you asked to interview him for the film?*

PB: I was hoping he would be as expansive as he was when I interviewed him for my book [*John Ford*].[2] He did tell me some good stuff; it's just that he was perverse and gave me that great sequence where he wouldn't answer any questions, which was pretty funny.

PT: *Did you have any clue that he would be so difficult that day?*

PB: No, but it didn't bother me particularly. I knew what he was like, and he did answer some of the questions. He just refused to answer some of them straight. He didn't like to get into philosophical conversations. He didn't get into that sort of stuff. It just wasn't his thing.

I rode with him by train to Flagstaff. He wanted to go by train—he loved trains. It was an overnight trip, and I hung out with him a little bit. When we got to Monument Valley, I said, "Well, I'd like to shoot with you, Jack." He said, "No, shoot some stuff with the Indians." I said, "Well, I don't have anything to shoot with the Indians." He said, "Just shoot some stuff with the Indians." I didn't know what the hell to shoot with the Indians. I can't remember if we actually did shoot anything with the Indians. He just didn't feel like shooting that day. We finally got him to do it the next day.

Did I tell you what happened when I showed it to Ford for the first time?

PT: *No, you haven't.*

PB: The AFI screened it for Ford. All of the actors were invited, and it was introduced by Governor Ronald Reagan. It was a special screening—very official. I was seated fairly close to Fonda, Stewart, and Wayne. We were sort of in the same area. Ford was seated elsewhere. When it was over, Jimmy said, "I'm not gonna go anywhere *near* him." He was terrified because he had made those jokes about Ford! But I went over, and I said, "So, what'd you think, Jack?" He looks at me and goes, "Good job on a dull subject." I stood there for a while, and people were coming up and congratulating him and saying how much they liked it. I said, "Well, I'll see you, Jack. I'm going." I put my hand out, and he shook my hand. And then as I started to pull my hand away, he pulled me really close to him, rather suddenly, and he looked at me and said, "Thank you." Very touching. That was the best review I could have gotten.

PT: *How did you get Orson Welles to record the narration?*

PB: I said, "Would you do a narration for a documentary I'm doing on Ford?" He said, "Sure, but you'll have to pay me." I said, "Well, how much do you want?" He said, "Five grand." So we got him five grand. I sent him the pages, and he did it without me there. I wanted to be there to direct him, but he just recorded it and sent it to me. He was in Palm Springs or somewhere. He wasn't in LA. And I was a little unhappy with it because he was slower than I wanted. I wanted him to talk faster, and he was a little slow and ponderous, but I couldn't do anything about it. For the revised version, we actually sped up his speech. They now have a way of speeding up the words without messing up the sound of his voice. You can't tell, but he actually speaks faster.

PT: *In the new version, you're on camera much more.*

PB: You never really saw my face in the other version. Since I've achieved a certain notoriety by now, I thought it would work to see me tell some stories, too. We couldn't decide if I should talk to the camera or to somebody sitting off-camera. At first we were going to do it to camera, and we tried it that way, but it looked sort of fake. So I played it to Cybill Shepherd's daughter, Ariel Shepherd-Oppenheim. She was sitting there.

PT: *You also added clips from an interview with Maureen O'Hara.*

PB: We borrowed that from a documentary that Lindsay Anderson made.

PT: *We also hear Ford and Katharine Hepburn talking privately late in his life; Ford's grandson, Dan Ford, taped the exchange accidentally.*

PB: Well, that was gold. Dan explained to me that he left the tape running when he left the room, and he didn't hear it until after Jack had died. I thought it was very touching. We had to get permission from the Katharine Hepburn estate to use her voice. We sent it to Katharine Houghton, her niece, who was in *Guess Who's Coming to Dinner,* and she approved it. She thought it was touching, too. It's very haunting. Ford was such a grouch, and you hear him being as warm as he could be to anybody—and it was to her.

PT: *I think you are the last connection to old Hollywood.*

PB: Well, I knew all of those guys. That's my great advantage.

PT: *Do you think that really helps?*

PB: Yes, very much so. I learned a lot from them in terms of goals and certain technical things, like Hawks saying if you cut on movement, nobody will notice the cut. Well, if you're hiding the editing, as opposed to trying to be flashy, so that you don't notice it, then you cut on movement. That was a tremendous thing to be told. And things like what lenses to use. A 40 lens is how the eye sees. It's not often used, but one of the best lenses around. I shot most of *Picture Show* on a 40 or a 28.

I learned by knowing them. Once you got to know the directors' personality and what they were like, the work becomes illuminated. You say, "Oh, that was Howard doing that," or "I betcha Jack Ford wrote that line." You get intimate, so that it's almost like you're on the set. I've had moments where I feel like I knew what it was like on the set that day.

PT: *Have you ever been tempted to make a documentary on another director?*

PB: Well, I was hoping to do something on Hawks. We have that footage that was shot of me interviewing him in Palm Springs for the BBC. It's not very well shot. Have you ever seen that?

PT: *I've seen excerpts from it but never the entire interview.*

PB: It was about an hour, and they cut it fairly badly, I thought. The clips were badly used.

PT: *Do you think you could reuse that footage now for a project of your own?*

PB: I don't think so because there's no one to talk to about Howard. Everybody's gone.

The Last Picture Show (1971, Columbia Pictures)

> Director: Peter Bogdanovich; screenplay: Larry McMurtry and Peter Bogdanovich (based on the novel by Larry McMurtry); producer: Stephen J. Friedman; executive producer: Bert Schneider

PT: *In* This Is Orson Welles, *you write about how* Citizen Kane *was an albatross for Welles and how* The Naked and the Dead *was an albatross for Norman Mailer—their first big success that eclipses their other work. Is* The Last Picture Show *like that for you?*

Sam Bottoms and Ben Johnson in *The Last Picture Show*. Courtesy Jerry Ohlinger's Movie Material Store.

PB: No, I don't feel that way at all. First of all, I had other successful pictures. People come up to me and mention *Paper Moon* or *They All Laughed* or *What's Up, Doc?* or *Noises Off*. When people come up to me, they don't just say *The Last Picture Show*.

What *The Last Picture Show* did was establish me. I didn't have to make another picture. I could have just lived off of that one, or I could have kept making the same picture over and over.

PT: The Last Picture Show *was produced by BBS, the company Bob Rafelson, Bert Schneider, and Steve Blauner had at Columbia.*

PB: Bob Rafelson saw *Targets*, and then Bert Schneider saw it. They told me they wanted to work with me. I brought them a script called *The Looters*, which Polly [Platt] and I had worked on at Cinema Center. Bert said, "No, I don't think that's very personal to you. That's just a genre picture." So I brought them *The Last Picture Show*. I had a very funny conversation. I said, "Well, I want to do a book called *The Last Picture Show*." He [Bert] said, "Well, send me a copy." I said, "Why don't you buy it?" And he was amused at that and said, "All right. I'll buy it." He called me about a week later, "Well, I *bought* it. Took me a few days to find it. But we want to do it with you." I said, "Great!"

There was a problem, though. Steve Friedman owned the rights. Bert said, "Little Stevie Friedman from camp? I went to camp with him. Is he as big a jerk now as he was then?" I said, "Yeah, he sure is." He said, "Well, I can take care of *him.*" Bert had to make a deal with him—Steve got a very good deal. He's billed as producer, when in fact Bert Schneider was the producer. Steve had nothing to do with the film at all.

PT: *Bert Schneider really supported the director.*

PB: That's correct. He made a suggestion that I didn't like. He said, "Why don't you end the picture when the kid drives out of town and then turns around and comes back?" I said, "And lose the scene with Cloris [Leachman] and Tim [Bottoms]?" He said, "Do you need it?" I said, "Bert, I made the picture 'cause of that scene." And he said, "Oh, okay." [*Laughs.*] That was Bert. He didn't push an issue like that.

BBS was very honest. They gave, I think, 10 percent of the earnings to the staff. Everybody who worked there had a piece of the action. That was part of the rules. They were very fair about the money, and I saw very good money on the picture. I got $75,000 upfront, but I owned 22 percent of the picture or something like that. There were a huge amount of profits, and I saw money. I mean, half of my points were bought for half a million dollars within a few months. Everybody benefitted from that picture. And it was made, really, just because they wanted to make a picture with me, and they liked the book and thought I could do something good with it. It was the easiest deal I ever made.

PT: *I was reading the piece Grover Lewis wrote for* Rolling Stone *about* The Last Picture Show.

PB: That was a controversial piece.

PT: *Lewis quotes Polly Platt about what drew you to the film: "He"—referring to you—"has a terrific nostalgia for his teenage years in the fifties—Holden Caulfield ice-skating at Rockefeller Plaza with wholesome young girls in knee socks, like that. . . . Somehow, he's managed to transfer those feelings about his own adolescence to the totally different experience of the kids in the film."*[3]

PB: Well, love is sort of the same no matter where you feel it.

PT: *But one of your hesitations about doing the film was because the setting was so alien to you.*

PB: I got interested because I didn't know how to do it. I understood the emotions, and that's what got me into it. Plus, the idea of treating it sort of like a foreign country. That's the external part of it. The internal part of it is that the emotions are the same. That's why people all over the world responded to the movie. In Australia or England or Italy, they all sort of had the same reaction to the picture. They understood the people.

PT: *The scenes I like best are those with Sam the Lion.*

PB: He's the heart of the movie.

PT: *There's that scene when Sam tells Sonny and Duane that he doesn't want them to come to the theater after humiliating Billy. I wonder if Sam is speaking for you—the way he is condemning contemporary manners and mores.*

PB: Well, it was in the book, but I certainly identified with it. Let's put it this way: I agreed with it. It was shabby behavior.

I changed one important element from the book in the contour of Sam the Lion. It's the big speech at the tank dam about racing horses across the dam. That was written at my behest because what was in the book was seeing how far he could pee off the dam or something. I just thought it wasn't going to work. We needed something romantic. So Larry [McMurtry] wrote a very nice, romantic piece. He gave it that poetic thing that it needed.

PT: *I connect Sam the Lion with Byron Orlok in* Targets: *two people from an earlier era.*

PB: Well, I was hanging around with those kind of people, you know?

PT: *You've always been drawn to people from past generations—Ford and Hawks and even Robert Graves, too.*

PB: The 1800s.

PT: *Sam the Lion and Byron Orlok are both very disapproving of the world around them.*

PB: Because I was too! I was disapproving! [*Laughs.*]

PT: *But you were in your late twenties and early thirties!*

PB: The older men were bewildered by what they saw, and I was saddened by what I saw. Now that I'm their age, it's even worse.

PT: *Do you think the innocence of the early years of Hollywood had been lost by the time you arrived on the scene?*

PB: Oh, yeah. It just got worse. It kept getting worse and worse, until it's now apocalyptic. It can't go on like this. They're [films are] being made for these teenagers, these adolescent or postadolescent men-children. They play video games, they look at pornography on the internet, they read *Maxim* magazine. Movies are made for them.

PT: *You have reservations about the freedom you were given to show sex and violence.*

PB: I think it's fucked up the movies pretty badly, actually. Now you can't have sex without nudity. Sex is equated with nudity and with slobbering mouths. It used to be much more interesting when it was oblique.

The thing that has hurt the most is women's roles in movies. The proliferation of pornography in society has destroyed women's roles because in order to be sexy, it means you have to take off your clothes. And mystery is part of the allure of women. Imagine if we could switch on Garbo and see her naked. It would be horrible.

PT: Picture Show *and* Saint Jack *are your only two films that are particularly explicit in that department.*

PB: I didn't necessarily like doing it in *Picture Show.* I found it difficult to do. I think it was effective. There is only seven seconds of nudity in the whole picture. It's very brief, and it's all in movement. It doesn't gloat. I think it's okay to be candid, but you have to be careful that it doesn't turn pornographic, which is what it mostly is nowadays. And violence has become pornographic, too. I told you Hawks's comment about Peckinpah, didn't I? He [Hawks] could kill and bury ten guys in the time it takes him [Peckinpah] to kill one.

PT: *This is in reference to* The Wild Bunch.

PB: Yeah. I had a lot of violence in *Targets,* but I think we did it pretty tastefully. You didn't see guts splattering around.

PT: *You don't ever take violence lightly in your films.*

PB: I guess even before I experienced a murder in my own family, even before that, I just . . . I don't know. To kill somebody is a big deal. I think you have to [take it seriously]. Otherwise you're making murder—which is the worst crime, to take somebody's life—you're making less of it. Therefore, you make less of life. That's why I hate all those pictures that make violence random and sort of boring.

PT: *That's the opposite view of most directors and studios these days.*

PB: Well, sensationalism is all they've got because they haven't got a lot of talent. So the sensationalism is what gets them in the tent.

PT: *Tell me the story of Bert Schneider calling you after* Picture Show *was reviewed in* Newsweek.

PB: I was at Warner Bros. shooting *What's Up, Doc?* and he calls me. He gets me in my trailer on the set. He said, "Are you sitting?" I said, "Okay, I'm sitting now." He said, "This is from *Newsweek.*" And he reads me the first line of the *Newsweek* review, which compares the picture to *Citizen Kane.* And I said, "Holy shit. Are you kidding?" He said, "No. Congratulations."

What's Up, Doc? (1972, Warner Bros. Pictures)

Director: Peter Bogdanovich; screenplay: Buck Henry, David Newman, and Robert Benton; story: Peter Bogdanovich; producer: Peter Bogdanovich

PT: *Did you want to follow* Picture Show *with a much lighter, G-rated movie?*

PB: It just sort of happened. I was asked to make a picture with Barbra Streisand, but I didn't like the script. I liked one thing in the script, which we stole, by the way, without telling anybody, which is that she knows everything. Her character has been to so many schools that she knows everything. But that's all. The rest of it was this sort of comedy-drama called *Glimpse of Tiger,* and I didn't like it. They said, "But Barbra really wants to make a picture with you." I said, "Well, I don't want to do that picture." They said, "Well, what would you do if you could do any kind of picture you wanted with Barbra?" I said, "Oh, you know, screwball comedy, like *Bringing Up Baby.* Screwy dame, square professor, she lightens him up, it all turns out all right." "Go ahead and do it." [*Laughs.*]

So there I was. It was not an assignment, but it was like *Okay, what do you do if you're going to make a picture with Barbra Streisand?* It's just like *What do you do if you're going to make a picture with Boris Karloff?* It's the same thing. I came at the tail end of when you did that for stars. Streisand was a *real* star. She had a certain quality that made her a star, and she played herself, so to speak, and Karloff was famous for his certain niche. Those were both star vehicles in a certain way.

Once I was committed to do this, then I was really going to go all the way and do it the way I wanted to in terms of the kind of picture I wanted to make. And I wanted to make it absolutely the opposite of the last one: a G-rated picture for the whole family that isn't a Disney picture and that's sharp and witty and funny. Like the old days. We had a Buster Keaton chase. And we wanted very garish colors. Polly and I discussed it. We said, "Let's make it really look ugly at the hotel," or "Austin Pendleton's [character Frederick Larrabee's] house we should make very abstract and all black-and-white." It was a little bit like a cartoon because the movie is a bit like a cartoon.

PT: *Was it fun to make?*

PB: We had a lot of fun making that picture, no question about it, but you had to. It was that kind of picture. You're either falling down laughing at something, or you were making up something and having fun with it. It was hard work. We did it in seventy-one days. We had seventy-two, but I came in a day under.

You know the story about when we were shooting the stuff when she crosses the street with the pizza?

PT: *No, I don't—you mean when Streisand causes the car crash?*

PB: The first shot of the morning was a high-angle shot looking down on the pizza as it comes in under frame. We pan up, and Barbra appears, following the pizza guy, and she crosses the street, and they go into the hotel. That was the shot. One shot. So I looked, and I said, "Jesus Christ, Frank"—Frank [Marshall] was my right-hand man, even though he got billing as location manager—"this is a boring fucking shot. Have we got a couple of stunt guys here?" He said, "We've got drivers, but no cars. You didn't order any cars." I said, "Go to Hertz and rent a couple of cars. Be sure to check off where it says insurance." [*Laughter.*] Frank said, "What are we going to do?" I said, "We're gonna wreck 'em."

So Frank goes and rents two cars from Hertz. I said, "Okay, now you guys drive down here and just barely miss Barbra. One of the cars stops short, and the other car will hit you in the ass, and you guys get out and fight about it." Then I said, "Now, Barbra, sweetheart, you're going to walk across the street, and no matter what happens, don't blink. Just ignore it. A guy is going to stop his car in front of you, and the other guy is going to hit him, but you just keep walking."

Then we took the cars back, and we said, "Oh, we're terribly sorry!" [*Laughs.*]

PT: *Howard Hawks phoned you on the set while you were shooting.*

PB: We were actually having a table read. I think it was before the read had started. The whole cast was assembled, and we were chatting. The assistant director comes over and says, "Peter, you've got a call on the stage phone. It's Howard Hawks." Everybody went, *Ohhh, it's Howard Hawks!* I went over, and I said, "Howard?" "Peter?" "Howard?" "Peter?" "Howard!" "Peter!" I said, "Hi, how are you?" I had sent him the script of *What's Up, Doc?*, and I had told him we had stolen a few things from him. Now, he calls me, and he says, "Well, you didn't steal the leopard." "I couldn't steal the leopard, Howard! I mean, it's too much identified with your picture." "Well, yeah, I guess. Well, you didn't steal the dinosaur." "No, I couldn't steal the dinosaur, Howard. Again, it's very associated with your picture. I just took the basic plot." "Yeah, well, it's okay. It's fine. Who you got in it?" "Well, Barbra Streisand and Ryan O'Neal. I know they're not Katharine Hepburn and Cary Grant . . ." "You're damn right they're not. Well, just don't let 'em be cute." "Okay, Howard. Thank you." "All right, boy. See you later."

PT: *What did Hawks think when he saw it?*

PB: He was very proud of it. [*Laughs.*] He took a lot of bows for it.

PT: *But that was fine with you.*

PB: Oh, yeah, I told everybody it was stolen from *Bringing Up Baby*, and then everybody said, "He stole it from *Bringing Up Baby*." [*Laughs.*] One of them said I stole it from *Bringing Up Father,* which was a comic strip at that time.

PT: *But Hawks felt you did a good job.*

PB: He went down to Rio, and it was playing there. With his own little camera, he took pictures of the marquee, showing what it looked like for me. Isn't that sweet?

PT: *It's such a buoyant movie.*

PB: It was done very, very quickly. The time from having that meeting in the office with John Calley to the time we were shooting was a very short time. I think it was about four months at most. I was finishing *Picture Show,* and then I went over and started *Doc.* It was a lot of fun. As I said before, I thought they were all going to be fun like that. It didn't turn out that way. But it doesn't really matter. I didn't have much fun making *Paper Moon,* and it turned out okay.

Austin Pendleton made a very interesting remark to me. As an actor, he said, he was playing with big stars like Barbra Streisand and Ryan O'Neal, and he was not a name. He was a New York actor who'd done a couple of pictures, but he wasn't a big name. But because of the way I shot it, he said to me years later, oftentimes in four shots—where you had Barbra and Ryan and Austin and Ken Mars all in one shot, all playing off of each other—it put the stars in the same kind of nervous position as the supporting players. So it sort of democratized everybody. It made everybody equal.

PT: *It's kind of an Otto Preminger approach.*

PB: It's true of any kind of shot with a lot of people in it. Austin said it made it so much more fun to do the scenes. The actors were sort of in it together. "Oh God, I don't want to be the one to fuck up." Ryan would say things like, "Oh, he's going to be so mad at me 'cause I fucked up."

PT: *There are an awful lot of scenes in hotels in your films.*

PB: That's very funny. I like hotels. [*Laughs.*]

PT: *Well,* Doc *takes place in a hotel. Later, you have a great hotel sequence in* Paper Moon, *and you shot at the Plaza and the Algonquin in* They All Laughed. *Much of* She's Funny That Way *is set in a hotel.*

PB: Hotels have always been romantic to me. I stayed by myself in a hotel for the first time when I was fifteen, going on sixteen, when I went to act in Traverse City, Michigan, in a season of summer stock. I took the train from Manhattan to Grand Rapids, got off and stayed at a hotel, and caught another train the next morning to Traverse City. I don't know. It's clean, it's impersonal, and yet it's warm and welcoming. It has a transient quality so you don't feel like there are any strings attached. Hotels are fun.

Also, I've spent so much time of my life in hotels because of shooting pictures. I have an option of renting a house or staying in a hotel, and I always stay in a hotel if I can. The maid comes and cleans up every day. You don't have to worry about anything. I just like hotels. You're perceptive to notice that. If could stay anywhere, I'd rather live in a hotel. I've had some of my most wonderful times in hotels. Dorothy and I lived at the Plaza basically through that period. I associate it with good times.

Hotels are also a great way to bring a bunch of people together, as we did in *Doc*. Everybody staying in the same hotel is a good dramatic device to get everybody together believably.

PT: *When you were making* Doc, *I wonder if you had any thought about how it might go over. The tagline on the poster—"A screwball comedy. Remember them?"—implies that there hadn't been a movie like this in a while.*

PB: There hadn't been. What happened was, they came to me as I was about to get into a limousine going to the airport to go to Denver for the first preview. It really was very dramatic! I was rushing, and the guys from the publicity and ad department were literally following me as I was going through the lot to get the car! They're talking to me about the campaign. They show me this ad with Barbra and Ryan. The artwork was okay, but the tagline was "Laugh Story." I said, "That's not gonna work. 'Laugh Story.'" They said, "You don't like it?" I said, "No, it's terrible." I said, "Why don't you just say, 'A screwball comedy. Remember them?'" And they said, "Okay."

PT: *It's one of my favorite taglines.*

PB: Well, I threw it over my shoulder as I was getting into the limo! I was referring back to an older generation, in a way, because there hadn't been a screwball comedy. Even the phrase was more '30s than '40s or '50s. It was a nostalgic thing, but "screwball" sounded funny, and I thought it would work even for people who didn't know what it meant.

PT: *Were you surprised that there was a ready-made audience for it?*

PB: I wasn't surprised. I was hoping that it would work for the whole family, and it did. It became a favorite for families everywhere. Adults can enjoy it as much as the kids. We were very conscious of making a G-rated picture and also avoiding any kind of contemporary reference. There are no contemporary references except the line, "Love means never having to say you're sorry," but it works in the context of the picture even if you don't know the line from *Love Story.* It's just a silly line.

People love that picture. They see it fifty times—one woman told me she saw it fifty times. That's overdoing it a bit.

PT: *Unless one is writing a book on your movies!*

PB: That's right. Fifty times! I know one woman who could quote the whole script.

We had a presentable version of *What's Up, Doc?* that I showed to the studio three weeks after we wrapped—*three weeks* after we wrapped. [*Laughs.*] We previewed it right after that, and the preview was 100 percent. I said, "I need to take three or four minutes out." They said, "What are you talking about?" We had a smash. I said, "Just a little bit here and there. Nothing in particular." And then we released it. So it came out very quickly. Now, *Picture Show* didn't open in theaters until October [1971], and in March [1972] we opened *What's Up, Doc?* at the Radio City Music Hall—and *Picture Show* was still playing on Third Avenue in one theater, where we were bringing down $40,000 a week like clockwork. So I went to New York, and on one side of town was *The Last Picture Show*—I stood at the back, and it played great—and then I went to the other side of town, and I went to the Radio City Music Hall. There was the marquee—which, by the way, was not in my contract—that said, "BARBRA STREISAND RYAN O'NEAL IN PETER BOGDANOVICH'S COMEDY *WHAT'S UP, DOC?*" It was a very thrilling moment for me because I used to go to Radio City Music Hall with my parents. It was a real kick to see my name like that, and they put it there. And the reason they put it there wasn't my ego—it was because it sold tickets. I was anointed by those reviews on *Picture Show.*

Also, the ads for *Picture Show* said "A film by Peter Bogdanovich" in fairly big letters—which I did not request, which was given to me by Bert

Schneider. That was because I had attracted attention in underground circles and I was known for *Targets* and for *Esquire.* Bert thought enough of me that he gave me that billing, which was a European billing that had never been used before on an American film. On *Doc,* I took "A Peter Bogdanovich Production," but they didn't use that on the marquee—they put "PETER BOGDANOVICH'S COMEDY" because it sold tickets. The other thing I can brag about is that I had two pictures—*two* pictures—in the top ten in *Variety* for several months in 1972.

It was a kind of career high point. I think the real dramatization of that high point was when I stood in the back of the Music Hall when *What's Up, Doc?* was playing—as Cary Grant had instructed me, "You listen and you watch while 6,500 people laugh at something you did—it will do your heart good!" That was amazing. That was really the high point of me and an audience.

A Western Called *Streets of Laredo* (and Another Western)

PT: *You were going to do a Western next—*Streets of Laredo.

PB: *Streets of Laredo* started with my saying, "I want to make a Western at Warner Bros." I wanted it to star John Wayne, Jimmy Stewart, Henry Fonda, Cybill, the Clancy Brothers, Ellen Burstyn, Cloris Leachman, and Ben Johnson. And they said, "Okay, who's going to write it?" I said, "Larry McMurtry." So I called Larry and said I wanted to do a Western with these people. Originally, Ryan O'Neal was in it, too. That was the list. I got him [McMurtry] $35,000 to write the first draft with me. It was a lot of money for him. I got paid something, too, but I had an overall deal at Warners for three pictures. None of them ever happened, but this was to be the first one.

Cybill was doing *The Heartbreak Kid* in Florida and Minneapolis, and at the time we started this whole thing, she was in Florida at the Fontainebleau [hotel]. Larry was in Texas, so it was easier for him to go from Texas and me to go from LA and meet at the Fontainebleau, 'cause I was going to go see Cybill anyway. So we met at the Fontainebleau, and the first conversation about the movie happened as we were sitting on a sunbaked balcony overlooking the Olympic-size swimming pool where Cybill was doing laps and Larry saying to me, "What kind of Western do you want to make?" [*Laughs.*]

PT: *That's quite a scene!*

PB: That's the scene. And I said, "A trek. You know, they start somewhere, and they go somewhere." He said, "Well, we might as well start at the Rio Grande. That's the lowest we can get and go north. What is there—a cattle drive?" I said, "No, *Red River* did that. We can't do that." Larry said, "Horses." I said, "Horses would be good." So it was horses. They have a horse farm. Then we started working out the relationships among the three main characters. He would say something, and I would say it back to him like Jimmy Stewart.

We worked out the basic characters for Stewart and Wayne, and we decided Fonda was the bad boy who was in trouble with the law for having killed somebody, and they want to hang him, and he comes to hide out with them on their pig and horse farm. Cybill has a scar on her upper lip from when she was about ten and ran into a barbed-wire fence, so she has a faded scar. I said, "We'll accentuate the scar," and somebody in the film will say, "What happened to your lip?" and she'll say, "Somebody bit me."

We sort of talked about how the characters were going to be, the sort of basic, general run of the picture. Why were the Clancy Brothers in it? There were four of them actually, the Clancy Brothers and Tommy Makem. They were a singing group, and I liked them. I told Larry, "Well, there's a funny story that John Ford told me. He had four cousins who came from Ireland to fight the Civil War. When he asked them, 'Well, what side did you want to fight on, Uncle?' They said, 'Oh, either side.'" [*Laughs.*] I thought that was funny, so I told Larry, "Let's put that in the picture." So he wrote the Irishmen into it.

Now that's how it started. Then we would talk on the phone a lot and take notes. I don't know if we met in LA or not—I can't remember, but I don't think we did. Larry went back to Texas, and we might have met in Texas once. In the time we were in Florida, we had worked out the basic plot—the characters, who they were—and then we continued to work that way for a little while until he started to write. He would send me five to ten pages at a time, and I would rewrite them and send them back. The rewriting would be shortening a scene or tightening it up and putting in the things that make it a screenplay, like "Int.," "Ext.," and some of the descriptions. We ended up with 350 pages. It just poured out of him, which is why I later suggested that he should write it as a novel. I remember Polly getting very angry at him, saying, "What does he think he is doing, writing all that stuff?" I said, "What does it matter? We can just cut it. It's great stuff."

PT: *You'd rather have more to work with than less.*

PB: Yeah, we could just cut it. It's not like they were bad scenes. But Cybill was going to be in it, and Polly was going to design it, so we were going to actually all work together again. We got the 350 pages down to about 150. I did most of the cutting. We got it to the actors. Fonda said that he loved it. Jimmy Stewart said [*Stewart's voice*], "Why do I let the horses go?" "Well, we're gonna make that clear, Jimmy." "Well, I just, I don't understand why I did that." "We'll shore it up, Jim. It's just a first draft." But then Duke turned it down. He said [*Wayne's voice*], "Well, it's kinda an end-of-the-West Western, Pete, and I'm not ready to hang up the spurs yet." I said, "But you don't get killed, Duke." "No, but everybody else does."

PT: *Is it true that Ford torpedoed the project?*

PB: He did. His daughter, Barbara, told me. He was in bed, and she read the script to him. And he told Duke not to do it. He said it would have been bad for his career.

PT: *It would have been the opposite, I would think.*

PB: Oh, yeah. It would have been great. But listen: Ford was malicious. Ford was also very nice. He gave me Ben Johnson—he fought to have Ben Johnson in *Picture Show*—but he wouldn't let me have those three on his deathbed. "This fuckin' Serbian prick is going to direct Wayne, Fonda, and Stewart? That's not going to happen." I called Jimmy, and I told him about Duke, and he said [*Stewart's voice*], "Well, if Duke's not gonna do it . . . uh, uh, why do I let the horses go?" [*Laughter.*]

PT: *I hate to hear that the rest of the cast began to drift away after Wayne said no.*

PB: Well, no—Jimmy was the only one who was vocal about it. But *I* drifted away from it. You can't replace John Wayne. They talked about Kirk Douglas, Burt Lancaster, several other people. I said, "It's not John Wayne."

PT: *In retrospect, do you wish you would have gone with one of them?*

PB: No! Because those stars had to be in it. It was written for them. I told Larry, "Forget it. Just write it as a book."

PT: *And he did:* Lonesome Dove.

PB: It's a brilliant book. I read the book while I was ill. I read it straight through in about three days. I mean, Larry wrote it with a vengeance. He was going to prove that his prose could be as exciting as movie action, and it is. He writes the action brilliantly, and the dialogue is, of course, unparalleled. He's just the best regional dialogue writer since Mark Twain. He's got an ear for it. It's extraordinary. He really found his voice with that book.

PT: *As you said a moment ago, the screenplay poured out of him.*

PB: And he wrote about four sequels to it. The title *Streets of Laredo* was my idea. It was not the best title. We had other titles, but just couldn't decide what to call it. The one I liked best was *Along the Brazos. Streets of Laredo* wasn't really our final title, but he took that as the sequel title for his book.

PT: *Now, Ford didn't live forever. Was there ever talk of reviving the project later on?*

PB: Not really.

PT: *Did this change your feeling about Ford?*

PB: No, it was typical.

PT: *It's a shame that you didn't make the film and a shame that—so far—you haven't done a Western.*

PB: Well, I came close to it with *The Last Picture Show!* [*Laughs.*]

PT: *You were offered the sequel to* True Grit.

PB: Yes, that's right—*Rooster Cogburn,* with [Katharine] Hepburn and Wayne. I turned it down because I didn't want to do a sequel to a picture I hated. But it would have been nice to work with them.

We wrote a Western that's quite good, a kind of modern Western called *One Lucky Moon.* It has horses and everything. Charming. I wrote it with Parish [Rahbar]. It's all about a kind of amusement-park Western town. People do live there, but people go there to see some shows, and they rob the bank, and they have a gunfight at the OK Corral.

PT: *How did you come up with the idea?*

PB: Willie Nelson wanted me to do a movie with him. Willie had an idea for a movie where the guy owns the town. There was a terrible script with gangsters and all kinds of shit. I threw the whole thing out. I said, "I think this is unusable, Willie. Somebody has a town, and somebody's trying to get it away from you—we'll use the town. I'll use that much." And the rest of it we made up.

Paper Moon (1973, Paramount Pictures)

> Director: Peter Bogdanovich; screenplay: Alvin Sargent (based on the novel *Addie Pray* by Joe David Brown); producer: Peter Bogdanovich

PB: *Paper Moon* was very solid. We had a cut of that picture very quickly. Three weeks after we wrapped, we had a cut of the picture, and it didn't change. We previewed it, and I took a minute out of the credits, out of the black, to move it along faster. That's the only thing I changed. It was shot very tight.

Frankly, that shoot was very difficult, sort of oppressive, because Polly was on the picture, and she was making trouble for me and Cybill. Cybill couldn't come on the set, so she wasn't down there much, and I was kind of lonely. I didn't enjoy the making of the picture much. I finished four days under schedule because I wanted to get the hell out of there.

PT: *Are there advantages to casting actors who haven't worked before, like Tatum O'Neal?*

PB: You can show them what to do, and they can just do it without having any hang-ups about it. Same thing with nonprofessional actors like we used in *Saint Jack* quite a bit and in *The Last Picture Show,* where we used just people who wanted to be in a movie. You don't have to give them the script. You just tell them what to say.

PT: *I know that you like to act out the scenes for the actors.*

PB: It makes it a lot easier if they're nonprofessional because some actors don't like that. If they haven't acted before, they don't have a problem with it.

Tatum O'Neal and Ryan O'Neal in *Paper Moon.* Courtesy Jerry Ohlinger's Movie Material Store.

PT: Paper Moon *starts with a close-up of Tatum O'Neal beside her mother's grave, and then you cut back.*

PB: That was a decision I made. I thought, *How can I open this movie?* I didn't want to start with a pan of the funeral. I just wanted to tell the audience that this movie is about this little girl. So we might as well begin with a close-up. What's she looking at? A grave. It tells you right away that this is the girl that the movie is about.

PT: *Why do you think those three early movies*—Picture Show, Doc, *and* Paper Moon—*caught on like wildfire?*

PB: I think I would have had the same kind of experience with *At Long Last Love* and *Nickelodeon* if they had been properly released in their right versions. It was as much my fault as it was anybody else's, but I was thrown by the studio's reversal of attitude after *Daisy Miller,* which was not a hit. I thought that if you make three hits in a row, it doesn't matter if the fourth one isn't a big hit. I made a lot of money for the studio for *Paper Moon,* so I figured, *What the hell?* I was wrong. You can't make *any* flops. [*Laughs.*] They don't trust you if you make a flop. It's that old thing that you're only as good as your last picture. So I was rattled on *At Long Last Love* and *Nickelodeon,* and I think both could have been popular pictures.

You see, the thing was that *Picture Show* (except for a compromise about length), *What's Up, Doc?,* and *Paper Moon* were exactly the way I wanted them to be, as were *Targets* and *Daisy Miller.* There was no need for me to go back and fuck around with those because they were the way I wanted them to be. Now, both *At Long Last Love* and *Nickelodeon* were *not* the way I wanted them to be. It shows you that even if you get conflict, you have to stick by your guns. If you don't, you're going to lose. That's why *Saint Jack* and *They All Laughed* are so good. Having learned that compromise is death, I didn't compromise.

PT: *When some directors say that they shouldn't compromise, they're talking about making very arty, odd pictures, like what Francis Ford Coppola has been doing in recent years. The pictures might be interesting, but their audience is limited. In your case, you had a track record that suggested that when you didn't compromise, your movies did well with the public.*

PB: Whenever the picture is emasculated or fucked around with, it doesn't connect. It has to be right. With *Noises Off,* they purposefully distributed it badly. Otherwise, it would have been a big hit. But they pissed it away on purpose. That's another story. There are pictures of mine that I felt would not be popular pictures, like *Daisy Miller* and, to be candid, like *Saint Jack.* But there were other pictures that I thought should have been and could have been popular, like *At Long Last Love, Nickelodeon, They All Laughed,* and *Noises Off.* And *Mask* would have been more popular in my version, too.

PT: *So many of the directors of your era were not trying to really reach the public.*

PB: The ones who were influenced most by the European cinema, which I think is a disastrous influence, those were the guys who somehow felt that success was equated with compromise and artistic failure. Like [Michelangelo] Antonioni wasn't commercial, so he was good. Well, to me Antonioni was a big bore.

I was just picking up the ball for American movies that were made for the whole family. *The Last Picture Show* wasn't, because you couldn't take the kids to see it, but adults could go to it without being scandalized.

PT: *You were different, in all ways, from your contemporaries.*

PB: Looking at the pictures made by my contemporaries—you are probably better at the history of my contemporaries than I am—but very few of them seem to deal with people. I mean, they all deal with stereotypes or gangster figures who are sort of stereotypical or aberrations of human behavior, like *Raging Bull,* but not real human beings. They're sort of monsters.

PT: *Your visual style is more like George Cukor or Leo McCarey—invisible.*

PB: There was a freshness they had that I'd be happy to be able to do. When I make a picture, I always say that I need to get the audience on my wavelength. Once they're on my wavelength, I can take them anywhere I want—as long as I don't break that wavelength.

PT: *I wrote a piece about Terrence Malick's* Tree of Life*—which I didn't care for at all.*

PB: I saw the piece you did—I thought it was very good.

PT: *You told me that, even as far back as* Badlands, *you felt that Malick wasn't on the side of the audience. But you're always thinking of the audience.*

PB: You know, Robert Graves and Alan Hodge wrote an extremely good handbook for writers in English. It's out of print, but it's a brilliant, brilliant book called—significantly—*The Reader over Your Shoulder.* The whole point of the book was that you want to be clear in what you want to say, you want to be clear to the reader over your shoulder. I never knew about that book until the '80s, but when I was making a picture, I was always thinking, *How is the audience going to react to this?* I have to take my best guess as to how they will react to it. If I like it, I hope they will. I can only go with what I like. If I don't like it, I'm not going to do it just because I think the audience *might* like it. In other words, I'm not going to pander to the audience. I think you have to make the picture you see, but make sure that what you're trying to convey is clear. Otherwise, it's muddy, and they won't understand it.

It's like writing a good sentence. Hitchcock used to compare shooting certain shots to language. Like the famous shot in *Notorious* where the camera shows the whole party and then cranes down to a key in Ingrid Bergman's hand. It goes from a wide angle shot down, down, down, down to basically an insert of Bergman's hand with the key. And Hitchcock said to me, "That's like saying, 'In this vast area, everybody's having a good time, but the key to the entire evening is contained in somebody's hand.'" The point is that it's very economical. You could have done it in cuts: close-up here, close-up there, and then go to the key. But that's not elegant. Anybody can do that. [*Laughs.*]

PT: *You cut in the camera, but does that mean you make a storyboard or shot list?*

PB: I never do a storyboard unless I have to for some practical reason, which is rare. I've done maybe three storyboards in my whole career. Usually I have about five to seven to ten days of rehearsal. We basically go through the script. Most of the time is spent rewriting and very little time rehearsing, and we kind of structure things and solve problems and so on. An idea of the scene sort of begins to form in my mind. But I don't usually make up my mind about how I'm going to shoot it until the night before in terms of reading the scene over and just seeing it in my mind and making notes for myself as to the shots. Basically, if I don't see a cut, it's all one shot. I figure out how to do it in one shot. If I do see some cutting, I have to figure out what it is. It's always based on the moments that are happening in the scene. Should it be a medium close-up or a close-up over the shoulder, or do we play it in one, or do we start on something and pull back? What is it? It's all that—what's the scene before, what's the last shot in the scene before, so what's the first shot in this sequence? How are we going to end it so that we know where we're going in the next one? All that I figure out the night before, if I haven't already been thinking about it. And I make notes for myself.

When I get on the set with the actors, I will many times discard some of the shots and combine things. And sometimes, just based on what the actors do, I'll change it even more radically. But at least I understand what the point of the scene is and what the emphasis is, so if I decide to shoot it differently, I don't overshoot. I just shoot what I need. I shoot up to the cut, and then that's it.

The most basic thing in my approach to movies is that each shot has to be a building block. If you can make it do double duty—do more than one thing—all the better. Each shot has its own meaning. It's not just functional.

PT: *And there's an order to the shots. That's why cutting in the camera is so critical.*

PB: Yeah, the order is planned beforehand so that it's smooth. You have to know what the scene is about. Otherwise, you can't make the scene. Once you know what the scene is about—and that might not happen until you're shooting it—then each shot is dictated by the meaning of the scene. So if there's an argument scene, but they're not really arguing because they're family, then you don't cut.

PT: *There are some examples of that in* Paper Moon*—long takes with Moses and Addie in the car. They are screaming at each other, but because you don't cut, as you've said, the audience still feels the two have a bond with each other.*

PB: That's what I was thinking of.

PT: *I wonder if Tatum O'Neal would have won the Oscar if she hadn't played a few of her scenes in long takes.*

PB: There were a couple of sustained scenes that she pulled off that made you realize that she was really good.

PT: *Preminger told you that every cut is an interruption.*

PB: Yup. [*Preminger's voice:*] "Every cut is an interruption!"

PT: *Do you think you were influenced by him?*

PB: Yes, certainly, but I think most of the great directors alternated between scenes that were cut up and scenes that played in very few shots, if not one. Ford was particularly perverse. He would sometimes avoid going to a shot you expected. You'd expect a close-up, and he wouldn't give it to you. He'd hold it back.

PT: *Most films today are shot much more willy-nilly.*

PB: Everybody just shoots a shitload of footage, and they say, "Let's use a close-up there. Okay, good. Is there a two-shot? We need a two-shot. But I don't think I shot a two-shot. Well, we can merge it in the . . . ." You know, it's just haphazard. That's why films look so tacky. The scenes don't add up. It's just a lot of shots.

PT: *That approach has a bad effect on the narrative, too.*

PB: Well, part of the narrative is the angle of vision. Where you're seeing it from is part of the narrative. I remember when we were cutting *The Cat's Meow.* Early on in the picture, there's a scene when Charlie Chaplin is standing outside the yacht. He hasn't gotten aboard yet, and he sees Marion Davies through the porthole. The editor [Edward Norris] cut it the way I wanted it, but there was something wrong with it. I said, "Did you use every shot?" He said, "Well, I didn't use this one." I said, "Well, you see. That's supposed to go in between here." I knew there was something wrong. If I shot it, it's meant to be used. It was a shot of the porthole that was sort of medium—it wasn't loose, and it wasn't tight; it was in between. It was meant to build to the closer shot. There was a reason for it.

PT: *You've quoted Hitchcock to the effect that he liked to watch his films without the sound on to see if he could still understand what was happening—as a kind of test.*

PB: Actually, Allan Dwan said that. Dwan said that he ran every talkie he made silent to see if it worked. He figured if it still worked—if you could basically follow the story—then he'd done a good job, and if you couldn't, he hadn't. Hitch may have done the same thing, but I remember Allan said it. I try to keep that in mind. Am I telling this visually? Can you follow it? That's why filmmaking has gotten so decadent, because the technique has been lost. There's close-ups when there doesn't need to be. A close-up means nothing anymore because virtually all films are shot in close-up.

Daisy Miller (1974, Paramount Pictures)

Director: Peter Bogdanovich; screenplay: Frederic Raphael (based on the novella by Henry James); producer: Peter Bogdanovich

PT: *One of the projects you were contemplating making after* Paper Moon *was an adaptation of John Galsworthy's "The Apple Tree."*

PB: A long short story called "The Apple Tree."

PT: *In an interview with Martin Rubin, you said that "The Apple Tree" had several points in common with* Daisy Miller.[4]

Cybill Shepherd and Barry Brown in *Daisy Miller.* Courtesy Jerry Ohlinger's Movie Material Store.

PB: Well, the big common point was that the man, the leading character, doesn't understand the girl, and she dies as a result of his negligence and misunderstanding. *Daisy Miller* is sort of more urban, and "The Apple Tree" is more rural. It's about an urban guy who goes into the countryside and spends some time there, and a wild girl in the country falls in love with him, and he falls in love with her, but she's so different from him that he can't go back for her, and she dies.

PT: *Did you ever have a script?*

PB: We had a deal at Warners to make it. James Costigan wrote a script, but it wasn't very good.

PT: *Do you still want to make it?*

PB: Somebody made it badly. It's a beautiful long short story. I had wanted to make it since I was a kid. I regret that I didn't. Cybill wasn't right for the part of the girl. That's one of the reasons I didn't do it.

PT: *You told me that when you settled on* Daisy Miller, *you first asked Welles to direct it, with Cybill as Daisy and you as Winterbourne.*

PB: I said, "Why don't you direct it with Cybill and me in it?" He thought about it for a day or so and then said, "No, you direct it."

PT: *I think you had a better feel for the material.*

PB: It would have been an interesting movie. But it wasn't his kind of thing.

PT: *I doubt he would have had the light touch you had.*

PB: Allan Dwan made a lovely comment. He said, "I've never seen a film like it. It's a bright, charming comedy, and then she dies."

PT: *So you directed* Daisy Miller.

PB: I was going to do something else actually. There was another picture that was being talked about. In retrospect, I kind of regret it because *Daisy Miller* was not going to be a commercial picture, unfortunately. The studio didn't know what to do with it; the critics didn't know what to do with it. It badly affected *At Long Last Love* and so on. Because I like the picture, I can't say I regret it, but it commercially was not a smart move.

PT: *What was the other project?*

PB: It was based on a book by Calder Willingham called *Rambling Rose.* It had a great part for Cybill. Ironically, Martha Coolidge made it some years later with Laura Dern. It was one of her best pictures.

PT: *Frederic Raphael worked on the script of* Daisy Miller.

PB: Freddie and I had a meeting, and we talked about doing an entirely different take on the story. We were going to make it more modern, I guess. That's not the right word. Something more intense, more emotional. He wrote a draft doing that, and it was completely wrong. It just didn't work. Cybill and I took the *Queen Elizabeth* to London to cast the picture. On the way, I rewrote the script completely, going back to the book entirely. I went directly back to the book. I used maybe two or three things from Raphael's script, including one line: "There ain't no Colosseum in Schenectady yet."

PT: *Welles told you how to start the movie.*

PB: I said to him, "If you were making the movie, how would you start?" He said, "With the little boy."

PT: *You're referring to Daisy's younger brother, Randolph, who was played by Larry McMurtry's son, James.*

PB: He had never acted before. He was named after Henry James, you know. He's very good.

PT: *What made you think of casting him?*

PB: I just thought he'd be good for it. He was a funny-looking kid. He's become an attractive man; he's a good singer. I'd met him a few times and said, "How about James?" So Larry came over with us. He was there for the whole shoot. I asked him to read the Raphael script for me because I couldn't bear to read it again. I said, "Do me a favor. Read this and see if there's any line that we could keep." And he said, "Just one: 'There ain't no Colosseum in Schenectady yet.'" He was the one who found it.

PT: *Barry Brown was made for the role of Winterbourne.*

PB: Well, Cybill and I thought he was so perfect; we thought he *was* Winterbourne. He was just like that. Very stiff, very reserved. He used to read the obituaries every morning. He killed himself at a young age. He also had alcohol problems.

PT: *He was previously in* Bad Company*—the fine first film directed by Robert Benton.*

PB: That's where we saw him. We liked him in that a lot. It's a nice picture. Benton didn't tell me Barry had a drinking problem.

PT: *It is so clear that Daisy is practically begging Winterbourne to, as he puts it in a line of dialogue, "reciprocate her affections." And yet it flies right over him.*

PB: He just doesn't get it. A lot of men don't get what women mean. That's what it's about.

PT: *It was only Cybill Shepherd's third film—after* The Last Picture Show *and Elaine May's* The Heartbreak Kid*—but she's brilliant. Many of her long monologues were shot in single takes.*

PB: Yeah, it was tough.

PT: *She speaks extremely rapidly in many of those scenes.*

PB: Well, it says in the book that she chatters. Some people said that she talked too fast, but I just think they're being self-conscious because they know Cybill.

Up until *Saint Jack, Daisy Miller* was the last picture of mine that was done without compromise. It's beautiful looking. I kept saying when we were looking at dailies over there, in Switzerland and in Rome, "It sure is beautiful, but I don't know who is going to want to see it." And nobody did.

PT: *You had made* Targets, Doc, *and* Paper Moon *with László Kovács, but here your cinematographer was Alberto Spagnoli. Why the change?*

PB: I decided that it was important to use an Italian crew as much as possible because they would work harder for me than an American crew imported. It would be a big mistake to bring everybody over and insult the country that you're shooting in. So we had actually another cameraman who was going to do it who had worked with Fellini. Then Fellini called him right at the last minute, so we lost that guy. So we saw a bunch of other cameramen. They all came in, one after the other, over a period of two days. We liked Alberto. It was very funny—we liked the way he looked! We thought he was attractive. Frank Marshall, Mae Woods [PB's assistant], and I were sitting around the room, saying, "Well, he's attractive. He's a good-looking guy. Yeah, let's use him." I think we saw a reel, too, that looked good. But he was nicely dressed and was a very hip guy. He died very young.

The deep focus was particularly difficult. I admire Alberto for doing it. I would say to him, in Italian, I learned the phrase, "Everything sharp." He said, "Si, si, si." Even in the night stuff, like the scene where Eileen Brennan [the socialite Mrs. Walker] cuts her [Daisy] off at the end, which has a lot of mirrors, I would say, "I want everything sharp, everything sharp, everything sharp." I knew he couldn't do it, but I kept saying it, and I thought, *Well, it will be close to sharp.* But he did it! When I saw the stuff, I said, "How did you do it?" He shrugged and said, "I don't know."

PT: *How do you usually work with the cinematographer?*

PB: I always set up the camera. Nobody else does that. I usually pick the lens and the angle and the size and what the camera does. That's not something I let the cameraman do. I sit on the camera until I get the shot the way I want it, and then I turn it over to him.

PT: *The camera operator must be key on your sets—to execute what you've laid out.*

PB: I had one of the best on *The Cat's Meow* [Marc Spicer]. He was brilliant. On *Targets,* Laszlo was the operator, and then on *What's Up, Doc?* he couldn't operate, but we had Bobby Byrne, who is brilliant.

PT: *You said in an interview with* Sight and Sound *that you wanted* Targets *and* Doc *to look "purposely ugly; in terms of the lighting and the clothes I tried rather strenuously to make them as ugly as possible."*[5] *But, you added,* Daisy Miller *should look beautiful.*

PB: The current world is garish and rather in bad taste, and the old world wasn't as garish and in bad taste. Those hotel rooms are grotesque in *What's Up, Doc?* We made them grotesque on purpose. The millionaire's house is so uncomfortable. Every place is sort of ugly. That's the joke. It was the same thing on *Targets,* to a degree, although the Karloff sections were softer.

On *Daisy Miller,* you're doing it in the period of the great Impressionists, you know? Strangely enough, because it was before film existed, there's no sense of black-and-white from that period. It needs to be in color. The Impressionists were painting, and you got your images through paintings in those days, as opposed to black-and-white newsreels. So it seemed right to do it with a kind of beautiful color. We shot the whole Switzerland sequence with a black stocking over the lens, which is an old trick they used to use to defuse everything and make it sparkle. We took it off for Rome. You can see the difference when you see it properly projected. The whole Switzerland sequence is kind of slightly hazy, with a romantic feel to it, and you get to Rome, it gets much more stark, more serious.

PT: *You love black-and-white, but you're not afraid to use color when it suits the story. For example, I would hate to see* They All Laughed *in black-and-white.*

PB: Well, it was very beautiful days, people were in love, and it wouldn't have worked in black-and-white. I have no predilection for black-and-white. I like it better because more movies that I like were made in black-and-white, but if color fits the story, I have no problem with it. It's great. What I object to is the forced use of color, not color itself. Like John Ford:

one should be able to make a movie in black-and-white, like *Wagon Master,* one year and make a movie in color, like *The Quiet Man,* another year.

PT: *Or* Mogambo.

PB: Or *Mogambo. Mogambo* should be in color, but *The Man Who Shot Liberty Valance* shouldn't. It's like telling a painter, "You may use every color you want, but not black or white."

PT: *Why haven't the success of some black-and-white films—like* Raging Bull*—allowed for more black-and-white films?*

PB: It's a business of what you would call poltroons—cowards.

Cybill Does It . . . to Cole Porter

PT: *I tracked down the record you produced:* Cybill Does It . . . to Cole Porter.

PB: Oh, Jesus.

PT: *I loved it! The songs are great, and Cybill has a lovely voice. I thought I should ask you about it since, after all, you produced and directed it. I mean, it is a part of your body of work.*

PB: I don't like it much. I didn't know enough to do it right. I think she sang it well and so on, but I think the arrangements are a little cute, and some of the stuff we did was a little too cutesy-pie.

PT: *Not knowing what a producer on a record does . . .*

PB: I didn't know what a producer does on a record either! Which is why I took such big billing. I found out that record producers take very small billing. Everybody made fun of the record because I took this huge billing.

PT: *But, in your ignorance, what did you do on it?*

PB: I picked the songs, I helped with the arrangements, and I coached Cybill. I listened to the album maybe two or three years ago, and I didn't think it was so hot. I thought Cybill was good. I just wasn't thrilled with the way I had done it.

PT: *If you had to do it over again . . .*

PB: I wouldn't do it.

PT: *Who is the male voice singing on "But in the Morning, No"?*

PB: Me.

PT: *I thought it sounded like you, but I wasn't sure.*

PB: Well, I made two albums, you know. They're not great, but I did them with a piano. The first one [*Monday Morning Quarterbacks*] we actually packaged. We did it privately, and we sent it out as a Christmas present. The second one we didn't even print up because we ran out of money. I sing standards, and Raymond De Felitta, who's a very fine writer-director, plays the piano beautifully.

PT: *You've also written a couple of songs over the years.*

PB: Well, Earl Poole Ball is a really good pianist, and we'd sit down, and we'd noodle around about a song. I'd write the lyrics, and then we'd put the music to it.

PT: *Was "One Day since Yesterday," from* They All Laughed, *the first song you wrote?*

PB: Well, I had a little bit of an involvement on *At Long Last Love* because one of the Cole Porter songs—"Poor Young Millionaire"—had no tune extant. It just had the lyrics, and we wanted to use the song for Burt. So Artie Butler and I sat down at the piano and came up with the tune. "One Day since Yesterday" was the first song we invented. It was based on something Dorothy had written to me in a card. It was the day after we first kissed. It was kind of a memorable occasion.

PT: *What did she think when she found out that you used the expression in a song?*

PB: I played it for her when she got to New York. She was thrilled. She laughed and cried. Mainly laughed.

PT: *It's a striking phrase.*

PB: Isn't it? It's great. She sent me a card that she had bought. She always found the right card, I don't know how. She and L. B., her sister, have this brilliance about picking the right greeting card. We had kissed on the beach, so she sent me a card with a shot of a girl in a dress silhouetted against the sky, jumping joyously right near the ocean. Inside she wrote, "Dear Peter, One day since yesterday, Love Dorothy." I thought, *What a great phrase.* So we wrote the song, we played it for her, and then we used it in the picture.

PT: *Where does your love of music comes from?*

PB: I don't know. I just always did like music. My father was a pianist. There was always music in the house—mostly classical. I loved the popular music when I was a teenager. Sinatra. Dean Martin. The hit parade. I like music as source in movies, but *At Long Last Love* is basically the only scored movie I made, and it's very well scored. The guys did a great job on the arrangements, I thought.

PT: *You often have characters sing in your films—there is Daisy singing "When You and I Were Young, Maggie" in* Daisy Miller *or the movie company singing "I'll Take You Home Again, Kathleen" in* Nickelodeon. *Why?*

PB: It varies. Different reasons. In *Daisy Miller,* it was kind of a scene of flirtation in a funny way, and he also falls madly in love with her, even though he doesn't know what's happening to him. In *Nickelodeon,* it was bittersweet because everybody is singing, but everybody has a different feeling about the girl. It's a way of being able to show different conflicting feelings during the course of the song.

The Gentleman Tramp (1976, Tinc Productions)

Director: Richard Patterson; screenplay: Richard Patterson; producer: Bert Schneider

PT: *Following* Daisy Miller, *you were involved in the making of a documentary about Charlie Chaplin, produced by Bert Schneider, called* The Gentleman Tramp. *A few years before that, you had put together a thirteen-and-a-half-minute montage of Chaplin's work when he was honored at the Academy Awards in 1972.*

PB: Bert asked me if I would shoot an interview with Charlie for a documentary. I said sure, but I didn't want to make a documentary. It was too much work. I said that I felt I had sort of done it with the thirteen and a half minutes! [*Laughs.*] I'd sort of summed it up, and I didn't feel like doing it again. But I said I would go over and interview Charlie.

So Cybill and I went over. We had Néstor Almendros shooting it. And it was the worst interview I've ever had. I mean, he made no sense. He was gaga. He would talk and talk and talk and make no fucking sense. It was just absolutely unusable. So we went outside, and the sun was setting. I said, "Let's get a shot of Oona [O'Neill] and Charlie walking off into the sunset." Néstor said, "Great idea." We all got ready, and we told Oona and Charlie what we were going to do. They were amused and sort of touched in a funny way.

We did it—and that was the last piece of film that Charlie Chaplin was ever in.

PT: *And you directed it.*

PB: Yeah, I directed it—I said, "Walk over there." [*Laughs.*] It was the last time that he was photographed that I know of. And that's the only thing that's in *The Gentleman Tramp* that I actually shot because the interview was unusable.

At Long Last Love (1975, 20th Century Fox)

Director: Peter Bogdanovich; screenplay: Peter Bogdanovich, suggested by the songs of Cole Porter; producers: Peter Bogdanovich and Frank Marshall

PT: At Long Last Love *was the first original screenplay you wrote without any collaboration.*

PB: Except Cole Porter, who was a big help! In fact, the credit I took on the picture was one of the bigger mistakes I made in my career. They hated it that I took "written and produced and directed"—they hated that. I should have just said what it says now: "Screenplay by Peter Bogdanovich, suggested by the songs of Cole Porter."

PT: *That's a little more modest.*

PB: Yeah, put it someplace else and mention Cole Porter.[6]

PT: *How did you get the idea for the story?*

PB: Cybill gave me the present of a book called *Cole,* which was a big coffee-table book that had all of his lyrics in it and photographs. It came out in the early '70s. I started reading the lyrics and playing the songs. I

Burt Reynolds and Cybill Shepherd in *At Long Last Love.* Courtesy Jerry Ohlinger's Movie Material Store.

thought this would make a musical, which is the way they used to do it. They'd take the work of one composer, and they'd spin a musical around it. *Singin' in the Rain* was Nacio Herb Brown and Arthur Freed. *The Band Wagon* was Schwartz and Dietz. *An American in Paris* was the Gershwins. You automatically constructed it around the songs you've got, to a degree.

For example, the song toward the end when they walk through Central Park, "I Loved Him (but He Didn't Love Me)," was the catalyst for the whole picture. I read that one, and it just gives you the whole plot. The whole plot sort of fell into place with that. We were in Switzerland or Rome making *Daisy Miller,* and one night I wrote that scene where they're walking in the park. "Well, he can't even speak English." "I know." "He snores." "I know." And they look at each other. All that was written on a yellow legal pad, and it was the first scene that I wrote for the movie.

PT: *It's the theme of the movie—mismatched lovers.*

PB: I loved that song. And there's no cut in that either.

PT: *Was the camera on tracks?*

PB: A crane. We craned up as they walked away. We're dollying with them the whole way, and then they walk up to the camera, and the camera cranes up as they walk down the hill. That was supposed to be Central Park. I think it's a pretty damn good match for Central Park.

PT: *Where did you shoot it?*

PB: I have no idea. In LA somewhere.

PT: *Even though the story takes place in New York, you shot everything in Hollywood?*

PB: Yeah. But that song was sort of the catalyst for the whole thing. And I had a devil of a time finding a recording of "I Loved Him." I found an obscure recording on the Evergreen label or Monmouth or some fucking thing. I found somebody singing it from some show, so I knew what the tune was. It's a nice tune. That arrangement is particularly good.

PT: *The scene shows off the vocal talents of both Cybill and Madeline Kahn. Madeline has a wonderful voice.*

PB: She's very good in the picture.

PT: *You discovered Madeline.*

PB: *What's Up, Doc?* was her first movie. She just was funny, and she didn't think she was funny. She was a serious and introspective person.

PT: *And yet she was capable of playing Trixie Delight!*

PB: She was sweet and funny.

PT: *Were you thinking of her when you wrote the character?*

PB: Yeah, they're all written for the people who did it. Except Burt Reynolds.

PT: *You told me you wanted Elliott Gould.*

PB: We talked about Elliott, and I got talked out of it, which was a mistake in certain ways because he was an accomplished singer and dancer. But Burt is very charming and adorable in it. It's one of the best things he ever did. There's a marvelous moment when he's at the piano, and he struts across and does a little leap and sings "It's De-Lovely."

Cybill was criticized, but I thought she was very good in it.

PT: *I agree. Was her character at all inspired by Grace Kelly in* High Society?

PB: No, it was just sort of a spoiled version of Cybill, basically. Everybody is sort of playing a version of themselves.

PT: *The supporting cast is also excellent. It was your fourth movie with John Hillerman and your third with Eileen Brennan.*

PB: It's nice because you can talk more shorthand. You know each other. You're used to working together. I wrote those parts for John and Eileen. Don't forget, I saw Eileen in the play that made her a star on Broadway, *Little Mary Sunshine,* which is a satirical musical. I knew she could sing and dance. And I knew Johnny Hillerman since we were both very young.

PT: *Of course, the idea of following several couples and their romantic doings anticipates* They All Laughed.

PB: Oh yeah, it does, very much so because I didn't get it right. [*Laughs.*] So I gave it another shot.

PT: *A different take on the same plot.*

PB: Very different. Because the people in *At Long Last Love* are completely superficial. They exchange songs like they would exchange greeting cards rather than writing something of their own. So the big misunderstanding at the time was that I was trying to do an Astaire–Rogers musical. It was kind of the anti-Astaire–Rogers musical. [*Laughs.*] It had no connection to that at all. I was thinking about it as a kind of comedy with music, in which the people sing instead of talk because that's the only way they can communicate.

PT: *No one can deny that the film has loads of visual style. You were working again with László Kovács, and the long takes are stunning.*

PB: Yeah, boy, they were long takes. When you do a musical number—I've seen it in the best musicals—they kind of pretty much do it in one piece or two or sometimes three. But generally they do it in a long piece. Lubitsch did because he couldn't cut. But even when you could cut, as he could by the time of *Merry Widow,* there's no reason to cut if you're doing a song number. There's no reason to cut unless they can't do it. The whole point is to take you into the song and not to cut away from it or cut into it or whatever. It's to get you into the song.

PT: *Here, though, you were also recording the songs on the set.*

PB: I know. It was an amazing experiment. The actors had a really tough job. Doing it live was not easy. They didn't even have an orchestra, like Lubitsch did. They only had an electric piano with the horn turned off. A little tiny speaker was in their ear and an antenna combed into the hair. Dear Millie Natwick said, "It sounds like grasshoppers."

PT: *The production designer was Gene Allen, who had often worked with George Cukor. Why did you hire him?*

PB: Well, because he was close to George, and he'd been the sort of man behind the throne in a lot of the color pictures, particularly *A Star Is Born,* which was brilliantly done. I had a very simple desire, which was to keep it all black-and-white and silver and gray. No color at all. Of course, nobody believes you when you say no color at all. They think you mean you want some color, but muted. No, no color at all, except for the green grass, the eyes blue, and hair blond. But other than that, everything we can control should be black-and-white or silver and gray.

PT: *Were you ever tempted to just shoot it in black-and-white?*

PB: No. That would have been perverse. [*Laughs*]

PT: *Was it your idea for the sets to have an art deco look?*

PB: Well, it's the '30s, you know? It's supposed to be 1935 or 1936. I can't remember. It was supposed to be either a year before or a year after *Paper Moon.*

PT: *Of course, it takes place in an entirely different world than* Paper Moon.

PB: Totally different world, but same era. You know what's interesting, somebody had the idea, and I sort of sketched it out: I think it'd be fascinating to run my pictures in chronological order, not by the year they were made but by the year they were about.

PT: *Oh, that would be fascinating.*

PB: Wouldn't it?

PT: *I guess you'd begin with* Daisy Miller?

PB: Yeah! [*Laughs.*] *Nickelodeon* would, I think, come after *Daisy Miller.*

PT: *It's interesting:* Targets *is one of the few films you made to have a truly contemporary setting. It takes place the year it was made. Even* Saint Jack *was set a few years before you shot it.*

PB: Five years earlier.

PT: *That is also true of* Mask.

PB: Yeah, '79, '80.

PT: *So it takes place in '79 and '80, but you made it in '84, and it was released in '85.*

PB: That's why I think it's interesting to show them in that order. There are so many different ways that they would suddenly appear very different. You're bringing it up to date. *Targets* would come in 1968. *What's Up, Doc?* would come in 1972.

PT: *Back to* At Long Last Love: *"You're the Top" is used as a kind of running theme throughout the film. Of course, you had already used it so memorably in* What's Up, Doc?.

PB: I like that song. [*Laughs.*] I first heard it on a plane trip. I was crossing the country for the umpteenth time. Unusually, I got bored, and I listened to the earphones. They were playing Ethel Merman singing "You're the Top." I just loved her version, I loved the song, and I said, "This is great. We'll begin *Doc* with it."

PT: *As in* The Last Picture Show, *you begin and end with the same image—in this case, a silver music box with four figurines atop it, representing the four lead characters.*

PB: You're back where you started. It has a certain completeness about it. You see the same image as in the beginning, but it has a completely different meaning.

PT: *The final shot dissolves from a shot of the two couples dancing in a ballroom to a shot of the music-box figurines.*

PB: We lit the dancers a certain way, and then as we shot that scene, the lights would fade—literally on the soundstage, where we were shooting—

and they would hold longer on Burt and Cybill, and they [the actors] were exactly positioned in a way that we knew would work with the music box. And when we made the music-box scene, we would start with the two figures in the middle sort of dark so that Burt and Cybill would look like they were dancing on the music box. And we'd bring the rest of it in that way. When you put it together in the lab, it's beautiful. Because it isn't random—your eye stays very carefully with the thing that you want the audience to see as you're going into the next image.

PT: *Tell me about the editor of* At Long Last Love, *Douglas Robertson.*

PB: Doug was married to Peggy Robertson. Peggy Robertson was Hitchcock's assistant for years. She became a good friend. It was going to be a very easy picture to cut. I'd rather have worked with Verna [Fields], but by then she was a hotshot over at Universal. It was going to be a lot of long, long takes, so it wasn't going to have a lot of cutting. So I didn't think it would be a problem, and it wasn't. He did a good job. He kept saying, "There isn't much for me to do except cut off the heads and tails."

PT: *What happened when the film was about to be released?*

PB: The trouble is, I fucked up, and the studio fucked up by rushing me into it. They were so sure that it was going to be a hit—they loved it—that they rushed me and said, "Oh, it's fine, it's fine, it's fine." But it's an original musical comedy. They usually go on the road with those for six months, but I had two previews, you know? The first one was a complete disaster. There was nobody left in the theater except the people from Fox. The sound was atrocious. The picture was out of focus because it was on a curved Cinerama screen, which I told them not to get, and it wasn't the right cut. Plus, you couldn't hear it—it's a musical! That was one of the complete disaster nights of my life. We flew there in a lightning thunderstorm in a small plane. We thought we weren't going to make it. We were sort of relieved we made it to the screening. It didn't matter so much that it was a complete disaster.

Then I recut and remixed it. We previewed in Denver, and it played well. Reasonably well. That was the cut I should have gone with. I should have tinkered with that. But then people said, "Well, you know, what you ought to do is you ought to lose this scene, you ought to lose that scene. It's going to really be good. It played well in Denver, but it can play even better if you lose this, you lose that." Everybody was talking at me, and I made a mistake. I cut a couple of things out that I shouldn't have cut out, and I left things in that I should have taken out. I was completely rattled. The version that was released at the [Radio City] Music Hall was the worst version. By the way, it did very well at the Music Hall—you can look it up. The grosses were very good, but they got such bad reviews they [the studio executives] were terrified to take it anywhere else.

I left town. Cybill and I went to Europe for a week or so, came back, stopped in New York. I went to the Music Hall, sat through it, and said, "I really fucked it up." I needed that break to gain some objectivity. I said, "This is the worst version of all." So I called [Fox president] Alan Ladd Jr. the next day, and I said, "Laddie, I just saw the picture. I know what to do now"—which was a sort of dark joke. "Can I do it? I'll pay for it." He said, "Yeah, go ahead." So I did a cut of it. Whether he let me pay for it or not, I don't know—I have a feeling he didn't. But that's where I recut the picture.

PT: *The kicker to the story is that there was another cut that you were not the author of! I saw it on cable several times in the late '90s, but you only became aware of it in 2011, and it was finally released on Blu-ray in 2013. This version restored almost everything you cut—it's like a director's cut, minus the director!*

PB: It's a mutilated child that's now been unmutilated. I did some research—I talked to the guy at Fox—and it turns out that this version that we're talking about has been around since 1980.

PT: *Who was responsible for it?*

PB: Well, there was a guy at Fox named James Blakeley. He probably did it because he was a big Cole Porter fan and used to work in musicals. It's kind of amazing. It has a bigger size to it than I had thought. It's very stately—it introduces the characters. It's well constructed. Jim died before I knew about what he'd done and could thank him profusely.

I wanted to integrate the songs with the dialogue. That's the hardest thing to do. To get the right balance between the musical numbers and the talking scenes. I don't think I ever achieved it, but James Blakeley did. It was the way it was meant to be. It was shot that way, but I just lost faith in it. I'm proud of this version, and I had been pretty unproud of the rest of the stuff. I didn't like any version until this one, but this one seems to work. It follows the story.

Two with Sackler: *Bugsy* and *Down*

PT: *Around this time, you were going to make a film about the gangster Bugsy Siegel, with a script by playwright Howard Sackler, who wrote* The Great White Hope.

PB: What happened was that [Richard] Zanuck and [David] Brown came to me and offered me the picture. It was called *Bugsy.* I thought it was quite a good script, and I had an idea to revise it. The construction was a little all over the place, so I thought—wrongly, as it turned out, but it was so long ago so, who knows?—to do it in flashbacks, à la *Citizen Kane,* with the various people telling what happened. We sort of juggled the time sequence a little bit, very much like *Kane.*

Sackler was a very good writer. It was fun to work with him, and he was very amenable to whatever I wanted. Then the picture didn't work out because Universal got scared after *Daisy Miller.* It was when Hollywood got scared of Cybill Shepherd and me being together on a picture. She was going to play Virginia Hill.

Bugsy would have been interesting. It's a love story—a damned love story. Warren [Beatty] did it years later with Barry Levinson.

PT: *You later worked with Howard Sackler on* Saint Jack *as well as on another as yet unmade project called* Down.

PB: *Down* was a very dark, cult-murder thing—funny and sexy and strange. A kind of Hitchcockian thriller. Howard Sackler wrote it on spec. He made the point that if you have power over ten people in a room, that's still power—even if it's only ten people. Sort of like the Manson family. I didn't make it because everybody was scared to death of it.

PT: *How did it begin?*

PB: It all started when Cybill and I took the train up from Los Angeles to San Francisco. It was a very sexy trip. We spent a weekend in San Francisco, and we just sort of saw a side of San Francisco that I hadn't seen when I made *What's Up, Doc?.* We started talking about doing some kind of a thriller that plays in San Francisco and has a train sequence, coming up and going down. So we set it between San Ysidro and San Francisco, so it's a little closer than LA.

Then we thought, *Wouldn't it be fun to get John Ritter as an innocent guy getting involved with Cybill, who was the femme fatale?* She said, "It's cool with me." We thought of a few sequences. Howard Sackler was living with us for a while, with his girlfriend. He was married, but it was him and his girlfriend. [*Laughs.*] He was living in one of the guestrooms with her. I started to tell him our story, sort of the idea for our picture. We talked back and forth with him, and then he wrote it. And I rewrote it.

PT: *When you say you saw a new side of San Francisco in that trip, what do you mean?*

PB: It had a film noir kind of feeling—back alleys and dark places.

PT: *This would have been one of your darkest pictures.*

PB: Yeah, very dark.

PT: Down *reminds me a little of Stanley Kubrick's* Eyes Wide Shut. *You put together an oral history of Kubrick for the* New York Times Magazine *shortly before the release of* Eyes Wide Shut.

PB: They paid me $10,000 to do it.

PT: *I don't know if you like* Eyes Wide Shut *or not.*

PB: I don't like Kubrick much. That's the funny thing.

PT: *You managed to suppress that in the oral history.*

PB: Yeah, I kind of kept that down. If you read the foreword I wrote, it's not effusive. It's just sort of documentary-like. I like the early films better. I like *Paths of Glory* and *The Killing.* I thought *Lolita* was really lousy. The book is so good, and the movie was such a compromise.

PT: *Howard Sackler was a great playwright.*

PB: He wrote a brilliant play called *Semmelweis,* about the guy who found out about sterilization and the doctors who were killing women in childbirth because their hands hadn't been sterilized. The guy was persecuted for it. It was a very interesting and well-written play. He made the mistake of directing it himself, and he cast the wrong people in it. We saw it performed in Buffalo. We went up there to see it and hung out for a few days. The play was good, but the production wasn't good, and it never made it to New York.

PT: *He was a Pulitzer Prize winner for* The Great White Hope.

PB: This was an even better play.

PT: *Back to gangster movies: you famously declined to direct* The Godfather.

PB: Yeah, I did. I didn't even know I was turning it down. They just said it was a best seller. They didn't tell me what it was. I turned down *Dog Day Afternoon,* too, which was not a gangster picture, but it was a crime picture. Sidney [Lumet] did a very good job. It was his kind of picture. It wasn't really my kind of picture. I was not interested in it because there were no women in it. [*Laughs*]

PT: *Except the bank tellers!*

PB: Yeah, but I mean there were no real women's parts. When it was offered to me, it was called *The Boys in the Bank,* and that just didn't click with me. I turned down the remake of *Scarface,* too. I turned it down angrily. I said, "Why the fuck are you remaking it? Release the old picture." They never spoke to me again.

PT: *It's true, though—you've rarely done a movie that lacked good parts for women.*

PB: That's what interests me more than anything else. It just was absent in *Dog Day Afternoon.* It was just the boys in the bank, really.

Nickelodeon (1976, Columbia Pictures)

> Director: Peter Bogdanovich; screenplay: Peter Bogdanovich and W. D. Richter; producers: Robert Chartoff, Frank Marshall, and Irwin Winkler

PT: *You've made several films concerning Hollywood. Some are quite cynical about the business—like* The Cat's Meow *or* The Mystery of Natalie Wood—*but* Nickelodeon *tells of a very joyful, innocent period: the silent era, before* The Birth of a Nation.

PB: Well, that's what appealed to me about it. It was the beginning of it all. It was a more innocent time, and it was a more innocent time for the country as well and for the world. So the beginning of the movies has a kind of innocence that appealed to me. By the time you get to the '20s, it's already a major force in the world.

Left to right: Ryan O'Neal, Brian Keith, John Ritter, and Burt Reynolds in *Nickelodeon.* Courtesy Jerry Ohlinger's Movie Material Store.

Nickelodeon is ironic because I'm telling a story about the innocence of the beginnings of the movies, but I wasn't having a particularly happy time making it. It was just the opposite of how I felt.

PT: *For starters,* Nickelodeon *was conceived as a black-and-white film.*

PB: We shot it with the idea that eventually it would be printed in black-and-white. We designed it so that it would eventually look good in black-and-white because it's got a lot of shadows and contrasts and so on, which you don't normally do with color.

PT: *Several years ago, you prepared a DVD which included the black-and-white version—it's a changed movie in black-and-white.*

PB: I thought it was a much better picture than it was in color. I think I made some mistakes with it. The tone is a little bit too slapsticky at the beginning. It doesn't seem as slapsticky in black-and-white, but I think it was a mistake to have it be quite as slapsticky as it is at the beginning.

When you read about the early days or talk to Dwan and Walsh, it is kind of slapsticky, it is kind of crazy. But you can always tell when

I'm not confident with a sequence if I add music to it, and there's that music that comes right in when Ryan runs down the street after he comes out of the courtroom. That means that I wasn't happy with that little sequence.

You see, the thing is, virtually everything in that movie was based on a real incident, whether it was Leo McCarey or Allan Dwan or Raoul Walsh. It was something that had happened to somebody, including the business with the air balloon. All this stuff was basically real.

PT: *And, of course, McCarey began as a lawyer, just like Ryan O'Neal's character.*

PB: He began as a lawyer. That was all McCarey. In black-and-white, it seems real. In color, it seems like a period movie that was made in the '70s. [*Laughs.*] That's the difference. It's the same old thing about black-and-white: it's more real.

PT: *You also wanted John Ritter instead of Ryan O'Neal.*

PB: Yeah, I wanted John Ritter and Jeff Bridges. Jeff would have done Burt Reynolds's part. But they wanted big names. It was really one of my pet projects, and it's sad that it got sort of fucked up. Jane [Hitchcock] was not right either. It was supposed to be Cybill. We wanted somebody who was threatening.

PT: *Yes, although I think Jane Hitchcock does a nice job . . .*

PB: She's very good, but she's in the Lillian Gish department, and we wanted somebody more in the Theda Bara department. [*Laughs.*]

Back to the Stage?

PT: *Following* Nickelodeon, *you almost made a return to the stage, courtesy of Thornton Wilder and Joseph Papp. There was an item in* New York *magazine: "In the fall, we understand, [Bogdanovich will] direct three one-act plays by Thornton Wilder for Joseph Papp at the New York Public Theatre. He may even act in one of the plays."*[7]

PB: I had been talking about wanting to do something on the order of what Orson did when he did his radio show: I wanted to introduce things on the stage. Like the Stage Manager in *Our Town.* Orson said, "Well, why don't you do the three Thornton Wilder plays? You can compare your head off." Which ones? And he told me the plays that would make a great evening. I read them, and I thought he was right. So I went to Joe with it; we had a couple of meetings, he said he would do it, and then he backed out.

PT: *You were going to do three of Wilder's one-acts:* Pullman Car Hiawatha, The Happy Journey to Trenton and Camden, *and* The Long Christmas Dinner.

PB: We were going to call it *Thornton Wilder's America, 1930.* The plays are wonderful, and they're done without props. It's very limited and stark. For a car, it's just a couple of chairs and a fake wheel and all of that.

PT: *Like in* Our Town.

PB: Yes, the same idea. I was going to get Cloris Leachman to play the mother in *The Happy Journey to Trenton and Camden.* She would have been great. It's about a mother and father and two kids going from one place to another. Very, very American—heartland America.

The Long Christmas Dinner, of course, is the play that Orson stole the basic idea from for the breakfast sequence in *Citizen Kane:* the idea that the entire marriage was shown at breakfast, through a series of time lapses. Now the play tells the sixty-year history of a family with everybody dining at the table. When they come out of the white-canopied entranceway, they're born, and when they go off into the black-canopied entranceway, they die. Eventually, as they get older, they put on a gray wig. It's all very theatrical, but Orson said he'd seen it performed, and it was just devastating. By the time people are getting up to die, you're saying, "No, no, not him!"

PT: *Wilder is one of the giants.*

PB: I think Thornton Wilder is one of the great American writers and not often spoken of these days. Gore Vidal calls America the "United States of Amnesia." But he [Wilder] was one of the great novelists of that period and one of the great playwrights. He wrote three plays that were not only hits but classics: *Our Town, The Skin of Our Teeth,* and *The Matchmaker.*

Saint Jack (1979, New World Pictures)

Director: Peter Bogdanovich; screenplay: Howard Sackler, Paul Theroux, and Peter Bogdanovich (based on the novel by Paul Theroux); producers: Roger Corman and George Morfogen; executive producers: Hugh M. Hefner and Edward L. Rissien

PT: Saint Jack *was a turning point in your career.*

PB: Well, I certainly know what you mean—but I've had a number of turning points. [*Laughs.*] What I think *Saint Jack* represented was a return rather than a turning. It was a return to basics. And a step in another direction as well, the way I see it. Both *At Long Last Love* and *Nickelodeon* had been compromised rather a lot in how they were released—and also even in the way that they were finally cast and conceived and so on. There were problems with those two films of a kind that I hadn't had on the other ones up to that time. And that's why I stopped making pictures for three years. Some of the press thought it was because I couldn't get a job—this is nonsense. I turned down a lot of money during all the time that I was not working. I was constantly turning down pictures. I realized that I had to go back to basics. After having traveled around the world twice during those years and having an interesting time with Cybill, I realized I had to go back and make something the way we did *Targets.* Very low budget, down and dirty.

It turned out to be *Saint Jack,* and I think it was a great experience. And it was a particular decision inspired a little bit by [John] Cassavetes, of course, but also by [Ben] Gazzara when we worked together. We kept saying, "Let's try to avoid those obligatory scenes that every movie has. Let's see if we can do a movie without any of them." It was like trying to make an entire movie based on a premise that Howard Hawks once said to me. He said [*Hawks's voice*], "You know, there are scenes that an audience knows it's gonna get. And when you don't give it to them, they're so happy!"

PT: *How extensively did Howard Sackler work on the script?*

PB: He didn't really do much with *Saint Jack.* I'll tell you what happened there. He was living at the house, and we were working on the script. Cybill did the first draft—kind of more like a treatment—and it was about seventy pages. Then Paul Theroux took a whack at it, and it was terrible.

Left to right: Peter Bogdanovich, Monika Subramaniam, cinematographer Robby Muller (in a cameo), and Ben Gazzara in *Saint Jack*. Courtesy Jerry Ohlinger's Movie Material Store.

I tried to fix it up, and it still wasn't right. I gave it to Howard and said, "Read this and tell me what you think we should do with it." I think he looked at the book, too. Well, he found the construction. In the book, Denholm Elliott's character comes to Singapore once and dies. And everything that happens to him in the movie that you have now seen happened in one visit. Howard said, "Why don't you have him come three times? Then you have three times." Brilliant. So that gave us the clue. I think he did write a version of the script, but we had to change it quite a bit because he'd never been to Singapore, and there weren't any women in any version. There was a lot of rewriting that Benny [Gazzara] and I did later.

PT: *Still, the idea to hang the whole thing . . .*

PB: . . . on three visits from William Leigh. That was the solution for the construction. It was a huge contribution. I gave him [Sackler] first billing.

PT: Saint Jack *begins with a pan of a section of Singapore. You like to open by showing the landscape of the place.*

PB: I do that a lot, I know. I catch myself doing it. I don't know how else to do it.

PT: *I don't know if there's a better way to start a film than with a nice look at . . .*

PB: . . . where you are. Tell them where you are. Hawks said that all the audience knows about the geography of a place is from what you show them. I have always felt that the place is a character in the story, like Los Angeles was in *Targets* or San Francisco was in *What's Up, Doc?*. I mean, the place where it's set is very important. So in a lot of my pictures, introducing the place first is a kind of normal way of taking you into the story. Here's where we are, here's what's happening. I enjoyed beginning *Paper Moon* with a close-up, and we begin *Targets* with a shrieking bird. So, you know, those are different.

I've always regretted in *Saint Jack* that that first pan—which was an afterthought because I realized we didn't have any title footage and I thought we'd just do a 360-degree pan—but if I had to do it over again, I would have had it end up on Jack walking.

PT: *Right—you cut to him walking after the pan.*

PB: I had to cut to him.

PT: *Ben Gazzara did his best work in* Saint Jack *and, later, in* They All Laughed.

PB: I didn't meet him until John Cassavetes was shooting *Opening Night*, and he asked me to come down and be an extra. Peter Falk and I were the two main extras. I did a little scene at the end that John asked me to do, and then we went to lunch—John and Ben and Peter and I. Benny was being very like Ben: "Order whatever you want! John's paying!" He reminded me of Jack Flowers. So I called John, and I said, "There are two actors that I think could play Jack Flowers in this movie I'm doing. Ben Gazzara and you. Who do you think should do it?" He said, "I don't know." So I just decided on Ben because he was more gregarious and more Italian. He *is* Italian.

I had been a big admirer of his on the stage. I saw the first three things he did in New York—*End as a Man, Cat on a Hot Tin Roof,* and *A Hatful of Rain*—and he was electrifying on stage. Absolutely electrifying. I wanted to catch some of that electricity in the movie, which only really happened in *Anatomy of a Murder*, to a degree. He's very much like himself in *Saint Jack* and *They All Laughed.* It's very tailored to him. The dialogue was the kind of stuff that was comfortable for him to say.

We had to hold out for Ben. Paramount said they'd do the picture with me, but only with Paul Newman. I said, "I don't want to do it with Paul Newman. I want to do it with Ben Gazzara." Nobody would make it with me with him, except for Roger [Corman]. It revived his career. We gave him $15,000. The next picture he did—*Bloodline*—was for half a million.

PT: *While the English-speaking actors were very accomplished—not just Gazzara but also Denholm Elliott and Joss Ackland—many of the Asian actors had never done any acting before, including Monika Subramaniam as Gazzara's girlfriend.*

PB: No, none of the Asians had.

PT: *Monika is wonderful in the film. And that haunting last line she says to Gazzara: "I look for you in Ceylon."*

PB: You know where that comes from? One of the first nights I was in Singapore, after I got over the jet lag, I started hanging out with hookers because I was doing research for the picture. [*Laughs.*] There was this girl who was from Thailand, and she hardly spoke any English. I obviously didn't speak Thai. She stayed all night. I sort of got across to her that I thought she shouldn't do what she was doing, that I thought it was not healthy for her. She said she wanted to go back to Bangkok, and I gave her $5,000. She left the bordello she'd been working at and went back to Bangkok. As she was leaving, she looked back at me and said, "I look for you in Bangkok." It was very touching when she said it to me. There are a lot of things like that that happened to me with real hookers or real people. There was no detail about the prostitutes in the script. It was about a pimp, and there was nothing about the hookers. So I started meeting a lot of hookers, and we put some of them in the movie.

PT: *You told me that the British actors wrote a lot of their own dialogue.*

PB: Yes, for example, Denholm Elliott has that speech about trout fishing. It's in the alley when he talks about his dream of retiring. I said to Denholm, "Write something that you would like," and he wrote that speech. He was great. He was nominated for a British Academy Award. Should have won.

PT: *What made you decide to cast him?*

PB: I saw him in a movie called *Nothing but the Best.* It was a Clive Donner film with a good script by Freddie Raphael. Denholm was brilliant, and that's how I cast him for *Saint Jack.* I remembered him from *Nothing but the Best.*

PT: *But the other actors improvised, too.*

PB: Jimmy Villiers, who was twenty-fifth in line to the throne of England, played Frogget, and he made up that whole thing about the drink. Most of that dialogue was improvised with the actors in the room together after they got there. We read the scenes, and I said, "These scenes stink. Let's write something better. You guys come up with some thoughts. Let's improvise." We improvised it, and then we wrote it down.

PT: *You also have an important role in* Saint Jack. *Actually, I always wanted to ask you about something: When you deliver the speech about how the names of countries have been changed for the worse—like Ceylon being called Sri Lanka or Persia being called Iran—was that an opinion of yours?*

PB: That's my opinion. I thought they fucked up all the names. "Ceylon" is so beautiful and "Sri Lanka" sounds like a shriek. "Persia" is beautiful, and "Iran" is an ugly word. It was just the way I felt. Or "Thailand"—"Siam" had such mystery to it. "Malaya" is much more beautiful than "Malaysia." They improved everything to a disaster. I put that speech in. I wrote it. I think it was a good thing for him to talk about.

And then I thought, *We have a story about prostitutes and pimps, and it's interesting to have the CIA guy tell him where the word* hooker *comes from.* It's from General Hooker in the Civil War. I just think that's so interesting. The idea is to show that there's something going on there beyond what's on screen, and if you're curious, you'll find out. My mother used to always say, "If you have a thousand people watching something you've done, if one of them understands what you really mean, you're a success."

PT: *Robby Muller photographed both* Saint Jack *and* They All Laughed. *Among other things, both films feature an awful lot of nighttime shooting.*

PB: I like shooting at night.

PT: *Why?*

PB: Well, nobody's there to bother you. You're sort of doing this secret thing at night when nobody's there and the rest of the world is asleep, and you're up doing this conspiratorial event. It's wonderful. The night is beautiful to photograph. Also, [Jean] Renoir said to me, "When you make a picture, you should gather around you not associates, not collaborators, but conspirators!" I think that's a key, key thought. You're all conspiring to make this sort of forbidden thing.

They All Laughed (1981, Moon Pictures)

Director: Peter Bogdanovich; screenplay: Peter Bogdanovich; producers: George Morfogen and Blaine Novak

PB: *They All Laughed* was the most personal film I'd made to that time. I felt that I had been liberated on that film while I was making it because I took a lot of the things that I had learned on *Saint Jack* and carried them over, including the same director of photography.

PT: *And the location shooting.*

PB: Well, they are two island movies—Singapore and Manhattan both being islands.

PT: *So many of your pictures have been shot on real locations.*

PB: Mostly, yeah.

PT: *In some cases, as in* Saint Jack, *the places no longer exist.*

PB: Most of the locations we shot at are gone—gone forever. But the picture is a documentary of Singapore circa 1973. You see, I also think that the place where the story takes place is a character in the story. People live differently in New York than they do in Singapore. They live differently in Hays, Kansas, than they do in Washington, D.C.

PT: *You often go to great lengths to capture a place. I think of the opening shot of* To Sir, with Love II, *which shows the city for a few seconds.*

PB: Yeah, we went over to London just to get a few shots!

I've noticed that one of the things I like to do with the actors is put them in scenes in streets in the real locations and let the locations feed the scene in a way. I've noticed that some directors—notably, John Huston

Dorothy Stratten and John Ritter in *They All Laughed.* Courtesy Jerry Ohlinger's Movie Material Store.

and Elia Kazan in the old days—show you some shots of the locations at the beginning with no characters. Just shots of Paris or Manhattan or whatever. Kazan would show a bunch of interesting places, picked for their interest, and then he would go into the story. You never had the sense that the characters were in any one place. They set this up in the opening of the picture—atmosphere or what poets call "kindling." It's the wind and the trees. All of that stuff is setting up something. But they don't ever pay it off! Because from that point on you could have shot the rest of the picture in a studio.

Some directors don't seem to know how to integrate the place with the characters.

PT: *Let's go back to* They All Laughed.

PB: *They All Laughed* was a very personal project because it began as an idea I had a few years before. In fact, I had an idea for the title for a totally different plot. [*Laughs.*] I liked the title *They All Laughed.* I always thought it'd make a good title for a romantic comedy. So at one point I had one that I was going to do with Dudley Moore and Cybill. The idea was that

Cybill was going to play a jewel thief who was going to be a stowaway on an ocean liner, and Dudley, who plays the piano beautifully, was going to be a pianist in the lounge. It was a good idea, kind of an old-fashioned '30s comedy, but I didn't make it. I talked about it with Blake Edwards and mentioned how much I liked Dudley. When George Segal quit *10,* Blake remembered what I'd said and hired Dudley Moore.

PT: *I didn't know that.*

PB: Well, nobody does—except Blake. Anyway, I had this idea that I wanted to do something about the romantic life: the difficulties of romance, men and women at that time in history, at that moment. And I wanted to make it in the form of a comedy that was sort of bittersweet. I wanted to use things that happened to us, to all of us, to Benny and me and whoever I knew who had been through similar kinds of ordeals in terms of romance and love.

I wanted to use that and make it very personal, but I decided I didn't want it to be what didn't exist then, but I didn't want it to be one of those "artistic" films, one of those independent films. I wanted it to be a picture for everybody that was basically a romantic comedy with a bittersweet touch. In other words, make a very personal story but within what used to be known as "the rules of the game." By that I mean: you disguise your personal intentions by putting it within a genre. So basically we made it kind of a detective picture.

I had the idea to make them all private detectives because they could easily get involved in things—like show-business people get involved in things constantly. New picture, new show, new something. You lead a gypsy life, and you're constantly getting in touch with new people all the time. It's hell as a private life. And so same thing with private detectives—I guess. I never really did any research on private detectives. It was a fantasy private-detective agency, grounded in a kind of reality in Manhattan. It was done with a lot of realistic backgrounds because we didn't build anything except the office in the space of the actual building.

The deal that we made to make the picture—with Time-Life Films and David Susskind—was with a totally different script than we shot! He went crazy when he read a version of the script we shot. But there never was a final version of the script we shot except when we said, "Cut, print." The whole picture was not improvised because I wrote it, but most of the dialogue was written at the last minute or rewritten a lot or

Ben Gazzara and Audrey Hepburn in *They All Laughed.* Courtesy Jerry Ohlinger's Movie Material Store.

expanded or contracted or just written the night before on almost the entire picture.

PT: *How closely did the characters correspond to the actors playing them?*

PB: The picture's really about the people who are playing the parts. In other words, it's actually about Audrey [Hepburn] and Ben [Gazzara]—who had an affair—and it's about John [Ritter] and Dorothy [Stratten]—and John is me. I'm also Benny a little bit, too, so it's complicated. I was right in the middle age-wise. And then Audrey's character is totally based on Audrey. It's absolutely her biography. She's in a loveless marriage; she's staying in it because of the kid; and she fell in love with Ben Gazzara (and another after him). Even the clothes Audrey wore . . . everybody thinks Audrey Hepburn, and they think of Givenchy. The thing is, what she wore in the picture is all her wardrobe. When I'd hang out with Audrey, that's what kinds of clothes she'd wear. It's exactly what she wears in the movie: peacoat, slacks, shirt, scarf. Very simple. And Dorothy's story—except for the fact that her husband was lethal as opposed to somewhat benign—was also Dorothy's story. She was caught in a situation where she was in a loveless, hopeless marriage and was looking to get out.

PT: *It was personal not only for you, but for everybody involved.*

PB: It was. It was personal for everybody. And everybody knew it. It was easy to play.

PT: *Among the supporting roles, your daughters, Antonia and Alexandra, play Gazzara's daughters. Blaine Novak and George Morfogen were friends of yours. The woman who plays the secretary at the detective agency—wasn't she your secretary in real life?*

PB: Yeah. [*Laughs.*] Her name was Linda Ewen, and I said, "That's hard to say. Make it MacEwen." So I just called her MacEwen all the time. Blaine was working as a distributor—kind of an independent, arty distributor who worked with Cassavetes on *A Woman under the Influence.* He helped me quite a bit on *Saint Jack* for the distribution. I thought he was a character, and I wrote the part for him and put him in it. Of course, a lot of Blaine's stuff is really the way he talked, and he came up with a couple of really good lines, too. George was a dear old friend of mine. He was one of the producers. I thought that Blaine and George can work as the producers, Linda can be in the picture, and we can all work together.

Sean Ferrer—who played Jose—is Audrey's son, and he became my assistant. I said, "Let's put Sean in it." We had this character, sort of. But we said, "Let's have Sean do it." So all that dialogue when Colleen says, "How old are you?" and he says, "I'm nineteen, but I'll be twenty soon," . . . well, the day we shot that, he turned twenty. It was his birthday. That dialogue when they're walking and she says, "I think it's so sexy having that car follow us"? That was based on that I had a limo following Dorothy and me on July Fourth when we were trying to find a place to watch the fireworks from on Riverside Drive. We had the car following us along as we walked.

PT: *So even some of the actual incidents in the story were taken from real life.*

PB: The stuff about my daughters and the divorce and all that stuff—everything they say to Ben, they said to me at some point. None of it's made up; it's just sort of changed in terms of what they say. For example, Colleen [Camp] and that whole "feel my finger" thing is just a kind of variation taken to an extreme on something that Colleen did to me! She said, "I'll relax you, feel my finger," and it got to be very funny, so I put it in the picture.

PT: *Can you say what Dorothy Stratten meant to the movie?*

PB: That picture was inspired by Dorothy. It really didn't fall into place as the movie it became until I fell in love with her and then decided to put her into the picture. The character that she plays had about one or two scenes and no dialogue. It was just a case he was following at the beginning, and he comes to the conclusion that she's cheating on her husband and that was the end of that. That's how it was in the first few drafts, and that's the version that Time-Life bought. I rewrote it very heavily in the first three months of the year. The big breakthrough in terms of the overall script was when I came up with the idea of Christy [Colleen Camp] being a beard for John to go shopping in the shoe store.

PT: *It's your favorite scene in the picture.*

PB: It's a great scene. It's so funny. It's such a marvelous device to get them together. It was an idea I had, and I floated it to George and Ben and Blaine. Everybody said, "I don't know if you can do that." George said, "It's very difficult, but if you can do it, I think it would be very dynamic and powerful." So I went to California and wrote it.

PT: *What I like best about the scene is its joy.*

PB: There are some photographs of Dorothy and me during that scene which are just wonderful. We're both watching something off camera, and we both have exactly the same expression. The inspiration is from her and from all the women in the picture, really, the four leads, but predominantly Dorothy because I was crazy about her.

It's the kind of movie that you either connect with or you don't. And there are people who don't get it. Of course, you see, it was never seen ever the way it was really intended because Dorothy was murdered. So it changed what was supposed to be a kind of funny-on-one-side and bittersweet-on-the-other comedy . . . it sort of made it basically rather sad. It was tough for people at that time to look at it. I used to say that the picture would only work again when everybody was dead. It wouldn't be sad—you know what I mean?

PT: *It'd be like an old movie.*

PB: It'd be like an old movie. And now that John died, it's just very painful.

PT: *John and Dorothy were magical together.*

PB: Oh yeah, they were magical. They adored each other. She was very happy with me, and he was happily married, had a new child. Everybody was happy. Things turned a bit dark for Dorothy in May, but I didn't know about that.

PT: *One of my favorite moments is when John asks Dorothy to marry him.*

PB: That took the longest I've taken with John to get a line reading. He didn't know what I wanted. "Dolores, will you marry me?" The idea was that he just finally *had* to say it. John did it wonderfully, finally, but we did a lot of versions of it until we got it right. I had a certain thing I wanted to hear. It was like a getting-this-off-my-chest kind of line reading.

PT: *And the characters hardly know each other!*

PB: [*Laughs.*] Well, the point of that is that the two biggest close-ups are earlier, when they kiss in the alley. Obviously, it's an electric kiss. It's just overwhelming for both of them. She runs away from it, she's so taken with it. That's what the point of that moment is. A kind of romantic love is very quick. It was real—that's what happened with us.

PT: *Colleen sings "I Don't Think I Could Take You Back Again" again as John is proposing to Dorothy. The music is fit to the action.*

PB: It was very hard to do. I can't believe we did it this way, but we did: we had a Moviola on the set, and we had the lyrics typed out, and I sort of guessed approximately how long I'd be in each place with the lines of the song. I figured by the number of words in the tune approximately—within a word or two—where the cuts would be. And that's how we shot it. So that the main action only took a certain amount of time. And I timed it in such a way that it would work that way. All those cuts there were fitted in like a mosaic into that song.

PT: *There's a striking cut in this scene—right after Colleen finishes her first song but just before she starts "I Don't Think I Could Take You Back Again," you cut to an unexpected high-angle shot.*

PB: Yeah, when she goes to the new song.

PT: *That's the sort of shot that most directors would open a scene with. Why did you choose to put it where you did?*

PB: It felt right to go to a wide shot at that point. You know, Hitchcock always said to never use an establishing shot to establish. Use it for dramatic effect. It was a kind of establishing shot. It showed the place from a different perspective. It just felt right to go there. At first, I was worried that it was such a sharp change of angle, and you couldn't be in it for very long. It's not held very long, that shot. But I thought it worked. It's kind of exciting—it changes gears there.

PT: *It indicates to the audience that the tone of the scene is about to change.*

PB: Well, high-angle shots usually give a fateful effect. Fate is watching.

PT: *That's what happens in the scene. The two people who are meant to be together . . .*

PB: . . . finally get together.

PT: *Why did you decide to make Colleen's character a country singer?*

PB: Originally, when I first wrote it, she was going to be a jazz singer in New York. You know, like Andrea Marcovicci doing jazz standards. Something like that. And then I spent some time in New York, and country music had become slightly in fashion in New York. I thought that was sort of funny because it came so late to New York. [*Laughs.*] It just seemed funnier to me than the other, which seems kind of conventional, and it also went better for Colleen because she could kid it more.

PT: *Her scenes are like musical interludes.*

PB: What I like about those sequences is that they're integrated into the plot as opposed to stopping the story. Even the first one—for a minute you're seeing her singing, but then Ben comes in, and there's this whole thing, so you don't watch the entire song. The songs are very much part of the story.

PT: *I love the New York shown in the film.*

PB: Well, it's my hometown. I grew up there, so the streets are all familiar to me and have a warmth to them. And Dorothy was there, and we were having a great time making the picture and living together. It was just a glorious time. It was the peak of my life, really.

Every day was beautiful. I don't think it rained once. I guess it did a few times because we went inside to shoot the office when it was raining. It was just gorgeous. It was warm without being too hot.

PT: *Was this your first time back in New York since the early '60s?*

PB: For any length of time, yeah. *Once in a Lifetime* was a big flop, and it was just discouraging, so we left with our tails between the legs. We sort of turned against the city, which was stupid, but that's the way I felt. "I'll be back, New York!"

I always loved New York in movies. New York always looks great in movies. There's not a bad angle—just turn the camera on, and it will be good. [*Laughs.*] I always felt that way about every New York picture I saw, from *Naked City* to *It Should Happen to You* to *The Marrying Kind* to *Adam's Rib* to *North by Northwest.* Whenever I went to New York, I stayed at the Plaza because of *North by Northwest.*

PT: *I'm sure you're not advocating tobacco use, but I like all the cigarette smoking in* They All Laughed.

PB: Well, it's an interesting piece of business. It defines character. I hadn't thought about it particularly. In *They All Laughed,* Benny says, "You gotta quit. These things are killing people." So we tried to be on the side of morality there. He says, "Yeah, I quit," and he's smoking. That was something I did. I'd smoke, and then I'd quit, and then I'd smoke, and then I'd quit. In *They All Laughed,* we went to grass, too, of course. We threw that away, and people were sort of amused by that. We didn't make a big deal about it—they just were smoking a joint.

Leo McCarey used to talk about paying off a joke. That's how we came up with the ending of *Paper Moon.* I realized we hadn't paid off the $200. "You still owe me $200." That was all through the beginning of the picture, and then we get to the end, and we didn't deal with it. I thought, *That's how we'll get them back together.*

PT: *You also pay off Dorothy chewing gum when she has to take it out in the last scene with John.*

PB: Before they kiss. They're holding the gum in their hands. Dorothy was cute because she did chew gum. When she first takes the gum out of her pocket, she looks around to see if anybody's watching and then slips it into her mouth. I told her to do that because she thinks it's a little rude to chew gum—she's an old-fashioned girl.

PT: *Is there a trick to juggling multiple storylines, as you do in* At Long Last Love *and* They All Laughed?

PB: No, you just follow your instinct, really. Even on my first picture, I had two stories that were parallel. I noticed it made it easier to tell the story if you could cut away and come back.

PT: *Why do you think that is?*

PB: Because you can skip the boring parts. [*Laughs.*]

PT: *Was it a challenge figuring out how to introduce everybody and how they relate to each other at the start of* They All Laughed*?*

PB: I called Frank Capra—he was in Palm Desert—and I said, "Would you come and look at this picture? I finished it and would love to get your opinion before I do a final cut. I'll send a car for you." He said, "Well, I will, if you don't mind if I tell you the truth." I said, "Well, I want you to tell me the truth." He said, "Well, I told the truth to another fellow. He did the same thing—he asked me to look at his picture, and I told him the truth: I didn't like it. He wasn't very happy with me." I said, "Oh, really? Well, I'd love you to tell me the truth."

So I sent the car, he came down, sat in the projection room, ran it, and came out. He said, "Well, it's a good picture, kid. Your first reel is too fast." And that's all he said. [*Laughs.*] It was enough. Which meant that the rest of it he liked! I looked at it and what he meant by "too fast" was that I was crosscutting between characters too fast. I wasn't staying with one group of characters long enough. So I actually recut the picture somewhat. For example, if I was with Ben and I went to Blaine and then I came back to Ben, I would put the two Ben parts together so that it would be longer before we cut away.

One of the things that I think bothered people in the Florida preview—that was before I showed it to Capra—was that it was too fast in going from couple to couple. I picked up on that, and I slowed it up a bit, but I think Frank felt it needed to be slowed up some more.

I also tried to make it clearer by starting the picture with the sequence that comes about forty-five minutes into the picture. I actually began the movie, before the credits, on the street where Blaine signals Ritter, and then he [Blaine] goes underneath the window, and the girl chases him to the elevator. We go upstairs, they go inside, and the door closes. It says "Odyssey Detective Agency." Then we cut to the bridge.

PT: *To establish right away that they are detectives.*

PB: Yeah, because everybody was saying, "We don't know what they're doing." Other people have said that's one of the things they like about it.

PT: *It's one of the things I like about it.*

PB: And it's one of the things I like about it. But I tried this other way, and it didn't work because when you showed it to the audience, it was slapstick too fast. It was too early in the movie to get away with some of the things we did. It was a mistake. It didn't work, so we put it back the way it was originally.

Reading and Meeting Robert Graves

PT: *I recently came across a quote of Robert Graves in* Life *magazine that I think you will appreciate: "The supply of good women far exceeds that of the men who deserve them."*[8]

PB: "The supply of good women far exceeds that of the men who deserve them." Boy, is that accurate.

PT: *You first became aware of Graves through Orson Welles, who recommended that you read* The Greek Myths *and* The White Goddess.

PB: He said it to me in the mid-'70s.

PT: *Graves was a very important writer to Welles.*

PB: Very. Robert Graves and Isak Dinesen were his two favorite writers.

PT: *Why did he recommend them to you?*

PB: He said, "You ought to read . . ." Well, of course, I didn't. I told Cybill, "Why don't you read these and tell me what the gist of it is?" Two fat books. She went through them rather quickly. She was a speed demon as a reader.

PT: *Did she give you a report?*

PB: I said, "Boiling it all down, what does it come to?" She said, "Well, before men were in charge, it says women were in charge." I said, "That figures."

PT: *When was it that you read them yourself?*

PB: It wasn't until after Dorothy was killed that I started reading books that I had put aside for a rainy day. I started reading those two [*The Greek*

Myths and *The White Goddess*] starting sometime at the end of 1980 and read them really a lot. I also read books that people would tell you were good for you when you have a tragedy in your life or you're very fucked up. I read Francis Bacon, Montaigne, some of the Bible, the Book of Job, Emerson. Nothing helped. I found nothing that really said anything to me that helped me—except Graves.

The world that he resurrects in *The White Goddess* and in *The Greek Myths* is a world where what happened to Dorothy wouldn't have happened. So I enjoyed luxuriating in that world, and I wanted to know more about it—the matriarchal period in civilization. It ran from about 10,000 B.C. pretty smoothly up to about 3,000 B.C., and then the battles began.

PT: *You found it helpful to immerse yourself in the world he evoked.*

PB: That's right. It helped me emotionally. Also, don't forget, I was looking for an answer as to what the unicorn was. I had told Dorothy that she reminded me of a unicorn. She said, "What's that?" I showed her a little plastic image of a unicorn. She said, "Oh, that's what a unicorn is. I've seen that, but I didn't know what it was called. Did it ever exist?" And I said, "I don't know."

I found the answer in *The White Goddess.* It turns out the unicorn was a calendar beast, representing the calendar that the Druids elaborated, the Irish version of which is what Graves had in *The White Goddess* and which I put out in the calendar [*The White Goddess Engagement Diary*].

PT: The White Goddess Engagement Diary*—which you published from 1991 to 1998 and breaks up the year in accordance with Graves's research: thirteen months, each twenty-eight days long, plus a day —you had already been using it in your own life, right?*

PB: By '82 or something, I started using the calendar for myself. I would take modern-day calendars and re-mark them with the old tree calendar. I did that for a few years, just for myself. As my mother-in-law used to say, "You ruined another calendar." I kept ruining calendars by drawing over them. I found it made much more sense in terms of the cycles of the week and the cycles of the month. It flowed. It was based on natural history and based on nature and not on some arbitrary decision made in Rome in 44 B.C. The publisher didn't do anything to publicize it. I was paying for half of the costs, which was expensive.

PT: *You were trying to get to the bottom of things.*

PB: I got to the point where I was so thrown by what had happened that I didn't accept anything on face value any longer. Somebody would say, "A, B, C, D, E." I'd say, "Why is it A, B, C? Why isn't it C, B, A?" It turns out there was a reason. What is Monday, Tuesday, Wednesday, Thursday? What the fuck do those things mean? It turns out there was a reason. When you go back into ancient history, you find that almost everything leads back to a battle of the sexes. Virtually everything. The days were originally all female with a male protector, and now they're almost entirely male. Things like that.

PT: *When did you decide that you wanted to meet Graves?*

PB: Early in '81, I sent a telegram to Majorca to him, saying that I wanted to meet him and discuss in person events relating to—I sort of wrote in code—"Duir Ruis Saille," which are Dorothy's initials in the tree language. "Duir" is oak, "Ruis" is elder, and "Saille" is willow. It was unnecessary to put it in code, but I did. I left my number and said I'd like to arrange to come over to see you. His youngest son, Tomas, called me and said, "We got your telegram. You're more than welcome to come over, but my father doesn't speak." I said, "What do you mean he doesn't speak? He can't speak?" He said, "No, he can, he just chooses not to speak." I said, "Wow, that must be painful for you, for his children." He said, "Yes, there are many things we wish we would have talked to him about when he was speaking. But you're welcome to come over. My mother's here. My brothers and sister would all be happy to talk to you about *The White Goddess* and *The Greek Myths* and whatever you want to talk about." Then there was a pause. He said, "Oh, how extraordinary." I said, "What?" He said, "Well, my father is sitting here, and he just said, 'Yes.'" So I said I better get the fuck over there.

I went over to Majorca. I'd never been there. They welcomed me really graciously. I met Robert. He didn't talk. He sort of ignored me. He looked at me and was somewhat disdainful. He was more interested in eating cookies that his grandchild was feeding him. Beryl, his wife, would read Shakespeare to him, and he'd listen. He'd get a massage and so on. He was there, but he wasn't there. It was weird.

PT: *Was it senility?*

PB: Once, when he was sitting in the study where he wrote, surrounded by his books—he published over 150 books in his lifetime—his daughter, Lucia, asked him, "Daddy, why don't you speak?" And he gestured at the books and shook his head, as if to say, "I've said it all." There's nobody else like him. You talk about great writers of the twentieth century. He is *the* great writer of the twentieth century. People don't realize what an extraordinary body of work he created.

His family was very warm and welcoming, and I became quite friendly, particularly with his wife and then widow. He died four years later, the same year as Orson, actually, and I saw him once more in that time.

PT: *I wonder if you would have discovered Graves had it not been for Welles.*

PB: I don't know if I would have. I knew of Robert Graves, but I don't think I'd read anything of his.

PT: *Did Welles know what he had done for you by getting you started on Graves?*

PB: I always thought Orson figured I never would read the books. I think that he was amazed that I did.

PT: *Did Welles know you had gone to see Graves?*

PB: Yes, and he wasn't thrilled. Orson was pretty grim toward the end. He wasn't real friendly. The last conversation we had was friendly, and a couple others were not unfriendly. But he was not a happy camper.

PT: *What do you think we can learn from reading Graves?*

PB: Well, a better understanding of the relations between men and women, which is at the base of all our problems today. It all goes back to the battle of the sexes, believe it or not. Civilization, as he says, was thrown off kilter by man's violent takeover of women's primary functions.

In fact, ironically, women were much better treated in movies in the teens and '20s and '30s and even into the '40s and '50s than they are now. There were many female stars. And women got top billing in the '20s and in the '30s and in the '40s.

PT: *Many of those movies featured women who had the upper hand—like* Bringing Up Baby.

PB: Oh, yeah. She's the one who's right. Same thing in *The Awful Truth.* You know, America was kind of thought of as a de facto matriarchy in the '40s, and women were sort of in charge, in a funny way. Apple pie and mom were the symbols of America. You see it in a film like *The Searchers,* where Olive Carey has that speech about Texicans and one day this place will be a better place because of it. She exits, and John Qualen says, "She was a schoolteacher." She speaks the theme of the picture in a way.

PT: *Your work was always very sympathetic to women.*

PB: I think, generally speaking, the women in most of the pictures I've made are very strong. And I think the point of view is often from the women's perspective. *They All Laughed,* which I made before reading Graves, was of course the furthest I ever went with that. That's a movie about the sisterhood if ever there was one. It's a kind of instinctual sisterhood as opposed to a theoretic one or a didactic one. It's like a "we're all in this together" kind of thing. I have seen that with certain women. And I've also not seen it. But I chose to show it at its best because the film is a bit of a fantasy. And, of course, in that movie they do maneuver the entire situation, which is actually the main point in Shaw's *Man and Superman.*

PT: *You have talked about making films based on several Robert Graves novels, including* The Golden Fleece.

PB: Well, *The Golden Fleece* is the first great adventure story that ever existed. The zodiac is named after incidents in the narrative. It turns out to have been real as opposed to fictional. Every time it's been depicted in movies or previous to Graves, there were sort of supernatural elements involved, with weird animals that didn't exist. It was sort of fantasized. The truth is that it was an actual adventure in 1225 B.C., or something like that. It was about 1,200 years before Christ. It is representative of a religious and political climate that existed at that time in that period which was all about the matriarchal versus patriarchal civilizations. It's very interesting because most people don't even know that went on. The battle of the sexes turns out to have been real. The background to the story of Jason and the Argonauts has political and religious significance.

It's an absolutely fascinating story and very hard to do, very hard to do. With CGI [computer-generated imagery], it could be done. There are about thirty-seven accounts of the adventure. Graves reconciled the thirty-seven accounts that exist in literature and threw out things that were obviously fantastic and transformed into realistic terms those that were fantastic because he understood what they meant. They might have been symbols for something. It's a brilliant, brilliant, brilliant novel. It's riveting, and it's such a great adventure story. I had a great beginning of a script. It's about thirty pages. The beginning is dynamite.

PT: *What are the others?*

PB: There's a science-fiction book he wrote which is sort of fascinating called *Seven Days in New Crete.* The American title was *Watch the North Wind Rise,* so I'm calling the picture *Seven Days to the North Wind.* It's a time-machine story. A guy materializes from now to a thousand years into the future. But there's no technology in the world that he's brought into. It's a part of the world where no technology exists; they live in a kind of prehistoric social order. It's kind of an experiment, a thousand years hence. And he's brought into it for seven days, and it's what happens to him in those days. It's very perplexing, kind of suspenseful, funny, complicated—very strange.

And then there's a very good book of his called *Wife to Mr. Milton,* the story of Marie Powell. Marie Powell was sixteen when she married John Milton, the English poet, who was then thirty-six. And it's basically a triangle love story between him and her and a Royalist soldier that she falls in love with. It takes place during the English Civil War, which hardly anybody knows about. I think it's a fascinating moment in history because it affected America so much. When the Civil War was ended, about forty years later the Puritans were thrown out of England—the ones who had won the Civil War originally and then on the Restoration were ousted. They came over and started New England. I had a new title. I didn't like *Wife to Mr. Milton* for the movies—it's good for the book. I was going to call the movie *Brave Old Days.* It's a chapter title from the book.

He's a great novelist, but he's never acknowledged as such because he never wrote in the same style twice.

PT: *When readers think of Graves's books, they usually think of* I, Claudius.

PB: A lot of them are out of print. *I, Claudius* is in print, and *Claudius the God* and *Goodbye to All That* and *The White Goddess.* His novels are fascinating—they're really, really fascinating. *King Jesus* is great.

PT: *Were you ever interested in making a film based on* King Jesus?

PB: Yeah, I was interested in that because it's such an interesting story the way Graves tells it. You'd have to combine *King Jesus* with another book he did with a Hebrew scholar named Joshua Podro, *The Nazarene Gospel Restored.* He did a nonfiction rewrite of the four gospels. [*Laughs.*] Basically, telling the story of Jesus, straight through from the beginning to the end, based on the Bible, and giving you the Bible sections that relate to the biography of Jesus, but then transforming them into what he thinks really happened.

People were outraged by it. They only printed three thousand copies in the U.S. It's one thousand pages, but it's riveting. It taught me a huge lesson, that book, because I read the whole thing. At the end of the argument, before he does the actual *Nazarene Gospel,* the actual biblical text revised, the book sort of stops, there's a break, and in the break he summarizes the entire two-thirds of the book—in three pages. And I thought, *If Graves can summarize that book in three pages, I don't need more than a paragraph to write this fucking scene.* It taught me concision as a writer.

PT: *You also had an option to adapt* The White Goddess.

PB: I didn't know how to do it, but I thought maybe it could work as a cartoon. An historical cartoon. But Mrs. Graves—Beryl—didn't like that idea. I was thinking of doing it with Chuck Jones. Make it real simple.

PT: *Did it get any further than just thinking about it?*

PB: No, just thinking about it. I discussed it with Chuck briefly.

The Waxing and Waning of Moon Pictures

PT: *20th Century Fox was the original distributor of* They All Laughed, *but you formed your own company to put it out yourself. Why did you call it Moon Pictures?*

PB: That was because of Robert.

PT: *What do you mean?*

PB: *The White Goddess* had a lot to do with the moon—moon cycles and monthly women's cycles. The moon controls liquid, and we're 90 percent liquid. It's a very important influence on our lives, and I just liked the sound of it. We had several versions of Moon Pictures. We had Ivy Moon; we had Holly Moon.

PT: Who the Devil Made It *is copyrighted to Ivy Moon.*

PB: Ivy is the symbol of resurrection, so it was resurrecting the moon. [*Laughs.*]

PT: *Your previous production company was named for the street where you and Cybill lived—Copa de Oro.*

PB: In Bel Air, yeah. And Saticoy was the street we [PB and Polly Platt] were on in Van Nuys.

PT: *Your first several films were Saticoy Productions.*

Back to Moon Pictures: in addition to distributing They All Laughed, *you had other plans for the company. Films were announced in* Variety: Paradise Road—*"a comedy set in contemporary Las Vegas to be shot in black-and-white"—as well as adaptations of Thornton Wilder's* The Bridge of San Luis Rey *and Robert Graves's* Watch the North Wind Rise, *which you are said to have described as "the least expensive science-fiction film since Roger Corman stopped making them."*[9]

PB: We went down to Texas to raise money. Unfortunately, Steve Friedman, who was the nominal producer of *The Last Picture Show*—he has his name on it, but he had nothing to do with the picture except that he owned the book—had gone down there, taking bows for *The Last Picture Show,* and had raised a lot of money, and everybody had lost it. So when I came down after him to try to raise money in Texas, they were leery of the whole thing. I couldn't raise enough money. We were trying to raise $20 million, and we only got $8 million. Thanks to Steve Friedman, who was an asshole.

PT: *In the end, the only film produced under the banner of Moon Picture was Martha Coolidge's* City Girl.

PB: I lost my shirt on that. Colleen came to me and said, "Martha has run out of money, and she's making her first movie." She made a documentary called *Not a Pretty Picture,* about when she was raped. I was interested in women's problems and women's issues. They showed me some of the movie—it was called *Anne and Joey*—and I thought it was rather charming. The girl was good, and the guy was good. They needed about a half-a-million dollars to finish it, so I put up the money. We did finish it. It became quite good—I helped her in the cutting—and we ended up calling it *City Girl.* We did a few previews, and we kept getting it right. Just when we got it right, we ran out of money. We never could afford to pay for the music rights.

PT: *I've never seen the movie.*

PB: It was never released, but she has it—I gave it back to her. I'm sure it'll end up in some archive. It's worth seeing. It's not a bad little picture. But it cost me a lot of money.

PT: *It's too bad that it spelled the end of Moon Pictures.*

PB: Yes! [*Laughs.*] The beginning of the end! We almost did a couple of other pictures. We almost did *Rosebud County,* which ended up being done on TV. It was a script that Larry [McMurtry] wrote. He wanted me to do it, but I wasn't going to direct, so I got Jonathan Demme to do it. We tried to get Barbara Stanwyck, but she said she hated the script because it was nothing but cuss words.

PT: *Why were you interested in making a film of* The Bridge of San Luis Rey?

PB: It's a good book. Allan Dwan had written a draft of it. The widow of Benedict Bogeaus—Dolores Moran—had the rights at that time. She was the other girl in *To Have and Have Not,* Dolores Moran, so we talked about Howard [Hawks]. She had the rights. We bought them for about five grand and had them for about a year or so. I didn't want to direct it. I wanted to produce it. The problem was that they weren't interested in anybody else directing it.

PT: *You designed the logo for Moon Pictures—it's very stylish.*

PB: There was that moon with the river running through it. I came up with that at three in the morning one night when I was doing some kind of Robert Graves work. I knew what it meant at the time, but I've since forgotten. But I think it has something to do with an E and an O: E is autumn, and O is spring.

PT: *The plan was for you to produce other people's pictures—which was also part of the deal when you had the Directors Company in the 1970s.*

PB: With the Directors Company, we had a clause in there that said we could produce anybody's film for a million and a half as long as we stayed with that budget. We didn't even have to tell the studio. I was going to do one with Orson, with Nick Ray, with King Vidor. We were going to do a whole bunch of pictures, but Billy [Friedkin] and Francis [Coppola] disbanded the company.

The Killing of the Unicorn and What It Means

PT: *In the meantime, as you were distributing* They All Laughed *and trying to set things up with Moon Pictures, you were writing a book about Dorothy Stratten:* The Killing of the Unicorn. *You write that one way you dealt with the tragedy was to gain knowledge—to figure out what happened.*

PB: I had to do quite a bit of research. I talked to a lot of people. I interviewed people. I did find out what had happened. That's why I said that to [Bob] Fosse when he was making his stupid movie [*Star 80,* about Stratten]. I said, "You don't know the story. How can you make a movie?" He said, "Well, we think we do." I said, "Well, I don't know it, so how the fuck do you know?" That was the most superficial movie ever made. It's dreadful. People occasionally come up to me and say, "I love your movies. I particularly like *Star 80.*" I say, "I didn't make that." They get confused. They don't know what they're saying.

PT: *Was it therapeutic to write the book?*

PB: I guess it was. It didn't end the sorrow. I had to do it—I just had to do it.

PT: *How was it working on it each day?*

PB: It was the hardest thing I ever had to do. It used to take me three or four hours a day to just get myself to where I could sit down and start doing it. Very, very difficult.

I wrote about five times that length. It was much longer, and it went on a lot of tangents, which the editor thought were unnecessary. He was probably right. It should be a tight book. John Dodds was the editor. His wife was Vivian Vance, who played Lucy's friend on *I Love Lucy,* and she had died. So he was sympathetic to somebody in mourning. It was so painful to write that I would write it, and Iris Chester [PB's assistant] would type it up, and I just didn't even read it. I would just send it to him. It was hundreds of pages.

PT: *It's your best book.*

PB: It's the only one that's really important, I think. But the other ones are all right. They reproduce what existed with human beings who happened to be movie stars and directors.

PT: *It's not that I don't love the other books . . .*

PB: No, I was putting them down, but I shouldn't. They're valuable, but *The Killing of the Unicorn* is sort of an outcry against the whole fucking mess.

PT: *You write about a conversation you had with John Ritter in which you said that women were essentially superior to men. Do you still feel that way?*

PB: Yeah—they have more sophisticated bodies and more sophisticated minds.

PT: *They're also more interesting to watch on-screen.*

PB: Well, I think so. And more interesting to talk with. Orson used to say that. He said women are better conversationalists than men. I said, "Why do you say that?" He said, "Well, women tend to jump around in a conversation. Men sort of beat the subject to death."

PT: *Do you ever reread* The Killing of the Unicorn?

PB: About two or three years ago, somebody who was trying to help me get out of a depression or something said, "You ought to reread the book." And I thought, "Well, I don't know if that's going to help." Maybe it's like shock therapy or something. So I read it in one night, and it was devastating. It just brought it all back. I don't know that it was that healthy. I was just overcome. I had to stop occasionally and just sob. It was just so heavy. I'm glad it's there. It certainly chronicles the ten months we spent together.

PT: *How was the book received?*

PB: The book got generally bad reviews. It was a best seller for a while, but the reviewers kind of tried to kill it. There was a sort of whisper campaign among the bookshops that it was against pornography, and, you know, they make money with pornography, so they weren't too happy about the book. Gloria Steinem said to me, "You know, when the suffragettes used to march at the turn of the century for women's rights, people would throw things at them. But there was one man who marched with them—he got the most rotten eggs thrown at him." Because you become a traitor to the cause. I think the whole world won't work right until there's equality of the sexes—that's what I think.

PT: *The response you got from feminists was positive, though?*

PB: Gloria Steinem was in touch with me, as was Catharine A. MacKinnon, who is one of the great female lawyers. She is amazing. She has written some brilliant books about women's law and women in general. I love her—we became very good friends.

Andrea Dworkin and Kitty MacKinnon drafted an ordinance about pornography and the harm it does to women who participate in it. It passed in a couple of places, and then it was considered unconstitutional or something.

PT: *You supported the ordinance publicly at the time.*

PB: Yeah, I did—and I got into a lot of trouble.

PT: *Do you regret it?*

PB: No, I don't regret it, but I was not popular at that point.

PT: *Did you hear from average readers about the book?*

PB: Well, I got about four hundred letters—all from women, not one from a man. I was also going to make a movie about her [Dorothy].

PT: *Tell me about that.*

PB: That was an interesting idea. I was going to use outtakes of her from *They All Laughed.* I was going to begin the story with Lee Marvin playing a former FBI agent who's now a private detective. He gets a call from a director whose girlfriend has been murdered and is asked to get involved to find out what really happened. [In the story,] Hefner's magazine was called *Lucky's* magazine. It was going to tell the story from the point of view of the FBI agent. I did hire a former FBI agent to look into it. He was an interesting character, an older man, older than Lee, but I liked Lee for the part. It was not anything like *Laura,* but the idea was that the private detective falls in love with the image of Dorothy, and the only time you see her was in outtakes from *They All Laughed.*

PT: *That's riveting.*

PB: It was a good idea.

Mask (1985, Universal Pictures)

> Director: Peter Bogdanovich; screenplay: Anna Hamilton Phelan; producer: Martin Starger; executive producer: C. J. Kettler

PT: *So,* The Killing of the Unicorn *had been controversial, Moon Pictures had gone kaput, and you weren't able to properly distribute* They All Laughed. *Then, seemingly out of nowhere, you took an assignment from Universal to direct* Mask. *What drew you to it?*

PB: I'll tell you what happened. It happened during *They All Laughed.* Dorothy had never seen a Broadway show. Never seen a Broadway play. She'd never been to New York before. So she decided one afternoon that she was going to go to a matinee. I couldn't go for whatever reason. And she went to a matinee of *The Elephant Man.* She came back, and she just absolutely was bowled over. I mean, she was on Broadway, and it was a wonderful production, which I saw after she died. She was very, very, very, very, very interested in the real Elephant Man, the real person it was based on.

Dorothy and I used to go to Doubleday's Bookshop, which was on Fifth Avenue and just a few blocks from the Plaza. It's gone now. But it used to be open until midnight. We were working late many times, and we'd go for a walk up Fifth and go to Doubleday's and buy some books, all of which she devoured in that spring and summer. She read all these books, fat volumes like *Crime and Punishment, Great Expectations,* you know.

So one day we went, and I noticed she was leafing through a nonfiction book about this Elephant Man. It had a lot of very graphic photos, which I noticed because I came to stand next to her for a moment while she was leafing through the photo section. And I could not look at them. I said, "My God," and I walked away and did something else. I came back and saw that she was actually buying the book. She piled it up with other books that we were getting. I said, "You mean, you really want to get

Left to right: Cher, Sam Elliott, Eric Stoltz (back to camera), Harry Carey Jr., and others in *Mask*. Courtesy Jerry Ohlinger's Movie Material Store.

that? You sure you really want to get that book?" I thought to myself, *How can she look at those pictures?* And she said very, very determinedly, "*Yes.*" Like "Okay, back off." So I said, "Okay, okay," and laughed. And that was it, and I bought it for her.

She devoured the book. After she was killed, I was curious to know everything I could about her. So I went to see the play on Broadway, with David Bowie in it by this point. And I got it. The connection. Which was, when we'd walk down the street in New York, go to the park, or go down Fifth or wherever we walked—everybody stopped and looked at her. I mean, dogs stopped. You think I'm kidding. It was extraordinary. People just stopped and looked and turned. This was not because she was in *Playboy*. It was that she was so striking. And to such a degree, you have to understand, that it didn't photograph. She looks great in the picture—and in other pictures—but not as good as she really looked. That's what's so weird. She looked better than that. And I would say to her, "Jesus, everybody's looking at you." She'd say, "No, they're looking at you." I'd say, "Dorothy, they're only looking at me to see who you're with." She'd say, "Well, no, they're not." She'd be in denial. I pressured her and said, "Does that really bother you?" She said, "Oh yes, I hate it." "Why?" "Well, I always feel like there's something wrong with me, like I have ice cream on my dress or something. I don't know what it is." So it isn't just simply that she was unaware of her own impact, but that she felt uncomfortable by being set apart. Her beauty set her apart every bit as much as the Elephant Man was set apart by his ugliness. It was an entirely physical thing—not a thing from the soul—that people were reacting to. That's how she took it.

When I got *Mask,* it had a very poor script which took place over ten years of Rocky's life, and it just didn't work. There were some good ideas in it, but it was completely rewritten. I did nine drafts with Anna Hamilton Phelan. But when I got the one-hundred-page first draft, I wasn't really in the mood to make a picture, but I had to. I needed the money. I felt a little blessed that it came because it was the true story of a kid like that, and so it connected with me to Dorothy. That's the personal thing you felt in it.

PT: *But at first you weren't too thrilled about doing* any *movie.*

PB: George Morfogen had a great line. Around twenty days into the shoot—it was a sixty-day shoot—he said, "You made peace with the picture today." I said, "I did?" He said, "Yeah, you embraced it today." At a certain point I did. He was right.

PT: *It doesn't feel like a movie made by somebody who had taken a few years off.*

PB: No, it's very engaged.

PT: *After those twenty days, did you feel somewhat reconnected to your profession?*

PB: I think so. Something happened. There were some wonderful scenes in there.

PT: *For some reason, I always go back to the summer camp scenes with Rocky and Laura Dern's character—she is brilliant in the film.*

PB: She is brilliant. Well, it's a love story again, you see. I come alive with love stories.

PT: *What sort of work did you do on the script?*

PB: I basically did the construction with Anna Hamilton Phelan in an office. We did it—the producer, Marty Starger, was there too—for a month or two. And in fact the dialogue between Sam Elliott and Cher, most of that dialogue was not in the script. That was written while we were there, just before we shot it usually, or sometimes some of the stuff they ad-libbed in rehearsal.

PT: *Kind of like* They All Laughed.

PB: Not as much as *They All Laughed,* no. But we still ad-libbed, and there was a lot of stuff that we'd throw in just before we'd make it. Like that whole thing with the apple—remember when Laura Dern and Rocky are sitting under the tree and she cuts the apple and says, "See the star. It's supposed to be good luck"? That directly relates to *The White Goddess* because there's a lot in *The White Goddess* about the apple and what it means, why it's called the fruit of immortality, why it has sanctity—it has to do with the five-point star you find if you cut it crosswise.

PT: *In a number of the films you made after reading Robert Graves, you put references to his work—or mythology in general—in the mouths of your characters. In* Mask, *Rocky talks about the Trojan War in history class.*

PB: Well, I stick it in there hoping somebody will say, "What does that mean? Let me look that up."

PT: *Is that really your main motivation?*

PB: Yeah. It also gives a certain depth to the character. It gives them a certain complicated element. But also I hope people will say, "What does that mean?" Rocky gets the Trojan Horse story a little bit off, too—the thing about giving the apple to the winner of the Miss Goddess contest. Actually, if you look that up, the original version is that the goddess gave the apple to the man. But he wouldn't have known that unless he had Robert Graves, so he told the more conventional version of it.

PT: *You were able to get quite a lot of Robert Graves stuff in the picture. I'm thinking of the "celebration of New Year's Eve in July" bit at the camp.*

PB: Yes, that's right—with the holly and the oak tree in the background. It really is the middle of the year. Oak was the central tree, and holly was the beginning of the second half of the year. It connects with the sacred kings that River Phoenix talks about in *The Thing Called Love.* It's the same story, only that's the calendar version of it. The oak king and the holly king fought until Doomsday.

PT: *In an interview with Thomas J. Harris, you said that one of the things that appealed to you about* Mask *was that the script "had something to say . . . about the transcendence of a certain kind of death."*[10] *That aspect of the film was much more obvious in your original cut, which includes the funeral of the biker played by Harry Carey Jr.*

PB: Well, that's why the damn funeral was there. It was meant to set up Rocky's death.

PT: *After the funeral, Rocky says that Red is "everywhere" now.*

PB: Yeah, which comes from Sean Lennon, who said that about John after he was killed. Cher echoes it at the end: "Now you can go everywhere, baby." Which is a line I wrote. I wrote both scenes.

PT: *When did you decide to use so much Bruce Springsteen music in your cut of the film?*[11]

PB: Early on. Rocky was a fan of the Beatles and Springsteen and a couple of others, but those were his favorites. And since I knew Bruce and I liked his music, I thought there was a rough-hewn, working-class feeling to his music that would go well with Rocky, who came from a working-class kind of environment. I remember that "Born in the U.S.A." came out while we were shooting, and we would play it on the set between takes, so it was planned right away.

PT: *I love the opening shot, when the camera pans across freeways in Los Angeles, followed by cuts to Rocky's street and then Rocky's house, with Springsteen's "Badlands" getting louder with each cut.*

PB: At the end of the pan—like at about the last twenty seconds of the pan—you're starting to hear "Badlands" very far away, like you can hardly hear it. "Is that Springsteen? Holy shit, it is!" And then you cut, and then you hear it louder and louder and louder and louder until you just can't think it could get any louder, and then it gets louder in his room. All of that is Springsteen singing "Badlands." It's fucking one of the best openings I've ever shot. It was shot to that music; we shot it with that music playing. And when you see Rocky doing the guitar strum in the mirror in the beginning, he was doing "Badlands," and finally it's in synch.

PT: *Why did you decide to play Springsteen's "Promised Land" over the end credits?*

PB: I'll never forget it. I was driving along Mulholland in Los Angeles—it's a very curvy road—and I was playing Springsteen music, trying to figure out what to use for the end, and "Promised Land" came on, and it hit me that that's the ending. I was so overwhelmed with emotion—sobbing—that I had to pull over. I couldn't see to drive. I sat there and cried for about ten minutes. It so goes with the ending.

Illegally Yours (1988, United Artists)

> Director: Peter Bogdanovich; screenplay: Max Dickens and M. A. Stewart; producers: Peter Bogdanovich and Dino De Laurentiis; executive producers: William Peiffer and Peggy Robertson

PT: *On many of your recent films, you are doing what the older directors did: you find ways to express your own vision through someone else's story.*

PB: You make it your own. You find what really works for you, and you don't put anything on the screen that isn't real for you. Moment by moment, you take what you like and make it your own.

PT: *Were directors like Ford or Hawks very much involved on a script level?*

PB: Well, Ford and Hawks had a lot to do with the script. Particularly after the Fox years, I think Ford had a lot to do with the scripts. He didn't write it, but he influenced it. I didn't write *Mask*, but I was in the room. They did nine drafts with me.

PT: *There are other ways to inject your personality into a movie.*

PB: Constantly. You're always doing it. The mise-en-scène is part of the movie.

PT: *Even a picture like* Illegally Yours . . .

PB: Oy.

PT: *I hesitate to even bring it up—not because I think it's a terrible movie, but because you dislike it so much. But I was going to say that even on a movie as compromised as that one, you shot it your way.*

PB: Well, it was shot by me, and the pacing is all right. You know, there was originally supposed to be Rob Lowe, and his mother was going to be

Ava Gardner, and the Harry Carey part was Jimmy Stewart, and the rich guy was going to be Robert Stack. I wanted an all-star cast. Dino [De Laurentiis] just refused to pay for them. One of the things Rob and I were talking about was, "Ava Gardner plays your mother. Wouldn't it be nice to see Ava Gardner in a kind of flirtation with Jimmy Stewart?" And the father is Robert Stack, as a kind of military lunatic. But Dino just wouldn't pay for it. He had Rob Lowe—he didn't need anybody else.

PT: *You told me the original title was* Love Is a Gambler.

PB: Well, that is what I wanted to call it—*Love Is a Gambler.* But the original script that they sent to me was called *Double Duty.* And it was a totally different script. It had to do with people importing slave labor from Mexico. It was a very dark sort of black comedy about slave labor. I don't remember much more about it except that Dino agreed to do it, we got Rob Lowe, and then about a month before we were supposed to start shooting, Dino announced that he didn't like the script. I said, "It's a black comedy." He said, "Well, sometimes black comedy is not so funny." I said, "Well, Dino . . ." He said, "I don't want to make this script." I said, "Well, Jesus Christ. What are we going to do?" He said, "Well, write something else."

So we wrote a completely new script. We had to throw out the slavery thing, which he didn't like. Then we scouted locations in Wilmington, where he had studios. Half the picture was supposed to be shot there. While we were shooting in St. Augustine, I get a communication saying that they didn't want us to come to Wilmington—just stay there, find new locations there. So while I'm shooting, I have to find a whole bunch of new locations. It was a disaster. He kept pulling the rug out from under me: no cast, no script, no locations. I mean, I'm good, but I'm not that good!

PT: *It sounds awful.*

PB: It was horrible. He ripped the film to shreds and took out a whole thing we had about marijuana, which was sort of funny. It was a whole subplot with a bushel of marijuana that got swept up on the shore and everybody got stoned. It was very funny, but he took all of that out.

PT: *Were you rewriting the script with the original writers?*

PB: No, no. We brought in another writer, who didn't do a very good job, and then I was sort of scrambling to rewrite it while I was shooting. I was rewriting it myself, just trying desperately to get something on paper and then had the actors contribute. I had Kenny Mars write some of his own stuff, and it was overwritten, and then I had to cut it out. It was just a nightmare, a complete nightmare. If I'd been smart, I would have just said, "Shove it," and walked off the picture. But I needed the money, and I think he would have sued me if I'd walked off. Plus, I was hoping to make *Texasville* with them [De Laurentiis's company] because he bought *Texasville* for me. We had to buy it away from him eventually.

PT: *There were sound reasons for you to do it, but it just wasn't what you signed up for.*

PB: It was not at all what I signed up for. It wasn't the same script, it wasn't the same locations, it wasn't the same actors—nothing. And the cut was wrong.

PT: *Do you think a director's cut would make any difference?*

PB: No, I wouldn't even know how to begin to recut it. There are some things I like in it; like the opening is good.

PT: *I think Colleen Camp is good in it, as are some of the other actors carried over from* They All Laughed, *like Linda MacEwen and George Morfogen. And I think you were also able to sneak in some interesting literary references, like when Rob Lowe quotes several lines from William Blake's "Why Was Cupid a Boy."*

PB: And there's the numerology with the dice.

PT: *Yes, there's that line, "Twenty. That's two. That's love," which you reuse in* The Thing Called Love.

PB: Yeah, "Eleven. That's two. That's love." Just to throw people off a little bit.

PT: *Would it have been that much better with the original script and cast?*

PB: It would have been a pretty good picture. I mean, Jimmy Stewart and Ava Gardner would have been interesting.

PT: *And Stewart wanted to do it?*

PB: We talked about it, but Dino wouldn't pay anybody. Everybody else got just minimal money.

PT: *I don't have a problem with Rob Lowe in the movie.*

PB: He's all right. There are some good scenes that we cut because they weren't played very well. He listened to me, but he was a bit scattered on the picture.

PT: *You knew him because he auditioned for* Mask.

PB: He gave a good reading. And I liked him. I saw him in a couple of pictures, and I thought he was a good-looking kid. I thought he would be interesting to use.

PT: *It's unfortunate that it turned out the way it did, but, as I say, I try to look for signs of your personality wherever I can.*

PB: Well, I was there! [*Laughs.*] I tried, but it was really painful.

PT: *You didn't have a good experience with De Laurentiis—putting it mildly.*

PB: He was the worst producer I've ever had.

PT: *Who was the best?*

PB: [Roger] Corman and Bert Schneider and, believe it or not, Marty Starger was good until the explosion about Springsteen. John Calley was a very good studio head on *Doc.* Bob Evans and Frank Yablans were very good studio people on *Paper Moon.* The best producer I had was me. [*Laughs.*]

Texasville (1990, Columbia Pictures)

> Director: Peter Bogdanovich; screenplay: Peter Bogdanovich (based on the novel by Larry McMurtry); producers: Peter Bogdanovich and Barry Spikings; executive producers: Jake Eberts and William Peiffer

PT: *What interested you about doing* Texasville*?*

PB: I was actually kind of scared to do it. I did it because I thought that I couldn't really not do it. It seemed obligatory. I didn't think we'd necessarily do well by comparison because the first film [*The Last Picture Show*] is more romantic simply because it's about young people. Even though mainly the sex is funny, young love has a sort of poetic, touching

Jeff Bridges and Cybill Shepherd in *Texasville.* Courtesy Jerry Ohlinger's Movie Material Store.

quality, whereas middle-aged love sort of has to be treated as comedy. No matter how painful it is, if you're going through a midlife crisis, somehow it's funny—simply because it's hard to get serious about it. [*Laughs.*] Even though it's very serious. But I followed the cue of the book. The book is that way—a totally different tone than the first one. It's not as well constructed as a book as the first one, so it wasn't that easy to adapt. We had to lose a lot. But I think we found Jacy's character, which was a little buried in the book as it was. But, I mean, it's a very good book.

PT: *I love the opening pan: as radio broadcasts are heard, indicating the time period we're in, we survey Duane's property and end up on a close-up of Duane as he's shooting his doghouse.*

PB: Well, we began with a pan in *Picture Show* and ended up on the truck, so I thought we would try to do the whole opening scene in one shot. It's actually two shots, I think. I just thought it would be a good way to run the titles. Also, it's supposedly been thirty years since they were teenagers, so if you take a long, slow pan, it's like you're covering all the years in between. And what do you see at the end of it? You see a gun, and Duane is shooting a doghouse. That was funny. He went to Korea, he came back, and now he's shooting a doghouse.

PT: *The deep-focus photography is extraordinary. I think of the scenes inside the Dairy Queen—it's very, very bright outside and rather dim inside, but everything is equally sharp.*

PB: That was hard to do. It took forever. It took a lot of work. I said, "I want everything sharp," and the cinematographer took me literally, and I meant him to. Balancing the interior and the exterior was hard to do. It has a nice feel to it. You get the sense of the heat and the sort of claustrophobia of the place.

PT: *The cinematographer was Nicholas von Sternberg, whose father was Josef, the great director of* Morocco *and* The Scarlett Empress.

PB: He was Joe's only son. I thought it'd be nice to give Nick a chance. He did a good job. He just took too long.

PT: *There is also some of your most intricate editing in the picture—for example, the final scene with everybody grabbing at Sonny as he's standing precariously atop the high school stadium seats. Why did you conceive the scene that way?*

PB: That's the way it seemed it had to be. It was a desperate scene, and it needed that kind of editing. You're right, it's quite cutty, but that's the only way you could do it. They're a lot of people involved, and there's action, you know? Action needs that kind of work.

PT: *It's striking because usually your editing style is very leisurely.*

PB: Well, that's the point, Peter. If you're cutting every second, like most films today, when you really want to do something with it, when you want the editing to really have an impact, it's impossible to have an impact because you've been doing it all the way through. It's like yelling all the time in every scene—then when you really want to have someone lose their temper, they've been yelling all through the picture, and it's useless. When you need fast cutting, you use it. When you don't need it, you don't. Some scenes really require it, and others absolutely need the opposite. It's just what the scene needs. It's a huge vocabulary and grammar of film, and you're just trying to use it properly.

PT: *You released a director's cut of* Texasville *on laserdisc that's longer and more episodic.*

PB: I think that the director's cut—the version that's on Pioneer laserdisc that's about twenty-five minutes longer—is much more the picture that we made because obviously those twenty-five minutes were important, but most of that time relates directly to *The Last Picture Show* or stuff that doesn't quite work as well if you don't know the other picture. We sort of got maneuvered into a bad place—I'm talking about the production—because Columbia, under one regime, had originally agreed to release *Picture Show*—with five, six minutes added—in theaters before *Texasville.* It was not yet out on home video, so it was an ideal situation. But unfortunately another regime came in and killed that idea, so we sort of had to make *Texasville* self-contained, which was sad.

People who have seen the long version of *The Last Picture Show* and the long version of *Texasville* back to back—the guy who used to run the American Cinematheque ran it that way, and then Quentin Tarantino ran it that way, the two pictures back to back—said it was quite overwhelming. I've actually never seen it that way.

PT: *One of the best scenes in the director's cut is when Jacy watches and is quite moved by John Cassavetes's* Gloria *in bed, while Duane dozes off. Was that a tip of the hat to Cassavetes?*

PB: There are two reasons for it. I tried a number of different things to see what would work best for the story—it's Cybill's story because Jeff falls asleep—and I tried *Mogambo* because I loved Ava Gardner's strength in it. But that didn't work. Then, of course, that whole thing was cut out of the release version, so I didn't have to worry about it. But then for the director's cut, I had to address it, and we got the permission to use *Gloria.* Because there was a little boy in the scene, and she'd [Jacy] lost a little boy. I thought that would help connect her to the picture. Why is she crying? Because her son died, and there's Gena Rowlands with a little boy. And, of course, it was a tip of the hat to Cassavetes, who was the first person to read the script of *Texasville.* When I finished the first draft of it, I sent it to John first, and he said, "What a life. You gotta make this picture." He loved it.

PT: *Didn't you direct one scene in Cassavetes's* Love Streams?

PB: John called me and asked me to come down and direct a scene that he was going to be in. And he said he needed my help. Of course, I said that he didn't need my help—he had directed himself many times. And he made it a real issue and put it in such a way that I couldn't refuse, even though I felt it was ridiculous—he certainly didn't need me. I came down, and we shot a brief scene with Diahnne Abbott when she comes to the door and I think she gives him a flower, and they talk at the door for a minute or two. It was my idea for her to give him the flower, and there was a little bit more to it. John wanted me to have the car drive up and see her pick the flower. I think that's not in it. But I shot that, and there wasn't much to it. I really didn't do much in directing—they rehearsed it, they did it, I thought it was good; I didn't really comment. I thought they were excellent. I just encouraged them and put the camera where I thought it ought to go.

PT: *Why do you think Cassavetes insisted that he needed you?*

PB: It took me a while to realize why John had done that. It was basically for me. I had been in my house pretty much since Dorothy was killed, finishing that picture [*They All Laughed*] and then writing the book [*The Killing of the Unicorn*], and I hadn't been on a movie set since *They All Laughed.* This was '83, I think. He also knew I wasn't keen on directing anymore. He did it to make me come back on a movie set. Really, it was very sweet of him.

Noises Off (1992, Buena Vista Pictures)

> Director: Peter Bogdanovich; screenplay: Marty Kaplan (based on the play by Michael Frayn); producer: Frank Marshall; executive producers: Peter Bogdanovich and Kathleen Kennedy

PT: *What were the challenges about bringing* Noises Off *to the screen?*

PB: Well, the big problem with that one was how to do the play as a movie. The play is very theatrical. Virtually all of it takes place in a theater. Hitchcock had warned me that when you take a hit play, don't open it up—you ruin the very thing that you bought, which is the construction. That's what makes a play a hit. He's so right. In adapting *Noises Off,* I did the same thing that I had done—actually with more difficulty—on a Georges

Left to right: Denholm Elliott (back to camera), Marilu Henner, Nicollette Sheridan, Christopher Reeve, Carol Burnett, Michael Caine, and John Ritter in *Noises Off.* Courtesy Jerry Ohlinger's Movie Material Store.

Feydeau bedroom farce, which I still haven't made. I've worked on it; I've constructed a screenplay. The trick on *Noises Off* was to not open it up too much but to open it up just a little bit, mainly in the intermissions where the play takes a break.

PT: *Had you seen the play on stage?*

PB: I saw a production of the play in New York—it was a big success—sometime in the '80s, and part of the dynamic of the theatrical experience was, and is, "Are the actors going to survive this night?" Because it's really hell to play it, up and down those stairs and doors, and, you know, it's not easy. They're doing it without a cut, so to speak. Curtain up and then curtain down. So I thought if I did the same thing in the way I shot it, it wouldn't create the same tension in the audience because the audience knows obviously they got through it because it's a movie. But it would create the same tension in the actors that they would have on the stage, which would communicate itself, I thought, enough to bring some of that experience into the movie.

So, as you've probably noticed if you've looked for it, there's an enormous number of long pieces, long takes, where the shot goes on for pages.

We were averaging twenty-five seconds a page. That was the other thing. I said, "Don't worry about page length on the script." Because everybody worries about whether it goes over 120 pages (figuring a minute a page). I said, "You can't judge that on this picture because it's gonna play so fast and there's so much dialogue; it's got to go quickly." We checked how long it played in the theater, and it was about two hours. And I thought, *Well, that's two hours, including laughs, because in the theater you do sometimes stop for laughs.* In the movie, you don't. So I said, "It'll come out to be about 110 minutes, I'm guessing." Well, I was right. The script was 220 pages—they almost shit over there at Disney. They said, "Are you out of your fucking mind?" And I said, "Don't worry. Look at the screenplay for *His Girl Friday.*" It's 180 pages—and the picture's 90 minutes. So, luckily, Frank Marshall had worked with me before. He'd worked on *What's Up, Doc?,* which was 150 pages, and the first cut was 97 minutes. He knew what I meant about speed.

The toughest was the second act, where it's mostly dumbshow. That was extremely difficult because in the writing, if you read the play or the script, you'll see that it's just basics. But the actual choreography of it was so difficult that I said, "I can't do this on a movie schedule. They took weeks to do this in the theater, and we're gonna need somebody who was involved in the London or the New York production to come here and show us at least basically what the choreography was, and then we can adapt it to the movie." We can't make this up. We haven't got the time. We rehearsed for six weeks, and even then . . . we needed two weeks per act to rehearse. But there was still no way to do that second act. Everybody was a bit shocked that I said that, but I said, "I'm being candid. I can't do it. Nobody's good enough to do this in this time. It needs to be very carefully done, and it takes too long." So we brought in a woman who had worked as an assistant director in the London production for five years, and she helped us. She showed us the basic way it worked in London. I adapted it to a degree and figured out how to shoot it so it would play.

The trick for me in that picture was pace and where to put the camera. For example, in the first and last acts, we had a lot of stuff where the camera goes up to the balcony, to the second floor, and then down to the stage. On the first day of shooting, I wanted to do it, and they had a regular crab dolly there, and we tried it, and I said, "It's absolutely not going to work." We have to be able to get up there fast. Finally, Frank said, "Well, you know, you're talking about a Louma crane." And I said, "I don't even know what it is." "Well, it's remote control. It can move quickly because the guy swings the arm up. There's no operator on it; it's done remote control from down here." I said, "Get it." We got it. It was a special crane that takes three men to run it. It was very tricky, but that's how we did those shots.

It's really fun when you notice it because you realize, "Jesus, the actors really did this." I mean, they really had to do this, and there's a lot of long pieces. I forget, when I'm watching it, "Jesus, where did we cut?" I realize we haven't cut yet. We had to have really good farce actors. There's nobody better than John Ritter at that.

PT: *Michael Caine and Carol Burnett were also wonderful.*

PB: Michael had never done anything like it. He said, "You know, I've never done anything like this." I said, "You haven't? You should've." He said, "Well, I haven't!" [*Laughs.*] Of course, Carol is amazing. She does readings, and you say, "Is that funny?" And then you see it with an audience, and people scream.

PT: *Didn't you try to get Audrey Hepburn to do Carol Burnett's part?*

PB: Yes, she felt insulted. She thought I was saying that she was like that character. It could have been funny. She always wanted to play Madame Arcati in *Blithe Spirit,* which is the part that Margaret Rutherford played. That's why I thought of her. When I talked to Audrey about *Noises Off,* she said, "Did you think that was like me?" I said, "No, no, no, but you always said you wanted to play something not like you, like Madame Arcati in *Blithe Spirit.* So I was thinking of you in those terms as an actress."

PT: *Christopher Reeve was very funny, too.*

PB: He was very good in that. He was good at comedy. I could tell that from the first *Superman.* He was my only choice for that part. Nice guy to work with, too. He got very Methody on me. He got so much into the role of the self-involved actor that he was getting to be a pain in the ass! I said, "You're taking on the character a little bit here, Chris." He said, "I am? Oh shit, I'm sorry." I said, "Well, that's okay."

PT: *This was the first time you worked with Denholm Elliott since* Saint Jack.

PB: We thought of a lot of different people, and he was the one we decided to use. He wasn't the most obvious choice, and I wasn't sure if he was the right choice. It turned out that he knew he was dying of AIDS. I didn't know it, but he knew it, and I think it put a darkness over him, which was unfortunate. He's brilliant in it. Roddy McDowall wanted to play it, and John Mills wanted to play it. Both of them would have been interesting, but Denholm had a kind of drunken, dissipated quality.

PT: *You mentioned that you worked on a Georges Feydeau [1862–1921] farce that was helpful as you were preparing* Noises Off.

PB: I was going to do a whole series of Feydeau farces. Feydeau wrote bedroom farces—he sort of invented them—and *Noises Off* is a kind of chaste bedroom farce. I learned a lot about the timing from Feydeau. I read the translation, which was a literal translation that wasn't very good to read, but I got the idea of what was going on in French, and then I was able to retranslate it, so to speak. We only did it with one picture, but I had titles for all of them.

One was called *Joined at the Hip,* based on a play called *Un fil à la patte,* which means literally "A Girl Hanging on My Leg." Then there was another one called *La main passé,* and we called that one *After the Shuffle.* "La main passé" means "the hand passes," like in poker, so *After the Shuffle* was a good title. And then there was another called *Mushrooms,* which was about a couple of characters named "Mushroom." I had a friend of mine—a French professor—read all the Feydeau that hadn't been done as movies and tell me which ones were the most cinematic. He told me those three. And they were. The most elaborate one was *Mushrooms.* Maybe the funniest one was *After the Shuffle.* And we have a whole screenplay on *Joined at the Hip.* I worked on that for quite a long time with Irwin Shaw's son, Adam Shaw, who spoke very fluent French.

PT: *Did you Americanize the settings?*

PB: No, but everybody spoke English.

The Thing Called Love (1993, Paramount Pictures)

Director: Peter Bogdanovich; screenplay: Carol Heikkinen; producer: John Davis; executive producer: George Folsey Jr.

PT: *Among your work from this period, I think I like* The Thing Called Love *the best.*

PB: The Thing Called Love—I'm glad you like it. I like it. River [Phoenix] and I worked hard on that together. All the actors did. I had to fight Paramount to get Sandy Bullock. They didn't want her.

PT: *That's amazing!*

PB: Yeah, it is amazing. They just kept saying no. This was not [former Paramount CEO] Sherry Lansing; this was the previous administration—Brandon Tartikoff. They kept saying, "No, we don't want her." I said, "She's brilliant. She gave a great reading. I met with her, and she's great." "No." And *The Thing Called Love* is the movie that got her the job in *Speed.* Jan de Bont had a choice of a couple of movies to screen with her in it, and he picked mine, he was quoted as saying, because he had a feeling he'd like it. And he cast her from that. Anyway, River and Samantha [Mathis] were great. Everybody was good. It was a good cast. Anthony Clark started on that—he's a television star now. And I loved Dermot [Mulroney]. They were all really good. They did some wonderful scenes.

The thing about *The Thing Called Love* is that the script needed an enormous amount of work. They told me that they wanted me to redo it. It was completely rewritten as we went along with the actors. A lot of stuff was improvised and then written down and then learned. The actors and I all worked on that endlessly. I told them that I wanted to get their point of view. They were in their early twenties. I wasn't. I wanted to know their attitude, how they would react, how they would feel. I didn't want it to be phony. So they were all involved.

PT: *What was the original script like?*

PB: It just was kind of amorphous. It was sketchy. You didn't get to know the people very well. *All* of the scenes were rewritten.

PT: *Was the writer on the set?*

PB: The writer was on the set, and then they kicked her out and brought in another writer, Allan Moyle. I didn't think she had to go, but they didn't want her there. I thought that was mean. The actors and I wrote it, and Allan sort of took it down.

PT: *Why do you think you have an affinity for stories about young people?*

PB: I don't know, but I've always liked kids. I like people that age. I like people older or younger. I don't like people the same age. [*Laughs.*] My contemporaries get on my nerves.

PT: *And you have an affinity for stories about young love, particularly.*

PB: Well, I feel a connection with lovers, period. Falling in love or the troubles of love is something that obviously runs through a lot of my pictures.

PT: *You told me that the actors picked their own songs.*

PB: River found that song "Blame It on Your Heart." He found that song one night while he was looking around town [Nashville] and came back and said, "What do you think of this?" I thought it was brilliant. Everybody contributed. Sandy wrote her own bad song—so did Sam. They wrote their own bad songs, and then somebody helped them a little bit. Things like that. That whole scene where they make up the song while watching *The Man Who Shot Liberty Valance* . . . I said, "This is so obviously a Bogdanovich touch that it's a bit much." [*Laughs.*] But what the hell, I can't resist it.

PT: *The song at the end, "Big Dream," ties in with your preoccupations—there are lines in there about the gender of God being female.*

PB: When the people who wrote the song played it for me, I thought they were kidding. I thought they knew how I felt about Robert Graves and his historical books. I said, "What are they doing? Reading my mind?" The refrain in the song goes, "Makes me think maybe God's a woman, too."

PT: *But it turned out to just be serendipitous.*

PB: Serendipitous, yeah. Nobody wanted the song. They wanted songs that were more upbeat or more flashy. I said, "You know, when an audience first hears a song, they're not going to love it. It takes time to get to know a song and to get familiar with a song. So it has to be something that's a little surprising and a little revolutionary in the lyric, not so much the tune. It has to be something a little shocking or a little controversial."

PT: *In the director's cut, you put back in several moments that allude to Robert Graves, and you also have Samantha Mathis reading some Graves books and Virginia Woolf's* A Room of One's Own.

PB: It's a very important point. A woman should have a room of her own. That's what the picture is about. She sort of triumphs at the end on her own. Every so often a woman comes up to me and says it's one of their favorite films. It's empowering to women.

PT: *What is it about country music that appeals to you? We hear it throughout not just* The Thing Called Love *but also* The Last Picture Show *and* They All Laughed.

PB: I think the simplicity and straightforwardness of it I like. And the easy melodies. It's not music that I listen to for pleasure myself, at this point. I did for a long time. In fact, there's some country music in *Saint Jack.* One of the best moments is that "Okie from Muskogee" coming through on the loudspeaker right on the cut—that's what made it so powerful. "We don't smoke marijuana in Muskogee . . . ." That was Ben's favorite moment. Country music is very American.

PT: *Your sensibility is in evidence in* The Thing Called Love, *even though it was an assignment.*

PB: It's true even of a thing like *Noises Off.* I tried to serve the text, but it's also personal; I know those kinds of people, I know that kind of world. And I know it's not that exaggerated. [*Laughs.*] So it's hard to keep myself out of them. Some projects are more personal than others. Some projects you can invest yourself into more.

The Small Screen

Song of Songs (1994, Showtime)

> Director: Peter Bogdanovich; screenplay: Harry Mark Petrakis and John Petrakis (based on the short story by Harry Mark Petrakis); producers: Jeff Freilich, Scott J. T. Frank, Daniel Halperin, and David Wachs; executive producers: Norman Jewison and S. Howard Rosen

A Dime a Dance (1995, Showtime)

> Director: Peter Bogdanovich; screenplay: Allan Scott (based on the short story "The Dancing Detective" by Cornell Woolrich); producers: Stuart Cornfeld and William Horberg; executive producers: Sydney Pollack and Lindsay Doran

To Sir, with Love II (1996, CBS)

Director: Peter Bogdanovich; screenplay: Philip Rosenberg (based on characters by E. R. Braithwaite); producer: Richard Stenta

The Price of Heaven (a.k.a. *Blessed Assurance)* (1997, CBS)

Director: Peter Bogdanovich; screenplay: Joyce Eliason (based on the novel by Allan Gurganus); producer: Jack Clements; executive producers: Joyce Eliason and Frank Konigsberg

Rescuers: Stories of Courage: Two Women (1997, Showtime)

Director: Peter Bogdanovich; screenplay: Ernest Kinoy and Susan Nanus (based on the book by Gay Block and Malka Drucker); producer: Jeff Freilich; executive producers: Cis Corman and Barbra Streisand

Naked City: A Killer Christmas (1998, Showtime)

Director: Peter Bogdanovich; screenplay: Jeff Freilich and Christopher Trumbo (based on characters by Malvin Wald); producer: Jeff Freilich; executive producers: Andrew W. Garroni and Walter Gernert

A Saintly Switch (1999, ABC)

Director: Peter Bogdanovich; screenplay: Sally Hampton and Harris Orkin; producers: Sally Hampton and Iain Paterson

PT: *Following* The Thing Called Love, *television beckoned. In hindsight, it's the most prolific period of your entire career—you did one after the other.*

PB: The last few pictures hadn't been anything to write home about financially, so I wasn't getting a lot of offers. I got a couple of TV offers, and I just said, "Fuck it." One led to another.

The first thing that was offered to me was from Sydney Pollack, who had offered me a couple of things over the years as an actor, and I unfortunately rejected them stupidly. He was just trying to be a friend and also liked my work. He wanted to cast me in *The Electric Horseman,* and I said, "Why do you want me for this?" He said, "Well, I can't afford

George C. Scott, and I want somebody who'll intimidate the actors." But Ray Stark was so cheap that he didn't want to pay me anything, so I couldn't do it. Then Sydney offered me the Dabney Coleman part in *Tootsie,* and I just was not in the shape to do it. I should have done it. It was 1980, the year D. R. was killed. I don't know how I got through that year anyway.

So Sydney was doing a series at Showtime called *Fallen Angels,* which was a series of short film noirs—half-hour or forty minutes. And so they sent me this thing, which was called "The Singing Detective." That's another title that the story was known as. I said that I didn't like that title. Can we go back to the original title of the short story, which was "Dime a Dance"? Without the *a*. I put the *a* in. [*Laughs.*]

PT: *It's an adaptation of a short story by Cornell Woolrich telling of a killer who targets dance-hall girls in the 1930s.*

PB: They had a pretty good script, and I came in and redid it with the writer. We rewrote it, put in the ghost of the girl, and I picked all the music and rewrote a little bit of the story. We shot it in five or six days.

PT: *You shot it in color, but the design is in black-and-white. How did you achieve that look?*

PB: We actually painted everything gray and black-and-white. And the costumes are all black-and-white. It looks like the whole thing's black-and-white, except for the hair and the eyes.

PT: *So nothing was done optically—you just painted the sets?*

PB: No, the whole picture was painted to look the way it did. The only thing we did was not optically, but on a Telecine machine. It's much more supple and pliable than what you can use for 35mm. We shot it in 35, but then you can do this work on it once it's been digitized. So there was a high-angle shot when she comes into the dance hall, and she's walking across alone. The floor of wherever we shot that was sort of brown, and on the Telecine machine we grayed it out. Everything else was painted. I told the costume designer, "No color. Black-and-white only." So there was no color in the costumes, either.

PT: *It's such a dark film.*

PB: It's a gruesome story.

PT: *You also made a short film,* Song of Songs, *as part of another Showtime series,* Picture Windows.

PB: I thought that *Song of Songs* was one of the best things I'd ever done. I did some work on the script with the writers, and we restructured it a bit. The story was the same, but we restructured it.

We did a lot of long pieces in that. We had good actors, and we did it in five days, the whole thing. All on location. I guess we did one thing in the studio, the bedroom scene with her, where he follows her around while she's lighting candles.

PT: *Next was your first feature-length work for television:* The Price of Heaven. *It's based on a very good novella by Allan Gurganus.*

PB: Yes, and I met him. He's a nice guy and a good writer.

PT: *What appealed to you about it?*

PB: It's the story of racism. The Grant Show character is a sort of closet racist, but he changes as he comes to be human, and he comes to recognize Cicely Tyson as a human being. It's got a lot of interesting elements to it. My original cut had a lot of the music of the period, which they couldn't afford, so they put in this score. It's okay, but they overuse it.

Cicely was extraordinary to work with, I remember that, and she wouldn't let me see her any way but in the elaborate makeup and costume and that voice. Many of her big scenes are done in one. A lot of the more complicated shots are done in one. By the way, when I finally saw her as herself, after we wrapped, I was astonished: she was youthful and very attractive!

Grant Show was so good. You know, he was cast first as the young hitchhiker in *Thelma and Louise,* and his TV series—*Melrose Place,* a *90210* copycat—wouldn't let him go for those few weeks. Brad Pitt got the part and became a star. Grant is so good, he doesn't make a wrong move in my picture, and the role's got a lot of different colors to play.

PT: *How much control did you have over the editing of your work for television?*

PB: The cutting was pretty much the way I did it. I don't think anything was changed. It was shot the way it was cut. There wasn't much you could do except lose something, and they didn't.

PT: To Sir, with Love II *is my favorite of this group.*

PB: I thought it was a pretty good script. When we did a table read before we started, we realized we had some problems in the third act. Sidney was a little distressed, but he did everything I said, so we straightened it out. We got the writer in, and we fixed it up. I ran the first picture—I had seen it before—and I was pretty disappointed in it. It's pretty dated, and I thought we could do better. Ours holds up better because it's not dated.

Sidney and I got along very well. He was a little nervous about the way I shoot. He's directed movies himself, and he covers his stuff. He doesn't just take it one way. He said, "Well, what if it doesn't work?" I said, "It's going to work." We'd do a shot in his apartment, and it was all in one shot. He said, "Aren't you going to cover it?" I said, "No." He said, "What if it doesn't work?" I said, "It always does." [*Laughs.*]

He didn't ever give me a hard time. He let me do it. He wouldn't say, "Well, you've got to shoot coverage." He just was nervous about it. I remember toward the end of shooting—it was about twenty-four days—we were going to do a shot along the street, dollying in front of him, and I explained it to him. He said, "Yeah, I know, a walk-and-talk. I hate those." I said, "You hate them?" He said, "I hate them." I said, "Well, Sidney, I've been doing nothing but walks-and-talks all through the picture. Why didn't you tell me you hate them?" He said, "Well, you like them." I said, "Why do you hate them?" He said, "Because I don't know if I'll be good enough to get through it!" I said, "Well, you always do." He said, "It makes me nervous." [*Laughs.*]

PT: *Sidney Poitier is a magnetic screen presence.*

PB: He's a star. Cicely's a star. These are star actors.

PT: *Did you shoot on location in Chicago?*

PB: All in Chicago, the whole thing. And we went to London after we finished in Chicago. We shot that in a day. It's a good opening. We got Seal for that opening song, which was great.

PT: *When George Cukor worked on TV, with* Love among the Ruins *and* The Corn Is Green, *he said in an interview with* American Film *that he shot them exactly as he would a theatrical feature.*[12]

PB: I did too. I didn't make any compromises. It was a movie, as far as I was concerned. It was a quick, low-budget movie.

PT: *Next came* Rescuers: Stories of Courage: Two Women, *which told a pair of true stories about Christian women who protected Jewish families during the Holocaust. Was it your family's experience of escaping World War II that interested you in doing it?*

PB: Of course it was. Everybody was affected by World War II. The entire world was shaken. And I was on the earth at that point. I remember when Roosevelt died. I remember the war years: bomb shelters and air raids and all that shit.

Rescuers was an amazing project because we did the whole thing in nineteen days with three different locations, including Quebec, Toronto, and a suburb of Toronto, with a train and tanks and explosions. I don't know, to this day, how we did it in nineteen days, but we did. It was brilliantly scheduled by the producer, Jeff Freilich, and we worked fast.

The actresses who played the rescuers—Sela Ward and Elizabeth Perkins—were wonderful and terrific to work with. I enjoyed them, and I really enjoyed making it. The first story was about a Hungarian boy named Michael. He's a grown man now. We showed him the movie with an audience, and he came up to me and said, "I don't know how you did it, but that's exactly the way it was." That was kind of the best review I ever got.

PT: *Then you made* Naked City: A Killer Christmas.

PB: That was mostly shot in Toronto in twenty-four days. It was fun to do. *To Sir, with Love II* and *Naked City* are both kind of crime pictures, with a little bit of a difference. But they're basically crime pictures, particularly *Naked City.*

PT: *I like the contrast between the holiday setting and the dark story.*

PB: The grisly subject matter—yeah, that was interesting. We shot on Sixth Avenue, and we shot down on Wall Street [in New York City].

PT: *When I first saw the film, it occurred to me that it might be the first time you'd done any shooting in New York since* They All Laughed.

PB: Yeah, it was . . . well, no, I also shot part of *Noises Off*—the opening and the ending—in Manhattan. But it was one of the rare times that I was in New York.

PT: *By this point, however, you had come back to live in New York, after many decades in California.*

PB: I think it helped me a lot to move back to my hometown. It gives a totally different kind of perspective on the time in Los Angeles and the time in New York. I lived in New York for the first twenty-five years of my life and then moved to California for a *long* time. Now looking back, yeah, it makes a big difference. I think it gives me more objectivity. You see, it's a monstrous business. It's hell. It's pretty much like any other kind of business. The merchandise happens to be humans as opposed to cars or cookies. We manufacture people, so to speak, with people. [*Laughs.*] It's very odd.

We were suddenly brought back to LA to do the Tom Petty documentary, and here we are. LA is just easier. Not necessarily better, just easier.

PT: *I think of* A Saintly Switch, *made for ABC's* Wonderful World of Disney, *as your contribution to the genre of Vincente Minnelli's* Goodbye Charlie *and Blake Edwards's* Switch*—the gender-swapping farce, with David Alan Grier as a tough-guy football player who briefly inhabits his wife's body.*

PB: I thought it was pretty funny. It was quite a good script. The woman who produced it was very nice. It was originally called *In Your Shoes.* We tried to get Dennis Quaid and a couple of people, and nobody wanted to do it because it was television. Hollywood actors were afraid of television in those days—more than they are now. I can't remember if it was Disney or me, but somebody said, "Why don't we get a black cast?" So we decided to do that. We got David Alan Grier, who was brilliant, and Vivica A. Fox. David made me scream with laughter when he was playing her.

PT: *Several of these films—*The Price of Heaven, To Sir, with Love II, A Saintly Switch*—have predominantly African American casts.*

PB: I was privileged to work with them. They were all such good actors. Sidney and Cicely are two absolute black icons. And, as a result, black people know who I am. In airports, they see my name—"Oh, Mr. Bogdanovich, you're the movie director." I couldn't figure it out.

Before I did *A Saintly Switch* for Disney, I had one meeting with the head of the division in New York. He said an interesting thing to me. He said, "You know, you're going to have a very good rating with this." I said, "Why do you say that?" He said, "Well, black people don't have that many shows made specifically for them." And that's what happened with *To Sir, with Love II:* we won the night—so did *The Price of Heaven* and *A Saintly Switch.* All because the black audience, which is huge, watched it. They saw the name "Bogdanovich," and they said, "That guy ain't black. That's for sure." [*Laughs.*]

PT: *Do you get recognized a lot in general?*

PB: A stewardess—a flight attendant, as they call them now—went nuts the other day. She was about a forty-five-year-old woman. She said, "Aren't you Peter Bogdanovich?" I said, "Yeah." "I knew it was you, I knew it was." She introduced me to the pilot and everybody. Then I was in a vitamin shop in Winston-Salem, and the guy says to me, "You look an awful lot like Peter Bogdanovich. You wouldn't be Peter Bogdanovich, would you?" I said, "Yeah." He said, "Oh my God. You're the most famous person I've ever met." [*Laughter.*]

PT: *Some of this must be due to your popularity on* The Sopranos.

PB: *The Sopranos*—and just generally being in the public consciousness for forty years. The forty years went by in about twenty for me. Time is completely relative. When you have a sudden death, like I had with Dorothy, time really gets warped. The time before the person died seems much shorter than the time since they died.

PT: *You cast Louise* [*Stratten*] *in almost all of your work for television. Did you always try to find a part for her?*

PB: I wanted to use her as much as possible. I usually found a way to get her in it. She was happy to do it, and I was happy to have her with me. She did a good job. She did a lot of different kind of things.

PT: *She played a wide variety of parts.*

PB: Yeah, from a cop to a pregnant girl. I think she's particularly touching in *A Dime a Dance* as the girl who gets murdered and comes back in dream flashbacks.

PT: *My favorite was when Louise played your on-screen girlfriend.*

PB: [*Laughs.*] In *Song of Songs.* That was fun.

PT: *Good casting. You're not asked about your television work too frequently, are you?*

PB: The funny thing is that *Price of Heaven* won the night. It was the most watched show that night in the time slot. *To Sir, with Love II* won its time slot. So millions of people saw them, but not the cognoscenti.

PT: *You were able to work in a variety of different styles on TV.*

PB: As you call them back to me, I remember we didn't compromise on them. I didn't act like I was slumming. I did my best work—the best I could within the time frame, and the time frame didn't bother me. It was nice to work fast.

The Cat's Meow (2001, Lions Gate)

> Director: Peter Bogdanovich; screenplay: Steven Peros (based on his play); producers: Julie Baines, Kim Bieber, Carol Lewis, and Dieter Meyer; executive producers: Michael Paseornek and Wieland Schulz-Keil

PT: *What is the story behind* The Cat's Meow?

PB: Orson had told me the essential story that the movie depicts, which is the rumor—but it was confirmed to Orson by Charles Lederer, who was Marion Davies's nephew, Marion Davies having been William Randolph Hearst's mistress—that Hearst had meant to shoot Charlie Chaplin because he was having an affair with Marion and instead by accident shot [film producer, director, and screenwriter] Thomas Ince. That's the story that Orson told me when we were doing the book [*This Is Orson Welles*]. And I asked him, "Did you ever consider having that story in *Citizen Kane*?" Which is only peripherally based on Hearst, anyway. And he said, "No, we had it in, and we took it out." And I said, "Why did you take it out?" And Orson said, "Well, I didn't think Charlie Kane was a killer."

PT: *He probably had a few other reasons for taking it out!*

PB: No, because Orson went on to say that if he had left it in, he thinks there would have been no Hearst blacklist because Hearst wouldn't have copped to it being about him.

PT: *Then, decades later, you received a script about this incident.*

PB: I don't know what year it was—it was at the end of the '90s—but the Telluride Film Festival had a cruise for a bunch of movie fans. A number of people, like Paul Schrader and Chuck Jones and Roger Ebert and me, would entertain them with Q&A stuff once a day. On the ship, Ebert spent the entire week deconstructing *Citizen Kane* for about two hundred passengers. And at lunch, one time, I said to Roger, "Do you know this story about Ince and Chaplin and Hearst?" And he said, "No." I told him the story, and he had never heard it. He said—quote—"Sounds like there's a movie in it." Or something to that effect.

I get home to New York—I'm living in New York at that time—and on my desk is a script called *The Cat's Meow.* And in thirty-five years or whatever it had been since Orson told me the story, I had never told anybody the story.

PT: *Talk about serendipity. What was your reaction to the script?*

PB: I read the script, and I thought it needed work. One of the things we did was to cut the first forty pages, which was introducing Marion in her studio and introducing Charlie in his studio, and I think introducing Ince as well, and then going to the yacht. I said, "Look, let's just begin at the yacht, with everybody arriving." And it ends with everybody leaving the yacht.

PT: *Why did you decide to film the present-day funeral of Ince in black-and-white and the flashbacks in color?*

PB: Preminger did it in *Bonjour Tristesse.* I thought it was a wonderful idea, and we wanted to try it. It was funny how that came about. If I had suggested it as an artistic device, it would have been rejected out of hand, or it might have been controversial. But the way it happened was we were shooting in Berlin and in Greece. All the exteriors were done in Greece—a small fishing village on the coast—but we couldn't do the funeral there. But when we were shooting in Berlin, it was December, and December in Berlin does not look like Beverly Hills any time in color. I said, "This is not going to look like Beverly Hills. It will look like Germany." They said, "Well, what are we going to do? We have no choice." I said, "Well, I'll tell you what. We could shoot it in black-and-white. That would solve everything because people won't notice the look of the weather." And they said, "What a good idea." So I got my way on that.

PT: *The funeral also contains one of your best dissolves—you transition from Ince's casket to Hearst's yacht.*

PB: Well, it's his tomb, isn't it? The yacht is his grave. It's as simple as that.

PT: *Being in show business yourself, did you see yourself in the characters?*

PB: I guess you could say that. I certainly had experienced a lot of the things that they were experiencing. I certainly had observed that kind of stuff going on in show business and in business period. Movies were, are, and always will be a rather cutthroat business because you're dealing with a lot of money and fame. There are ways that people can be sabotaged. There are a lot of "appointments in Samarra," you know? I felt I could understand the story very clearly.

PT: *Kirsten Dunst was wonderful as Marion Davies.*

PB: She had so many moments that were brilliant. She was the reason the picture got made, you know.

PT: *Because she was a rising star at the moment.*

PB: She had just done a picture called *Bring It On,* which was a big hit. I'm in Germany and don't even know about the fucking picture. I was in Berlin preparing the picture, but we didn't even know if we were making it or not because we didn't have a star—we didn't have her cast. The head of the studio called me up, and he said, "Kirsten Dunst wants to do the picture. She wants to play Marion Davies. She has always wanted to play a '20s movie star." I bit my tongue and *didn't* say, "Who is Kirsten Dunst?" [*Laughs.*] I just said, "Okay, well that's interesting. How old is she?" He said, "I don't know how old she is, but she wants to do the picture. She's probably eighteen or nineteen." "Well, the character is twenty-five." "Well, she can do it." That's how it happened. I hadn't seen her in anything.

PT: *You lucked out.*

PB: We had one conversation on the phone. I said, "She stutters a little bit, but I don't want to make a big deal out of it." I told her, "See a few movies of Marion Davies's. See *The Patsy, Show People,* and *Not so Dumb,* all directed by King Vidor." I told her to see those three pictures, and I think she did. I didn't meet her until she came to Germany.

PT: *You write in* Who the Hell's in It *that there was talk of casting Marlon Brando as Hearst.*

PB: Brando was suggested, and I said, "Let's give it a shot." We didn't know who to go to. They did, and he [Brando] came back and said that he didn't want to go up against Orson Welles. Which is ironic because *Kane* really isn't about Hearst. Then we got Christopher Plummer. He agreed to do the picture. He would have been very good, and unfortunately pulled out after Kirsten was in and after Eddie Izzard was in [as Chaplin]. Chris pulled out because he had done three pictures in a row and was flat-out exhausted. He apologized profusely. By this time, we had Kirsten and Eddie, and we were ready to go, and the studio said, "Well, who do you want?" I said, "Well, Ed Herrmann looks the part." They said, "Let's take him," and that was it.

PT: *What do you think Welles would have thought about your having made a picture based on the story he told you?*

PB: I think he would have been very pleased because everywhere I went I said that he told me the story before I read the script!

The Small Screen Redux—and a Grammy

The Mystery of Natalie Wood (2004, ABC)

> Director: Peter Bogdanovich; screenplay: Elizabeth Egloff (based on the books by Suzanne Finstad and Warren G. Harris); producers: Richard Fischoff and Randy Sutter; executive producers: Gerald W. Abrams, Suzanne Finstad, Robert Sertner, and Frank von Zerneck

Hustle (2004, ESPN)

> Director: Peter Bogdanovich; screenplay: Christian Darren; producer: Terry Gould; executive producers: Orly Adelson and Mark Shapiro

Runnin' Down a Dream: Tom Petty and the Heartbreakers (2007, Warner Bros. Records)

> Director: Peter Bogdanovich; producers: Skot Bright and George Drakoulias; executive producers: John Berg, Tony Dimitriades, and Diarmuid Quinn

PT: *Why did you return to television after* The Cat's Meow*?*

PB: *The Cat's Meow* was supposed to come out in September of 2001, and you know what happened in September 2001, so it got pushed back six months because of 9/11. That fucked us up in the distribution. *The Cat's Meow* was supposed to return me to the silver screen, and it didn't.

So I needed to work, and I did *The Mystery of Natalie Wood.* It was the worst script I'd ever read. We spent several weeks redoing it completely from start to finish, with the writer, and then I did some rewriting over in Australia, where we shot it in thirty-six days.

PT: *Both* The Cat's Meow *and* Natalie Wood *are very dark takes on Hollywood.*

PB: It's the truth as opposed to fiction.

PT: *Yet* Nickelodeon, *which was also based on truth, was much less dark.*

PB: There's innocence in *Nickelodeon.* And the innocence is all gone by the time of *The Cat's Meow* and *Natalie Wood.*

PT: *The setting of* Natalie Wood *is much closer to your era than the other two . . .*

PB: I knew her. Before I made the picture, I ran a lot of her films. I hadn't thought she was that good, but when I saw the films again, she was superb. She was really good in every picture she did. Sometimes the pictures weren't very good or weren't as good as she was, like *Love with the Proper Stranger,* which is a nice film, but it isn't as good as she is in it. And the same thing with *West Side Story:* she's awfully good, and I don't like the picture that much. *Rebel without a Cause* is not one of my favorite films, but she's again really good. *Inside Daisy Clover* has problems, but she's brilliant in it. I was struck by how good she was, and I was sad that I didn't realize it when she was alive and I could have told her.

PT: *And you knew her, you say?*

PB: I knew her to say hello at a party. I didn't really know her. She looked at me rather suspiciously and not very friendly, actually.

PT: *I wonder why that was.*

PB: Because I was hot and she wasn't at that point.

PT: *Do you remember that she was one of the copresenters for Best Director at the Oscars the year you were up for* The Last Picture Show?

PB: Was she?

PT: *Yes, with Frank Capra.*

PB: Oh, really? God, I have no memory of that.

PT: *It's an odd coincidence. So she dies tragically, and years later you make a movie of her life.*

PB: In Australia!

PT: *I mean, who would have guessed?*

PB: Yeah, you can't guess life. It gets out of control.

PT: *Why did you shoot it in Australia?*

PB: Same question I asked. They said because the dollar is worth two dollars there. Oh—so that's why we did it. I don't think you'd know. I think we did a pretty good job.

PT: *You stage her death in such a way that we see what happened—her falling overboard and being in the water—from her perspective.*

PB: The thing that I thought might work—although it was a daring idea—was to be with her throughout that death scene. We don't know exactly what happened, but we followed the coroner's report. Based on the abrasions and bruises and so on, that is what they think happened. So I couldn't think of a movie where you had the leading character dying for twenty minutes. I don't think it's twenty minutes, but it's about ten minutes. It's from the time she falls in until the end of the picture. I couldn't think of one as a precedent, and I said, "I don't know if the audience is going to stand this because it's very painful."

PT: *It's powerful because the entire film is seen from her perspective—from beginning to end.*

PB: I think you're right—you put your finger on what I was trying to do—I wanted it to very much be her view of the story.

We did a couple of interesting things on *Natalie Wood* which haven't been done really to the degree that we did it. We got a bunch of people who really knew Natalie—in most cases not famous people, a few famous ones, but not too many—talking to me off-camera. You don't hear me. I ask them questions, and they answer. And we'd have been talking about

Natalie. And we don't see them for long, but they function as a very interesting kind of narrator. They take you in and out.

PT: *What are the advantages to framing the story that way?*

PB: The TV trade term for what we did is "cradle-to-grave" biopic. Natalie started acting when she was four. We made her five because I just said we can't deal with four. But in fact she was four, and she died at forty-three. There's a lot of ground to cover, but with narrators we could skip—we could jump ahead without it seeming to lose anything.

Then we also did the most daring thing that I think we got away with: we used clips of the real Natalie. Clips from her movies and also from newsreels and magazines and photos. They're of the real Natalie Wood, the real R. J. Wagner, the real Warren Beatty, and so on. What happened is, we got lucky in the casting: there are three girls that play Natalie in various ages, and they all look like her. But the last one, who goes from about seventeen until her death, Justine Waddell, an English actress, looks quite a bit like Natalie—enough to get away with showing clips of the real Natalie and have it not upset you.

What's interesting is that the clips—all the real Natalie—is kind of the public Natalie. It's all out front, it's all waving to the crowds or being photographed. Something that's public, even if it's home movies. And all the scenes that we do are all behind the scenes; they're all sort of behind closed doors or private stuff. We don't restage scenes from movies. We have some rehearsals. We see them getting ready to do a scene. But we don't see the scene restaged. The way it worked out is that there's a public Natalie—that's Natalie Wood at various ages—and then there's the private Natalie, and that's the scenes we made. I think it works filmically. The real Natalie stuff kind of enriches the scenes that we made and vice versa. Because you say, "That's what she was going through when she had these pictures taken."

PT: *What was it like directing scenes with fictionalized versions of people you actually knew, like Sal Mineo and Warren Beatty and Henry Jaglom?*

PB: It was very, very weird. That was one of the reasons I was reluctant to do it at first, and all the way through it made me nervous. It's tough. It'd been done to me, and I wasn't thrilled with it, so I had ambiguous feelings about the whole project.

PT: *The same year that* Natalie Wood *aired, you made a film about disgraced Cincinnati Reds player Pete Rose for ESPN—*Hustle, *starring Tom Sizemore as Rose.*

PB: It's a good story. Again, it's true. The guy cheated and got caught. It's a sad story. He finally admitted to it. I thought Sizemore was brilliant—difficult but brilliant.

PT: *Like* To Sir, with Love II *and* Naked City, Hustle *is another crime story.*

PB: It is. It's a story of betrayal, too. I liked the idea of the perversion of baseball, which is such an honest game. I was thinking once of making the Black Sox story, when they threw the World Series. I thought about doing that at one point. And there was a sequence in *Mask* where we shot in Dodger Stadium in LA. We took about a day and shot a whole sequence. I cut it out of the picture because I thought it was stupid. But it was very well shot, and it was interesting. It was a bunch of reaction shots from the players seeing Rocky in the stands. It was very interesting visually. I always thought that baseball was a very subtle game in terms of looks and gestures. I always kind of wanted to do that—a real baseball picture, which *Hustle* isn't, because you don't see much of the baseball.

PT: *You spent several years on* Runnin' Down a Dream, *a supersize documentary about Tom Petty.*

PB: Music people love it. Musicians love it because it's all about the music. I've had musicians like Ben Harper come up to me and say, "That's a helluva documentary." I just spoke to Tom [Petty] the other day. He said that people still mention how good it is to him. It won a goddamn Grammy, for God's sake. I had complete access; I loved Tom, I loved the music. It was exciting to do something I hadn't done before. And it was exciting to use all that digital editing equipment, which is the only way that that film could have been done.

Did you know that I had been nominated for a Grammy before?

PT: *No, I didn't!*

PB: Orson and I were nominated in 1992 for Best Spoken Word Album [*This Is Orson Welles*]. Caedmon [Records] put out four cassette tapes of Orson and me talking. It was nominated for a Grammy seven years after Orson died, and we lost to Magic Johnson.

I just think it's funny that Orson Welles lost to Magic Johnson.

She's Funny That Way (2015, Lionsgate Premiere)

Director: Peter Bogdanovich; screenplay: Louise Stratten and Peter Bogdanovich; producers: Holly Wiersma, Logan Levy, George Drakoulias, and Louise Stratten; executive producers: Wes Anderson, Noah Baumbach, and Cassian Elwes

PT: *What was the genesis of* She's Funny That Way?

PB: It began, really, with something that I did more than once, but it happened first in Singapore on *Saint Jack.* The first night I got to Singapore, I thought, *This is a movie about hookers and pimps and all of that, and there's not one of them in the book.* I got a cab—the cabdriver was named Andrew, and he became my transportation captain—and I asked where do you find girls in this town. He took me to a brothel. There were about twenty-five girls lined up for me. I picked one, got in the cab, and went to the hotel. She was from Thailand. She spoke no English. She was sort of brown and very, very sweet. We made love, quite a bit, and she stayed all night. I said that I'd pay for the whole night. Somehow she explained to me through gestures and movements that she came from Bangkok, and she'd come with a boyfriend, and he put her on the street. Would she do it for him? So she did, and then he dumped her. She asked me what I did. I tried to explain that I made movies. I did a gesture of winding up a camera. Then I opened the Singapore newspaper to the movie ads, and I pointed to one. She said, "Ohhh." There was a picture of Burt Reynolds. And she said his name in Thai! [*Laughs.*] That's how she figured it out. "I make those," I said.

PT: *Including two starring Burt Reynolds!*

PB: Right! I said, "Do you want to do what you're doing? Are you happy doing this?" She said no. I gave her $5,000 to promise me she wouldn't go back and would go back to Thailand. She couldn't believe that I gave her that much money. She told me where she was going to work in Bangkok, if she could get back there. I said that I would come to see her in Bangkok. She left in the morning, and that afternoon I called to see if she could come back, and she wasn't there. She had already left.

There was another girl later on in our stay—Benny [Gazzara] was already there—we had had an escort come up to the hotel, and she was young, and she had a child out of wedlock. She was disgraced in her hometown. A boyfriend had brought her down . . . the same shit again. I told her she could stay at the hotel, and we would give her a part in the movie. And I gave her an additional three or four thousand to go home after the movie was over.

There was a New York girl, too, that needed money. I said, "Why are you doing this?" She said she was angry at her father. She was nineteen. She said she was never good at anything. I said, "You really enjoy doing this?" She said, "No, I hate it." I said, "Well, get out of it," and I gave her some extra money, and I told her to do something else.

I thought it would be funny if a guy got caught doing that by his wife. I told that setup to L. B., and she said, "Let's write it." Then we wrote it over a period of a year. We wrote it together in a way I've never done a script before or since. We'd sit on a couch, and we'd try to figure out the basic structure. We talked out an outline and taped it on a tape recorder. Then we sent the tape to Iris Chester, and she typed it up. Then we'd look at that and take that breakdown and put it on cards. We'd start with card one. Okay, fade in, and I'd start to talk about what I think the scene ought to be. And she'd say, "Yeah, that's right, but what about this?" I would usually do the dialogue first, and then she would hold her nose if she didn't like something! It was a lot of fun to work with her. We were very close, and we still are, even though we're divorced.

PT: *The original title was* Squirrels to the Nuts—*an allusion to a passage of dialogue in Ernst Lubitsch's* Cluny Brown.

PB: It was Lubitsch's last completed film, and it's an absolute delight, with Charles Boyer and Jennifer Jones. It takes place in England, just as World War II is beginning. And Jennifer Jones is a plumber's niece. Her uncle sends her to fix a sink that's plugged up. And Boyer is visiting the person, an Englishman, Reginald Gardiner, when she comes to fix the sink. So while she's fixing the sink, he says to her, "Is that what you want to do, Cluny? You want to be a plumber?" And she says, "No, I have other things I'd like to do, but my uncle Arn says I don't know my place." And he gets very upset. He says, "That's just ridiculous because he doesn't know what he's talking about. What is your place? What is my place? What is anybody's place? You know what your place is? Your place is what makes you happy! If someone goes to Hyde Park and feeds nuts to the squirrels, it's all right. But if they feel like feeding squirrels to the nuts, who am I to say 'nuts to the squirrels'?" [*Laughs.*] She says, "Could you say that again?" And the other guy says, "Could you let her fix my sink?" Very funny scene.

The phrase becomes an issue in our picture as well. The leading character steals it from the movie, but we don't know it's from the movie until the end. But he steals it and uses it in his life with escorts. Anyway, it's a running gag.

PT: *It was easy to picture the movie when you had your original cast in the late 1990s: John Ritter as Arnold and Cybill Shepherd as his wife and Louise as Izzy. I know how those actors would play it. With a new, younger cast, I didn't know how it would work exactly, and maybe you didn't either.*

PB: I didn't, but they're really good. None of them had a problem with me telling them how to play it, luckily. A couple of times, Owen [Wilson] even said, "Okay, how would you do it?" He wasn't threatened by that at all. I would often say to Jennifer [Aniston], "Faster. Just keep it coming." And I'd run it for her. There's a certain rhythm to this, and you have to maintain that. Pauses are deadly, you know?

PT: *How did you cast Imogen Poots in the lead?*

PB: I met with—I don't know—three, four, five actresses in Hollywood. Sort of up-and-coming names. One of them was Imogen Poots. I met with all these girls in Los Angeles, and I met with a couple more in New York, and Imogen was shooting in Atlanta. They sent the script to her and said, "Peter would like to meet you. Would you come up to a meeting?" And she said, "In a second." So she came up to meet with me; we sat at the Palm Court at the Plaza Hotel—you know, the place where Audrey and her husband are in *They All Laughed.* It's still there. It's one of the few things that hasn't been destroyed at the Plaza.

So we met there one early afternoon, and five minutes after she sat down, I said this is the girl. I never auditioned her. I just talked to her. She's English and has an English accent, but she was so quirky and sort of unusual without trying to be—she wasn't trying to be cute or something. Not gorgeous but pretty and in some cases quite attractive. I just knew that she was the one. I didn't even tell the producers first. I said to her, before we broke up the meal, "By the way, don't tell anybody I told, but you're going to play the part."

PT: *Will Forte is so appealing—he could be your new John Ritter.*

PB: He's very good. He's very likeable, isn't he?

PT: *How did you think to cast him? I know the plan at one point was for Jason Schwartzman to play the part.*

PB: When we told Jennifer that we had lost Jason, she was very upset. She then came back and said, "I'll do it with Will Forte or Topher Grace." I knew Topher personally. I had met him and seen him in a couple of pictures. I didn't know Will at all, but the producers said, "Let's go for Will Forte first." I knew enough about him, and I checked him out a little bit. He looked the part. I said, "Fine."

PT: *You cast several parts very late in preproduction or after shooting had started.*

PB: We couldn't get anybody to agree to do the movie star, Seth Gilbert. We had a lot of trouble with that part. We offered it to a number of people, who either turned it down or couldn't do it. We must have offered it to eight or nine people. Basically, I don't think anybody understood it. They just didn't get what was funny about it. Then I even made the character bigger in another draft while we were in preproduction. I added a whole bunch of stuff to that character to make him more palatable to actors. Still, we couldn't get anybody. Finally, we were shooting, and we needed the character the second week. We were going to shoot the Sardi's sequence, starting on Monday through Thursday. George Drakoulias suggested Rhys Ifans, who he had worked with on Noah Baumbach's picture *Greenberg.* And he was in *Notting Hill,* which I had seen as well. I said, "Of course, it's going to have to be a different kind of movie star—not a matinee idol but more of a rock star." So I said, "Well, if he'll do it, I'll use him." He said he would do it. He loved the part. He flew in from London Saturday, I met with him Sunday, and we were shooting Monday.

PT: *Was that nerve-wracking?*

PB: It was a bit nerve-wracking, but I figured something would happen. We got lucky with this picture. We got what's called dumb luck, where you have something that you think is good and then you lose that person, and the person you get you think is a not necessarily desired substitute and turns out to be a hundred times better than the person you had. That happened three or four times on this picture, and I started to recognize it happening, so I said that's what's going to happen with Seth Gilbert, too—we'll get somebody, and he'll be better than anybody we've had. And he was. Rhys was better than anybody we could have in the part. He just brought so much to it. He understood it. He had the wit. He's a very good comedy actor.

PT: *Some of your regular actors also make appearances—George Morfogen as the detective and Austin Pendleton as the judge.*

PB: We wrote the detective and the judge for George and Austin.

PT: *This picture took you back on location in New York. Was it pregnant with emotion and history, or were you just trying to get through each day and each setup?*

PB: Pretty much the latter. I was very happy to be making a picture in New York again. That was wonderful. And particularly happy to be making it with L. B. That was great, having her here and doing the picture together in the same town that we'd done a picture with her sister, you know. That was sort of meaningful and made it really fun to have her on the picture, in a producing capacity as well as a writer.

Preproduction was very strenuous. The producers had certain ideas about casting that they felt very strongly about, which is that even the little supporting roles had to be actors who were known. I wanted to use unknowns, but I think in every case they were right.

PT: *Michael Shannon even logs an appearance as a police officer.*

PB: He wanted to be in the picture. I had cast him in *To Sir, with Love II.* He was playing the part that eventually was played by a guy who also became a name, Michael Pena. What happened was, we were in rehearsals for a couple of days, and Sidney Poitier took me aside and said, "I don't like that actor. I want you to fire him." I said, "I think he's doing a good job." He said, "No, he's very weird." I said, "Well, he's just finding the part, Sidney." He said, "Peter, get rid of him—he's weird." So I had to fire him. I felt terrible because I liked him. Anyway, years later, now he's a name. He got nominated for an Oscar for *Revolutionary Road.* He's brilliant. And my producer was in touch with him and said that he had talked about me and the Sidney Poitier incident on Letterman. I saw it, and it was quite funny—he didn't blame me; he sort of blamed Sidney. The producer said, "Do you want to be in Peter's new picture?" And he said, "Yeah, I'll do a cameo." I gave him the cop, and he did it.

PT: *You premiered the film at the Venice Film Festival.*

PB: There was a press conference, and they asked me about Hollywood, what did I think about Hollywood today, and I said, "Well, I don't want to bite the hand that doesn't feed me, but . . . ." That got a big laugh, and then I went on and said that Hollywood was in decadence.

Having seen it [*She's Funny That Way*] with an audience for the first time, really—and there was a big audience, it was a thousand people—the laughs were gigantic. Most of Jennifer's stuff got huge laughs. They thought she was very funny. Rhys went over very well, very funny. Owen they loved. We were standing there, and this applause just went on and on and on. I'd never had anything like that, and Owen said to me, "What do we do? Do you think you should give a speech or something?" I said, "I don't think so." He said, "Well, maybe this is like the way they applauded for Stalin—they were afraid to stop."

There were several audiences: two for the press, the one I was at, and then there was another one after that, which I heard was equally welcomed and people were laughing a lot. If you have three or four or five audiences that laugh in the same places, you generally have a hit.[13]

PT: *How did the ending go over? You finish with Izzy being whisked away by her new beau, played by Quentin Tarantino.*

PB: The audience loved Tarantino showing up. You could hardly hear a word he said. They were so into reacting to him. I think that's part of why the picture's having such a good reaction: it has a wild finish. [Samuel] Fuller used to say, "Save your money for the finish, kid." David Chase was there with his wife. He saw it, and he thought it was a funny finish. I said, "Well, it's a cheap trick, David, but it works." He said, "Well, you know, movies are all a cheap trick." And I said, "Well, that's really cynical," but anyway.

By the way, I think not to be discounted in terms of the reactions is the fact that the world right now is in a really terrible place. I mean, everybody wants to have a laugh, and the sillier, the more improbable, the better.

You know, I'll tell you something: it just reminds me of 9/11. We were in New York when that happened, L. B. and I, and I think it was on a Tuesday that it happened, and Broadway closed for the night and for the next night—for at least two nights. On Thursday or Friday, they started performing again, and we had tickets to see *42nd Street,* which is a Broadway version of the old Warner Bros. musical, and we went to see it. And I'm reminded of the desperate kind of wanting-to-laugh feeling that the audience had on that Thursday or Friday after one of the worst calamities in American history. That's sort of where we're out now—I mean, the world is in fucking chaos.

I agree with the sentiment expressed at the end of *Sullivan's Travels,* when Preston Sturges has Joel McCrea say, "There's a lot to be said for making people laugh. Did you know that that's all some people have? It isn't much, but it's better than nothing in this cockeyed caravan." And it's true, you know? I'm a big fan of comedy as a kind of tonic.

PT: *It would be nice if* She's Funny That Way *ushers in a bunch of new comedies from you—it's been too long.*

PB: It's been way too long.

PT: *We need more of your pictures.*

PB: I know. I need more of my pictures, too.

The Great Buster (2018, Cohen Media Group)

> Director: Peter Bogdanovich; screenplay: Peter Bogdanovich; producers: Peter Bogdanovich, Charles S. Cohen, Roee Sharon, and Louise Stratten

PT: *Looking back on your films on filmmakers, you directed a documentary on John Ford—twice, actually, since you reworked it in 2006—and you made a thirteen-and-a-half-minute tribute to Chaplin at the Oscars. What prompted you to do a documentary on Buster Keaton?*

PB: Charles Cohen, who owns the Keaton films, asked me if I would do a documentary on Buster Keaton, and I said yes. I liked the idea. I loved Buster. I saw him when I was kid. My father took me to the Museum of Modern Art, where I saw Keaton and Chaplin—you know, all of those guys.

PT: *People always want to choose between Keaton and Chaplin. Did you prefer one or the other?*

PB: I appreciated each for what they were, but when I was younger, I think I preferred Chaplin. As I've gotten older, I prefer Keaton. He's not sentimental; therefore he's more modern. He deals with dark subjects in a funny way.

PT: *Did you reacquaint yourself with all of Keaton's pictures?*

PB: I looked at them all—all of the shorts and the features.

PT: *How did you select the clips?*

PB: We fought our way through it. [Film editor] Bill Berg-Hillinger is very, very important on this picture. He is a really brilliant editor who had good ideas. We worked very closely together on it.

PT: *Bill had worked on* Runnin' Down a Dream, *right?*

PB: He did the final cut on the Tom Petty. We had already burned through four editors on that picture, and he just knew how to do it.

PT: *In the Keaton documentary, though, you adopted an unusual structure: you tell the whole story of his life, up to his death, but then you go back in time to offer appreciations of some of his masterpieces of the 1920s—you know,* The General *and* Steamboat Bill, Jr., *and so on.*

PB: Well, there's an old show-business maxim: "Always leave 'em laughing." You don't want to end it so sad. I didn't like ending with his death, and I didn't know quite how to get back to the pictures. Then I realized that the Venice Film Festival had done a tribute to him about a year before he died, so that was a way to get back to the features again. I thought, "Well, let's put all those at the end."

PT: *Why did you decide to do the narration yourself?*

PB: I thought, "Who shall I get to do it? Well, why don't I do it?" That was it. Interestingly enough, Thierry Fremaux, the director of Cannes, saw it, and he thought the narration was great because it made the film even more personal.

PT: *You open the film with a clip of yourself—you were discussing Keaton on Dick Cavett's talk show in the early 1970s.*

PB: L. B. found that. She saw it, and we tracked it down. I thought it was kind of an interesting opening. A little bit arrogant, but I thought, *What the hell—I made the film, why shouldn't I be in it? Saves me the trouble of directing the narrator.*

PT: *You can justify it because Frank Capra is on the same panel on Cavett as you were—also talking about Keaton!*

In making the documentary, did you find things in Keaton's life or career to connect with?

PB: Well, I was particularly interested in how he shot the pictures. His choice of where to put the camera is pretty fucking impeccable, and that's what makes him such a good director. Chaplin was fascinating to watch, but he wasn't much of a director in terms of the camera. You couldn't learn much from him. As he said, "*I'm* interesting—my shots don't have to be."

But Keaton was not only interesting; he also really knew how put a movie together. Look at that chase with the cannon in *The General.* The construction of that is brilliant.

PT: *Several interviewees in the film knew Keaton, like Norman Lloyd, but how did you pick the other interviewees, like Quentin Tarantino and Johnny Knoxville?*

PB: Anybody who I thought had something interesting to say about Keaton, whether they knew him or just had a comment to make. It was sort of scattershot. People would suggest people, and I would say, "Fine, let's do him." I didn't know what I was going to get. As usual, when you make a documentary, you shoot it, and then you write it. In fiction, you write, and then you shoot. But until you know what you have in a documentary, you can't really write it or cut it.

We interviewed a lot of people. I was very, very open to it. Even Werner Herzog. We just said, "You want to talk about Keaton?" He said, "Yes."

PT: *And you got some good stuff from him.*

PB: He was sort of funny when he says tragedy is very funny. His phrasing is funny. I liked him.

PT: The Great Buster *reminded me a little of the spots you did in the '80s on* CBS This Morning, *where you spoke about older pictures and showed clips.*

PB: We did one hundred shows. Five minutes every Thursday at quarter to nine. It was fun to do. Only about a million people saw it, but that's a lot of people. The rentals at video stores in the New York area particularly went up. People would say, "What happened? Why does everybody want to see this movie suddenly?" "Bogdanovich talked about it." "Oh, I see."

PT: *Louise helped with those, didn't she?*

PB: She was very important. She did all the clips. I would write and shoot it, and then L. B. would cut it, and I'd come down and look at it on Wednesday. At midnight or something, we'd satellite it to New York, and it would run at quarter to nine on Thursday.

The Other Side of the Wind (2018, Netflix)

> Director: Orson Welles; screenplay: Oja Kodar and Orson Welles; producers: Frank Marshall and Filip Jan Rymsza; executive producers: Peter Bogdanovich, Jon Anderson, Dominique Antoine, Jens Koethner Kaul, Carla Rosen-Vacher, and Beatrice Welles

PT: *Around the same time* The Great Buster *was released, you were onscreen in* The Other Side of the Wind, *one of Orson Welles's final projects in which you had the costarring part. Way back in the '70s, Welles had cast you as an on-the-rise director called Brooks Otterlake, who is positioned as a kind of rival to an older director played by John Huston.*

Orson asked you if you could finish the picture if something happened to him, which is what ultimately happened. Did you ever think it would come to that?

PB: No, I didn't. In fact, when he said that to me, I said, "Why do you say that, Orson? Nothing is going to happen to you." He said, "I know, but if it does . . . ." I didn't think it would come to pass, but after he died, I had no choice but to try and make it happen. He died in 1985.

PT: *Was it an ongoing effort to finish it?*

PB: We spent quite a long time with Showtime. Three different regimes at Showtime said they would do it, and we couldn't get the three or four people who owned the rights to come together on it, so we never did do it with Showtime. That took a number of years.

PT: *How did it finally come together?*

PB: Filip [Jan Rymsza] somehow managed to get Oja [Kodar] and Beatrice Welles, the lover and the daughter, on the same page, so to speak. That was a big breakthrough. I don't know how he did it, but he did it. And I think Frank [Marshall] and Filip got Netflix into it, and I had nothing to do with that. Once we had Netflix, we were home.

PT: *Did you have a sense of the state of the film before you started? The quick-editing style is so complex.*

PB: Well, Orson had said he shot everything he needed, and it just needed to be edited, which was almost true. It was a big job. The editor, Bob Murawski, was very good. He respected Orson and knew how to get into that tempo. He knew what to do. It was a bit challenging. Orson's style on that picture was very much like *F for Fake,* really. He said to me that he had to do that kind of style because he couldn't move the camera. They didn't have the equipment, and they didn't have the kind of Hollywood technicians, so he decided to put it all into the editing.

PT: *Had you seen many of your scenes as Otterlake?*

PB: I hadn't seen almost any of it.

PT: *What was it like to look at it?*

PB: I didn't really see it in pieces. I saw the whole film at one point. My first remark was, "What happened to that actor? He's pretty good."

PT: *You're great in it.*

PB: While we were shooting it—I only worked on it for about ten days—Orson and Oja were both raving about my performance, and I didn't see it until recently.

It was a weird experience, seeing myself in my thirties while I'm in my seventies. It made me a little ill to think I should have been acting more. The heart of the movie is the Huston–Otterlake relationship. Somebody said to me, "You're playing Prince Hal [from Welles's film *Chimes at Midnight*]." It's basically that story again. Orson had done that story a number of times. Betrayal is a running theme in his pictures. It's questionable whether Otterlake betrays Huston. He doesn't give him money.

PT: *While finishing* The Other Side of the Wind, *did you feel the presence of Welles?*

PB: Yes, definitely. I think he'd be happy with it. It got a good release. The press was generally very positive, and it's a very difficult movie.

PT: *It's a feather in your cap as an actor, too.*

PB: It makes up for all the movies I didn't do because I was waiting for Orson to come out with his film. He asked me not to do certain films. I was offered to be in [Samuel Fuller's] *The Big Red One.* I was offered a couple of other pictures. He said, "Don't do it. Let *The Other Side of the Wind* be your entrance in the leading-man department." You know, that didn't happen.

I told you what Orson said to me when he was directing me that one time. It was the greatest compliment I ever got. I can't remember what the scene was, but it was a close-up. He gave me a direction, and I did it. Then he told me another way to play it, and I did that. He gave me a couple more different pieces of direction, and I did them. And then he said to me, "Now I know how you get all those brilliant performances in your movies." I said, "What do you mean?" He said, "You show them how to do it, don't you?" I said, "Some of the time, yes." He said, "Because you're a brilliant actor."

Wait for Me

PT: *I think* Wait for Me *could be your* Chimes at Midnight *or* Rio Bravo—*in other words, the film where you sum it all up.*

PB: It feels that way to me. It's an attempt to take to the extreme the thing I like most in pictures, which is comedy and drama. So I take it further. It's comedy and tragedy. [*Laughs.*]

PT: *How did it come about?*

PB: While I was finishing *They All Laughed,* before Dorothy was killed, I was thinking about the next picture I was going to make, and it was going to be with Dorothy. And I wasn't sure who was going to play the lead, but it was very much a character like me, so it might have been John Cassavetes I was thinking of—someone dramatic who would be funny, theatrical, and real. It was about an orchestra conductor and a Dutch girl he meets when he goes to Amsterdam to conduct. She's a violinist, and he falls for her. He brings her home to Los Angeles. And it was called *The Return of the Count* because he's a count, some kind of middle-European count.

Again, I was going to do what I did on *They All Laughed,* which was I was going to take my own life stuff—with my kids and people that I knew who worked with me or whatever—and kind of change it enough to make it a romantic comedy about an orchestra conductor and a girl he falls for who doesn't speak English. Dorothy was going to play it. And, of course, when she was killed, that just went away, and I didn't have an idea for quite a while to do anything.

PT: *But then you had the idea for what became* Wait for Me*—a ghost comedy about a movie director called Charles Benedict.*

PB: The first idea I had had to do with ghosts. I started thinking about a ghost comedy. Not insignificantly, another one of my favorite films when I was ten, strangely enough, was a film called *The Ghost Goes West,* which was directed by the Frenchman René Clair. I haven't seen it in years; I don't know if it holds up. Probably not, but I loved it as a kid. I must have seen it ten times. It's about a ghost who talks to his nephew. I always kind of liked ghost pictures, but I didn't think they were done particularly well of late. So I had an idea about how to do this ghost picture. Again, it was very personal, but in this case I didn't disguise it. I sort of took it a bit further than myself and changed it a lot in terms of the plot, but the basic plot was about a movie director who, when the movie begins, is in deep shit, can't get work anywhere, is going bankrupt, has been married originally three times, has three daughters, three ex-wives, and the last one was killed in a plane crash six years before the movie starts—a plane crash which had killed two of his best friends as well.

I worked on that for a couple years, and John Cassavetes kept talking about it. I wanted John to play the director, and he loved it. And then, you know, he got sick and so on, and even when he was sick, he helped me with it. I just never could solve it. I didn't know what was wrong with it. I realized that it wasn't complicated enough, so I made it a movie director with six ex-wives and six daughters. [*Laughs.*] And instead of it playing all in Paris, I moved it around to about five different cities in Europe—Vienna, Salzburg, Budapest, Prague. I expanded it and rewrote it several times.

I have a version that I like now. It's pretty good.

PT: *The idea is Charles Benedict is inundated with ghosts of old friends and colleagues—and of his most recent ex-wife, Cynthia.*

PB: The ghosts have to be done visually in a different way than how you've ever seen them. The idea is that they're transparent, but they have to move differently. I want them to sort of move like smoke from one place to the other. They sort of disappear and then appear, dematerialize and then materialize. But they're always transparent. The way I want to do it is that there are an awful lot of ghosts who come in for a line and they're out.

PT: *Were you interested in ghosts before the tragedy with Dorothy Stratten?*

PB: I don't know if I ever really thought about it that much. I asked Allan Dwan about it, though, strangely enough, after it happened. He was ninety-something when it happened. I said, "Do you believe in ghosts, Allan?" He said, "Oh, yeah." I said, "You do?" He said, "Oh, sure. I think there are restless spirits who haven't finished their work on earth."

PT: *If you live long enough, you start to believe.*

PB: Because people die around you. He lost his wife.

PT: *Clint Eastwood's* Hereafter *shares some themes with* Wait for Me.

PB: I thought it was very good.

PT: *I loved it.*

PB: I couldn't understand why nobody liked it. Nobody said anything about it—it just sort of came and went. I thought it was one of his best films. I called Clint, and he called me back. I said, "I don't understand it. It's one of your best pictures."

PT: *I think the film speaks to anyone looking for answers after having lost someone.*

PB: Well, that's the tragedy of human beings: we don't know about something until we've been through it. I told Griffin Dunne and I told his father, Dominick Dunne, about *Wait for Me,* and they both wanted to read it. Now, they had a tragedy with Griffin's sister, Dominick's daughter, Dominique, who was strangled to death. They both read it, and they both said it was absolutely accurate. That was their words—not one thing isn't true.

PT: *River Phoenix inspired the ending.*

PB: Well, when River died, I was devastated, and then I realized I didn't have a third act and that his death would somehow inspire a third act.

PT: *The whole business in the script of looking for signs from the departed in license plates and such—does that come from personal experience?*

PB: I did it with Dorothy when we were in London. I pointed out to her where it said "D. R." in big letters somewhere. It was a sign—"D. R." something. And she shrieked. She had this shriek that was just otherworldly. It was mixed with joy and surprise and love of life. It was very unafraid.

PT: *I think we hear it in the shoe-store scene in* They All Laughed, *when the dog runs up and bites her.*

PB: You hear a little bit of it, but not the full-out shriek.

Anyway, back in LA, when we went to buy the kids some ice cream cones at Häagen-Dazs, the street was Dorothy Street, and we pointed to it, and she shrieked again. It became a kind of thing. After she was gone, license plates often say "D. R." L. B. and I used to tell ourselves, "Oh, there's a D. R. right there."

It was from Graves that I found out why people wear black at funerals. It started with the tradition of blacking your face and your hands—literally. The reason being that if the ghosts of the dead had something against you, they won't recognize you. Isn't that riveting? It gives you chills. When I found out about that in the '80s, I thought, *So that's why I didn't wear black to Dorothy's funeral.* The kids didn't either. I wore a gray jacket and slacks and a bright scarf.

And it struck me as right that I had put Ellen Burstyn in white at Sam the Lion's funeral . . . because we wanted to be recognized.

Acknowledgments

First and foremost, I thank my family: my parents, Del and Diane Tonguette, and my brother, Patrick Tonguette. I dedicate this book to the memory of my father.

For their friendship, or for help in matters large and small, I also thank David Baron, the late Dann and Judy Cahn, Tomm Carroll, Jean-Pierre Coursodon, Bilge Ebiri, Nick Dawson, Keith Gordon, Josh Karp, Dave Kehr, Vincent LoBrutto and Harriet Morrison, Joseph McBride, the late George Morfogen, Stephen R. Myers, Gerald Peary, Barry Putterman, Bob Rafelson, Jonathan Rosenbaum, Matt Zoller Seitz, James Stoller, and Louise Stratten.

I thank Iris Chester, Peter Bogdanovich's longtime assistant, for her diligent assistance over the course of many years, and Bill Krohn, the Los Angeles correspondent of *Cahiers du cinéma,* for first putting me in touch with Iris in 2003. In 2011, filmmaker Bill Teck interviewed me about *They All Laughed* for his documentary *One Day since Yesterday*—a fun and rewarding experience.

The Lilly Library at Indiana University furnished me with a number of rare documents from their exhaustive collection of Bogdanovich papers. I thank reference librarian David K. Frasier and former curator of manuscripts Cherry Dunham Williams.

I have benefitted greatly from the expertise—and extreme patience—of acquisitions editor Anne Dean Dotson at the University Press of Kentucky. I am grateful for the wisdom and guidance of Patrick McGilligan, who in addition to being among the great film biographers of his time, doubles as the editor of the press's Screen Classics series. Greatly appreciated, too, was the diligent and careful work of copy editor Annie Barva.

ACKNOWLEDGMENTS

Some of the material in this book first appeared in my article "Let Us Sing of the Days That Are Gone . . . Peter Bogdanovich: A Cinema of Silent Exchanges," *Senses of Cinema* 32 (July 2004). I thank my editors at that publication, especially Michelle Carey, Rolando Caputo, and Jake Wilson.

Notes

Prologue

1. Peter Bogdanovich, "A Year and a Day Calendar," *IndieWire,* December 22, 2011, at https://www.indiewire.com/2011/12/a-year-and-a-day-calendar-131732/.

2. François Truffaut, *Hitchcock* (New York: Simon and Schuster, 1983), 13.

Part 1: "Call Me Peter, Peter"

1. Peter Bogdanovich, *Who the Hell's in It: Conversations with Hollywood's Legendary Actors* (New York: Ballantine, 2004), 7.

2. Harold Hayes, introduction to Peter Bogdanovich, *Pieces of Time: Peter Bogdanovich on the Movies* (New York: Arbor House/Esquire, 1973), 15.

3. Ibid.

4. Pauline Kael, "The Rear Guard," in *Reeling* (New York: Warner Books, 1976), 617.

5. Studio executive quoted in Hayes, introduction to Bogdanovich, *Pieces of Time,* 20.

6. Quoted in Patrick McGilligan, "At Long Last, Bogdanovich," *Boston Globe,* March 30, 1975.

7. Quoted in Peter Biskind, *Easy Riders, Raging Bulls: How the Sex-Drugs-and-Rock 'n' Roll Generation Saved Hollywood* (New York: Simon and Schuster, 1998), 139.

8. Judy Stone, "All Because of Boris Karloff," *New York Times,* September 15, 1968.

9. Joseph McBride, *Hawks on Hawks* (Berkeley: University of California Press, 1982), 84.

10. Quoted in Stone, "All Because of Boris Karloff."

11. Herman Wouk, *Marjorie Morningstar* (New York: Little, Brown, 1955), 3.

12. Roger Ebert, "*The Last Picture Show,*" *Chicago Sun-Times,* January 1, 1971, https://www.rogerebert.com/reviews/the-last-picture-show-1971.

13. Peter Bogdanovich, foreword to F. Miguel Valenti, *More Than a Movie: Ethics in Entertainment* (Boulder, Colo.: Westview Press), xii.

14. George Steiner, "Night Words," in *George Steiner: A Reader* (New York: Oxford University Press, 1984), 313.

15. Peter Bogdanovich, testimony, "The Los Angeles Hearing," in *In Harm's Way: The Pornography Civil Rights Hearings*, ed. Catharine A. MacKinnon and Andrea Dworkin (Cambridge, Mass.: Harvard University Press, 1997), 351.

16. Biskind, *Easy Riders, Raging Bulls*, 139.

17. Clive James, "Hit Men," *New Yorker*, July 7, 1997.

18. "Revival of Oldtime Screwball Gags sans 'Social' Values Is Bogdanovich's Slant on WB's 'What's Up, Doc?' Film," *Variety*, October 20, 1971.

19. Vincent Canby, "*What's Up, Doc?*," *New York Times*, March 10, 1972.

20. Advertisement for *What's Up, Doc?*, *Variety*, March 29, 1972.

21. Gordon Gow, "Without a Dinosaur," *Films and Filming*, June 1972, in *Peter Bogdanovich: Interviews*, ed. Peter Tonguette (Jackson: University Press of Mississippi, 2015), 17.

22. Orson Welles and Peter Bogdanovich, *This Is Orson Welles*, rev. ed. (New York: Da Capo Press, 1998), xxix, emphasis in original.

23. "Bogdanovich Sets 3-Film WB Deal; Own 'Laredo' First," *Variety*, February 25, 1972.

24. Quoted in Biskind, *Easy Riders, Raging Bulls*, 140, emphasis in original.

25. Frank Yablans, "Bold Approach to Pix B.O.; and TV's Production Virility Yet to Be Tested," *Variety*, January 3, 1973.

26. Quoted in Peter Bogdanovich, *Who the Devil Made It* (New York: Knopf, 1997), 235.

27. Quoted in Barbara Grizzuti Harrison, "Peter Bogdanovich Comes Back from the Dead," *Esquire*, August 1990.

28. Bogdanovich, *Who the Devil Made It*, 15–16.

29. Ibid., 39.

30. Peter Bogdanovich, as told to Francine Russo, "Turning Point: Quick Cuts," *Time*, December 2, 2002.

31. Biskind, *Easy Riders, Raging Bills*, 209.

32. Peter Bogdanovich, *John Ford* (Berkeley: University of California Press, 1978), 109.

33. Tad Friend, "The Moviegoer," *New Yorker*, April 8, 2002.

34. Andrew Yule, *Picture Shows: The Life and Films of Peter Bogdanovich* (New York: Limelight Editions, 1992), 8.

35. Digby Diehl, "Q&A: Peter Bogdanovich," *Los Angeles Times*, April 2, 1972.

36. Wes Anderson, "A Pimp with a Heart," *Sight and Sound*, 1999.

37. "Dialogue on Film: Peter Bogdanovich," *American Film*, June 1986, in *Peter Bogdanovich*, ed. Tonguette, 93.

38. Vincent Canby, "'Daisy' Is an Unexpected Triumph," *New York Times*, June 16, 1974; *The* New York Times *Guide to the Best 1,000 Movies Ever Made* (New York: New York Times, 1999).

39. Quoted in Rex Reed, "Peter Bogdanovich and Cybill Shepherd," in *People Are Crazy Here* (New York: Delacorte Press, 1974), 275.

40. Bogdanovich, "Screenwriters and Preston Sturges," in *Pieces of Time*, 213.

41. John Leonard, "John Leonard's Television Notes," *New York*, April 8, 1996.

42. David Thomson, "Older, Sadder, Maybe Wiser," *New York Times,* April 7, 2002.

43. Barry Putterman, "Peter Bogdanovich," in *American Directors,* vol. 2, ed. Jean-Pierre Coursodon, with Pierre Sauvage (New York: McGraw Hill, 1983), 53.

44. Bogdanovich, *Who the Hell's in It,* 113.

45. Eric Sherman and Martin Rubin, "Peter Bogdanovich," in *Peter Bogdanovich,* ed. Tonguette, 12, emphasis in original.

46. Ibid., 16.

47. Lynn Hirschberg, "The Man Who Changed Everything" (interview), *New York Times Magazine,* November 16, 1997.

48. Quoted in Sue Reilly, "Haunted by a Lost Love, Director Peter Bogdanovich Pays Tribute with a New Film," *People,* February 8, 1982.

49. Quoted in Harrison, "Peter Bogdanovich Comes Back from the Dead."

50. Peter Bogdanovich, *The Killing of the Unicorn* (1984; reprint, New York: Bantam Books, 1985), 44.

51. Bogdanovich, *The Killing of the Unicorn,* 45, 53.

52. Ibid., 57.

53. Quoted in Reilly, "Haunted by a Lost Love."

54. Bogdanovich, *The Killing of the Unicorn,* 71.

55. Ibid., 215, 106 (quoting Stratten), 64.

56. Quoted in Friend, "The Moviegoer."

57. T. H. White, *The Once and Future King* (1958; reprint, New York: Ace Books, 2011), 183.

58. Bogdanovich, *The Killing of the Unicorn,* 221.

59. Quoted in Harrison, "Peter Bogdanovich Comes Back from the Dead."

60. Bogdanovich, *The Killing of the Unicorn,* 222.

61. Bogdanovich, *Who the Hell's in It,* 446.

62. Bogdanovich, *The Killing of the Unicorn,* 227.

63. Peter Bogdanovich, mailgram to Robert Graves, April 4, 1981, Lilly Library, Indiana University, Bloomington.

64. Peter Bogdanovich, email to the author, November 28, 2010.

65. Ibid.

66. Harrison, "Peter Bogdanovich Comes Back from the Dead."

67. Quoted in Wayne Warga, "Bogdanovich: Love, Comedy, and Tragedy," *Los Angeles Times,* December 13, 1981.

68. Reilly, "Haunted by a Lost Love."

69. Nina J. Easton, "The Next Picture Show," *Los Angeles Times,* October 15, 1989.

70. Vidor spoke these words in his short film *Metaphor: King Vidor Meets with Andrew Wyeth* (1980).

71. Thomas J. Harris, "Peter Bogdanovich Interview," in *Peter Bogdanovich,* ed. Tonguette, 99.

72. Armond White, "Directed by Peter Bogdanovich," *Film Comment,* March–April 1993.

73. Alex Simon, "Peter Bogdanovich's Year of the Cat," in *Peter Bogdanovich,* ed. Tonguette, 147.

74. Graham Greene, *The End of the Affair* (1951; reprint, New York: Penguin, 2004), 76.

75. Bogdanovich, *The Killing of the Unicorn*, 197, 202.

76. Todd McCarthy, "Trio of Projects on Tap for Peter Bogdanovich This Year," *Variety*, January. 11, 1983.

77. Bogdanovich, *The Killing of the Unicorn*, 197.

78. Bogdanovich, *Who the Devil Made It*, 437.

79. James, "Hit Men."

80. Quoted in Friend, "The Moviegoer."

81. Larry McMurtry, *Terms of Endearment* (1975; reprint, New York: Simon and Schuster, 1989), 403.

82. James, "Hit Men."

83. Peter Bogdanovich, email to the author, January 6, 2011.

Part 2. Q&A

1. Digby Diehl, "Q&A: Peter Bogdanovich," *Los Angeles Times*, April 2, 1972.

2. Peter Bogdanovich, *John Ford* (Berkeley: University of California Press, 1978).

3. Grover Lewis, "Bogdanovich's *Last Picture Show*," in *The* Rolling Stone *Film Reader: The Best Film Writing from* Rolling Stone *Magazine*, ed. Peter Travers (New York: Pocket Books, 1996), 165.

4. See Martin Rubin, "An Interview with Peter Bogdanovich," in *Peter Bogdanovich: Interviews*, ed. Peter Tonguette (Jackson: University Press of Mississippi, 2015), 28.

5. Jan Dawson, "The Continental Divide," *Sight and Sound*, Winter 1973–1974.

6. In fact, Bogdanovich *did* change his credit to "Screenplay by Peter Bogdanovich, suggested by the songs of Cole Porter" for the Blu-ray release of James Blakeley's cut of *At Long Last Love* in 2013.

7. "New Direction for Bogdanovich," *New York*, January 31, 1977.

8. Quoted in "Poet Ponders on Words and Women," *Life*, June 28, 1963.

9. Jim Robbins, "Bogdanovich Cites Thrift as Company's Bottom Line," *Variety*, November 5, 1981.

10. Thomas J. Harris, "Peter Bogdanovich Interview," in *Peter Bogdanovich*, ed. Tonguette, 99.

11. Bogdanovich intended to include songs by Bruce Springsteen in *Mask;* due to disagreements with executives, the songs were omitted from the version released in theaters but then restored nearly two decades later for a DVD release (which is also longer than the theatrical version).

12. "Dialogue on Film: George Cukor," *American Film*, February 1978, in *George Cukor: Interviews*, ed. Robert Emmet Long (Jackson: University Press of Mississippi, 2001), 118.

13. Like a number of Bogdanovich pictures since the 1990s, *She's Funny That Way* could never catch on with audiences due to its scant, barely publicized theatrical distribution in the United States.

Index

Screen Classics

Screen Classics is a series of critical biographies, film histories, and analytical studies focusing on neglected filmmakers and important screen artists and subjects, from the era of silent cinema through the golden age of Hollywood to the international generation of today. Books in the Screen Classics series are intended for scholars and general readers alike. The contributing authors are established figures in their respective fields. This series also serves the purpose of advancing scholarship on film personalities and themes with ties to Kentucky.

Series Editor

Patrick McGilligan

Books in the Series

Olivia de Havilland: Lady Triumphant
Victoria Amador

Mae Murray: The Girl with the Bee-Stung Lips
Michael G. Ankerich

Hedy Lamarr: The Most Beautiful Woman in Film
Ruth Barton

Rex Ingram: Visionary Director of the Silent Screen
Ruth Barton

Conversations with Classic Film Stars: Interviews from Hollywood's Golden Era
James Bawden and Ron Miller

Conversations with Legendary Television Stars: Interviews from the First Fifty Years
James Bawden and Ron Miller

You Ain't Heard Nothin' Yet: Interviews with Stars from Hollywood's Golden Era
James Bawden and Ron Miller

Von Sternberg
John Baxter

Hitchcock's Partner in Suspense: The Life of Screenwriter Charles Bennett
Charles Bennett, edited by John Charles Bennett

Hitchcock and the Censors
John Billheimer

A Uniquely American Epic: Intimacy and Action, Tenderness and Violence in Sam Peckinpah's The Wild Bunch
Edited by Michael Bliss

My Life in Focus: A Photographer's Journey with Elizabeth Taylor and the Hollywood Jet Set
Gianni Bozzacchi with Joey Tayler

Hollywood Divided: The 1950 Screen Directors Guild Meeting and the Impact of the Blacklist
Kevin Brianton

He's Got Rhythm: The Life and Career of Gene Kelly
Cynthia Brideson and Sara Brideson

Ziegfeld and His Follies: A Biography of Broadway's Greatest Producer
Cynthia Brideson and Sara Brideson

The Marxist and the Movies: A Biography of Paul Jarrico
Larry Ceplair

Dalton Trumbo: Blacklisted Hollywood Radical
Larry Ceplair and Christopher Trumbo

Warren Oates: A Wild Life
Susan Compo

Improvising Out Loud: My Life Teaching Hollywood How to Act
Jeff Corey with Emily Corey

Crane: Sex, Celebrity, and My Father's Unsolved Murder
Robert Crane and Christopher Fryer

Jack Nicholson: The Early Years
Robert Crane and Christopher Fryer

Anne Bancroft: A Life
Douglass K. Daniel

Being Hal Ashby: Life of a Hollywood Rebel
Nick Dawson

Bruce Dern: A Memoir
Bruce Dern with Christopher Fryer and Robert Crane

Intrepid Laughter: Preston Sturges and the Movies
Andrew Dickos

Miriam Hopkins: Life and Films of a Hollywood Rebel
Allan R. Ellenberger

John Gilbert: The Last of the Silent Film Stars
Eve Golden

Stuntwomen: The Untold Hollywood Story
Mollie Gregory

Saul Bass: Anatomy of Film Design
Jan-Christopher Horak

Hitchcock Lost and Found: The Forgotten Films
Alain Kerzoncuf and Charles Barr

Pola Negri: Hollywood's First Femme Fatale
Mariusz Kotowski

Sidney J. Furie: Life and Films
Daniel Kremer

Albert Capellani: Pioneer of the Silent Screen
Christine Leteux

Ridley Scott: A Biography
Vincent LoBrutto

Mamoulian: Life on Stage and Screen
David Luhrssen

Maureen O'Hara: The Biography
Aubrey Malone

My Life as a Mankiewicz: An Insider's Journey through Hollywood
Tom Mankiewicz and Robert Crane

Hawks on Hawks
Joseph McBride

Showman of the Screen: Joseph E. Levine and His Revolutions in Film Promotion
A. T. McKenna

William Wyler: The Life and Films of Hollywood's Most Celebrated Director
Gabriel Miller

Raoul Walsh: The True Adventures of Hollywood's Legendary Director
Marilyn Ann Moss

Veit Harlan: The Life and Work of a Nazi Filmmaker
Frank Noack

Harry Langdon: King of Silent Comedy
Gabriella Oldham and Mabel Langdon

Charles Walters: The Director Who Made Hollywood Dance
Brent Phillips

Some Like It Wilder: The Life and Controversial Films of Billy Wilder
Gene D. Phillips

Ann Dvorak: Hollywood's Forgotten Rebel
Christina Rice

Lewis Milestone: Life and Films
Harlow Robinson

Michael Curtiz: A Life in Film
Alan K. Rode

Arthur Penn: American Director
Nat Segaloff

Film's First Family: The Untold Story of the Costellos
Terry Chester Shulman

Claude Rains: An Actor's Voice
David J. Skal with Jessica Rains

Barbara La Marr: The Girl Who Was Too Beautiful for Hollywood
Sherri Snyder

Buzz: The Life and Art of Busby Berkeley
Jeffrey Spivak

Victor Fleming: An American Movie Master
Michael Sragow

Hollywood Presents Jules Verne: The Father of Science Fiction on Screen
Brian Taves

Thomas Ince: Hollywood's Independent Pioneer
Brian Taves

Picturing Peter Bogdanovich: My Conversations with the New Hollywood Director
Peter Tonguette

Carl Theodor Dreyer and Ordet: *My Summer with the Danish Filmmaker*
Jan Wahl

Clarence Brown: Hollywood's Forgotten Master
Gwenda Young